AGRICULTURE, ENVIRONMENT AND NANO-SCIENCE

ENV BOOKS SERIES

AGRICULTURE, ENVIRONMENT AND NANO-SCIENCE

Editor

Dr. Pawan Kumar 'Bharti'

Vice President (Executive)
Society for Environment, Health, Awareness of Nutrition & Toxicology (SEHAT)
1775, Sohan Ganj, Near Clock Tower, Delhi-7 (India)
E-mail: *gurupawanbharti@rediffmail.com*

Associate editors

Dr. E. Parameswari

Assistant Professor (Env. Sci.)
Horticultural College & Research Institute
Periyakulam, Theni (Dt), Tamilnadu- 625 604, (India)

&

Dr. Resham Bhalla

Associate Professor
Department of Zoology
LVH Arts, Science and Commerce College
Panchavati, Nashik-3, M.S., (India)

DPH

DISCOVERY PUBLISHING HOUSE PVT. LTD.
NEW DELHI-110 002

Published by:

Tilak Wasan

DISCOVERY PUBLISHING HOUSE PVT. LTD.

4383/4B, Ansari Road, Darya Ganj

New Delhi-110 002 (India)

Phone : +91-11-23279245, 43596064-65

Fax : +91-11-23253475

E-mail : discoverypublishinghouse@gmail.com

sales@discoverypublishinggroup.com

web : www.discoverypublishinggroup.com

First Edition: **2015**

ISBN: 978-93-5056-760-9

Agriculture, Environment and Nano-science

Printed at:

Infinity Imaging Systems

Delhi

ENV Books Series, India

Calls lengthy and error free chapters for further volumes of books on various environmental issues. (Send your manuscripts to envbooks@gmail.com)

Founding Editor (Editor-in-Chief)

Dr. Pawan Kumar 'Bharti'
Society for Environment, Health, Awareness of Nutrition & Toxicology (SEHAT-India)
1775, Sohanganj, Near Clock Tower, Delhi-7, India
E-mail:*gurupawanbharti@rediffmail.com*

Other Titles by Editor-in-Chief:

1. **Advances in Biotechnology and Ecological Sciences (2013)**
Bharti, P.K., Chauhan, A. and Ray, J. (eds.)
(ISBN: 978-93-5056-358-8).
2. **Advances in Agriculture and Ecology (2013)**
Bharti, P.K.; Chauhan, A. and Ezeaku Peter Ikemefuna (eds.)
(ISBN: 978-93-5056-362-5).
3. **Agriculture and Environmental Biotechnology (2014)**
Bharti, P.K. and Chauhan, A. (eds.)
(ISBN: 978-93-5056-479-0).
4. **Agriculture Development and Sustainable Environment (2015)**
Ray, J. and Bharti, P.K. (eds.)
(ISBN: 978-93-5056-759-3).
5. **Agriculture Ecology and Environment (2014)**
Bharti, P.K. and Olubukola O. Babalola (eds.)
(ISBN: 978-93-5056-480-6).
6. **Agro-forestry and Climate Change (2014)**
Bharti, Pawan K. and Singh, Narayan (eds.)
(ISBN: 978-93-5056-514-8).
7. **Aquaculture and Fisheries Environment (2014)**
Gupta, S.K. and Pawan K. Bharti (eds.)
(ISBN: 978-93-5056-408-0).

8. **Aquatic Biodiversity and Pollution (2013)**
   Bharti, P.K.; Chauhan, A. and Kaoud, H.A.H. (eds.)
   (ISBN: 978-93-5056-359-5).
9. **Aquatic Ecology and Biotechnology (2014)**
   Bharti, P.K. and Zaki, M.S.A. (eds.)
   (ISBN: 978-93-5056-451-6).
10. **Aquatic Environment and Toxicology (2013)**
    Bharti, Pawan K. (ed.)
    (ISBN: 978-93-5056-236-9).
11. **Biodiversity, Biotechnology and Environmental Conservation (2015)**
    Bharti, P.K. and Bhandari, G. (eds.)
    (ISBN: 978-93-5056-750-0).
12. **Biodiversity of Aquatic Ecosystem: *Significance, Threat and Conservation* (2013)**
    Bharti, P.K. and Kaoud, H.A.H. (eds.)
    (ISBN: 978-93-5056-297-0).
13. **Biotechnology, Agro-ecology and Environment (2015)**
    Chauhan, Avnish and Bharti, P.K. (eds.)
    (ISBN: 978-93-5056-757-9).
14. **Clean Technologies and Environmental Protection (2015)**
    Chauhan, A.; Sharma, S. and Bharti, P.K. (eds.)
    (ISBN: 978-93-5056-731-9).
15. **Climate Change and Agriculture (2012)**
    Bharti, P.K. and Chauhan, Avnish (eds.)
    (ISBN: 978-93-5056-148-5).
16. **Climate Change and Biodiversity (2013)**
    Bharti, P.K. and Chauhan, Avnish (eds.)
    (ISBN: 978-93-5056-360-1).
17. **Conservation and Cultivation of Medicinal Plants (2015)**
    Bharti, P.K. and Singh Narayan (eds.)
    (ISBN: 978-93-5056-740-1).
18. **Eco-toxicology and Eco-technology (2013)**
    Bharti, P.K. and Zaki, M. (eds.)
    (ISBN: 978-93-5056-313-7).
19. **Environmental Biotechnology and Application (2013)**
    Bharti, P.K. and Chauhan, Avnish (eds.)
    (ISBN: 978-93-5056-262-8).
20. **Environmental Conservation and Biotechnology (2014)**
    Chauhan, A. and P.K. Bharti (eds.)
    (ISBN: 978-93-5056-512-4).

21. **Environmental Health and Problems (2013)**
Bharti, P.K. and Gajananda, Kh. (eds.)
(ISBN: 978-93-5056-263-5).

22. **Environmental Pollution and Biodiversity (2012)**
Bharti, P.K.; Chauhan, Avnish and Kumar, P. (eds.)
(ISBN: 978-93-5056-149-2).

23. **Fisheries and Toxicology (2014)**
Zaki, M.S.A.; Bharti, P.K. and Chauhan, A. (eds.)
(ISBN: 978-93-5056-452-3).

24. **Fish Habitat and Aquaculture (2015)**
Bharti, P.K.; Gupta Kr. Sanjay (eds.)
(ISBN: 978-93-5056-744-9).

25. **Freshwater Ecosystem and Xenobiotics (2013)**
Bharti, P.K.; Zaki, M. and Chauhan, A. (eds.)
(ISBN: 978-93-5056-299-4).

26. **Limnology and Aquatic Science (2015)**
Sharma, S. and Bharti, P.K. (eds.)
(ISBN: 978-93-5056-735-7).

27. **Medicinal Plants: *Distribution, Utilization and Significance* (2015)**
Sharma, P.; Bharti, P.K. and Narayan Singh (eds.)
(ISBN: 978-93-5056-734-0).

28. **Microbial Applications and Environment (2014)**
Bharti, Pawan K. (ed.)
(ISBN: 978-93-5056-515-5).

29. **Microbial Ecology and Habitat (2014)**
Bharti, Pawan K. (ed.)
(ISBN: 978-93-5056-514-8).

30. **Natural Ecosystem and Climate Change (2015)**
Bharti, P.K., and Kh. Gajananda (ed.)
(ISBN: 978-93-5056-745-6).

31. **Prakriti me Aushadhi (*in Hindi*) (2012)**
Singh, J.R.; Bharti, P.K. and Bharti, B.
(ISBN: 978-93-5056-200-0).

32. **Seed Technology, Plant Growth and Cropping System (2015)**
Tyagi, P.K. and Bharti, P.K. (eds.)
(ISBN: 978-93-5056-738-8).

33. **Soil Characteristics and Agro-ecology**
Chauhan, Avnish and Bharti, P.K. (eds.)
(ISBN: 978-93-5056-758-6).

34. **Soil Contamination and Conservation (2015)**
Ezeaku, P.I. and Bharti, P.K. (eds.)
(ISBN: 978-93-5056-737-1).

35. **Soil Quality and Contamination (2013)**
    Bharti, P.K. and Chauhan, Avnish (eds.)
    (ISBN: 978-93-5056-361-8).
36. **Waste Disposal and Management (2015)**
    Bharti, P.K.; Tabassum, B. and Bajaj, P. (eds.)
    (ISBN: 978-93-5056-729-6).
37. **Water Resources and Agriculture (2014)**
    Bharti, P.K. and Ezeaku Peter Ikemefuna (eds.)
    (ISBN: 978-93-5056-481-3).

Preface

Nano-Science & nanotechnology has immense potential to enhance the quality of life through its applications in various fields like agriculture, food system and environmental conservation. Globally, it has become the future of any nation, but we must be very careful with any new technology to be introduced regarding its possible unforeseen related risks that may come through its positive potential. There is vast potential in nanoscience and nanotechnology in the provision of state-of-the-art solutions for various challenges faced by agriculture and society today and in the future. Climate change, urbanization, Pollution, sustainable use of natural resources and environmental issues like runoff and accumulation of pesticides and fertilizers are the hot issues for today's agriculture. These problems are further intensified by an alarming increase in food demand that will be needed to feed an estimated population of 6-9 billion by 2050.

The scenario of a rapidly developing and complex agricultural system is existing and greater challenges will be posed to the developing countries as, in the developing countries, agriculture is the backbone of the national economy. They face many critical issues such as lack of new arable soil, reduction of the current agricultural land due to competing economic development activities, commodity dependence, poverty and malnutrition, which need to be solved on a sustainable basis. Many technologies have been developed that have the potential to increase farm productivity and also reduce the environmental and resource costs related with agricultural production. These technologies have the ability to conserve land and water by increasing yields through the application of the same or fewer inputs, ultimately conserving the environment. Applications of nanoscience and nanotechnology in materials science and biomass conversion technologies applied in agriculture are the basis of providing food, feed, fiber, fire and fuels. In the future, demand for food will increase tremendously while natural resources such as land, water and soil fertility are limited. The cost of production inputs like chemical fertilizers and pesticides is expected to increase at an alarming rate due to limited reserves of fuel such as natural gas and petroleum. In order to conquer these constraints, precision farming is a better option to reduce production costs and to maximize agricultural production. Through advancement in nanotechnology, a number of state-of-the-art techniques are available for the improvement of precision farming practices that will allow precise control at nanometer scale.

This book updates the subject matter, illustrations and problems to incorporate new concepts and issues related to the role of nanoscience in environmental conservation and agriculture.

Thanks are due to contributors from different institutions and publisher for their interest in this book. We hope this book will provide a multi-disciplinary forum to explore emerging areas in the field of Nanoscience, nanotechnology, agriculture, ecology, environmental science, pollution control and bioremediation.

–Editors

(envbooks@gmail.com)

Contents

Pages: 1-9

AGRICULTURE, ENVIRONMENT AND NANO-SCIENCE
Edited by: Dr. Pawan Kumar 'Bharti'
ISBN: 978-93-5056-760-9
Edition: 2015
Published by: Discovery Publishing House Pvt. Ltd., New Delhi (India)

1

Nanosensors for Environmental Analysis

E. Parameswari; V. Davamani
S. Paulsebastian[1] and A. Rathinasamy

ABSTRACT

Nanomaterials are at the edge of the rapidly developing field of nanotechnology. Their unique size-dependent properties make these materials superior and indispensable in many areas of human activity. However these properties related to low dimensions are more important than size. Nanotechnology is based on the fact that some very small structures usually have new properties and behavior that are not displayed by the bulk matter with the same composition. This paper introduces the main concepts behind the development of nanosensors and most relevant applications in the field of environmental analysis. The nano structures that are currently used in the development of nanosensors: nanoparticles, nanotubes, nanorods, embedded nanostructures, porous silicon and self assembled materials.

The detection mechanism works when the target molecule is bound to the receptor fragment. In this case, the population of conduction ion channels

Horticultural College and Research Institute, Periyakulam, Tamilnadu, (India).

[1] Dept.of Environmental Sciences, Tamil Nadu Agricultural University, Tamilnadu, (India).

pairs with in the membrane is altered and this changes the membrane conduction. With this biosensor, picomolar concentrations of proteins have been detected. Nanosensors have been used to detect small organic molecules at pico and femto molar analyte concentrations. The sensor is highly effective for detecting single and multilayered molecular assemblies.

Nanosized cantilevers can therefore detect up to attograms, but the aim is to detect the mass of individual molecules. Gold coated silicon cantilevers that measures 2-6 µm long, 50-100 nm thick and had resonance frequencies in the 1 to 6 MHz range, total mass of a few femto grams of 11 mercaptoundecanoic acid vapours that was chemisorbed on the surface of gold coated cantilevers was monitored in air.

Key words: Sensors, Carbon tube, Nanotechnology.

INTRODUCTION

Biology has entered a new era with the recent advances in nanotechnology,which have recently led the development of biosensor devices having nanoscale dimensions that are capable to prove the inner space of single living cells. Nanoscience and nanotechnology deal with the study and application of structures of matter with at least one dimension of the order of less than 100 nm (1 nm = 10^{-9} m). This is the standard way of classifying what belongs to the 'nano' world. However, properties related to low dimensions are more important than size. Nanotechnology is based on the fact that some structures usually smaller than 100 nm have new properties and behaviour that are not exhibited by the bulk matter of the same composition.

This is because particles that are smaller than the characteristic lengths associated with the specific phenomena often display new chemistry and new physics that lead to new properties that depend on size. Perhaps one of the most intuitive effects is due to the change in the surface/volume ratio. When the size of the structure is decreased, this ratio increases considerably and the surface phenomena predominate over the chemistry and physics in the bulk.

Nanosensors provide new and powerful tools for monitoring in vivo processes with in living cells, leading to new information on the inner working cells, leading to new information on the inner workings of the entire cell (Vo-Dinh, 2003). Such a systems biology approach could greatly improve our understanding of cellular function, there by revolutionizing cell biology. In this article, we discuss several nanostructures that are currently used in the development of nanosensors, nanoelectrodes and nanodevices. In particular we focus on the main nanostructures, i.e. nanoparticles, nanotubes and nanorods. In each section we first describe the type of nanomaterial used and explain the properties related to the nanostructure.

SENSORS BASED ON NANOPARTICLES AND NANOCLUSTERS

Nanoparticles (NPs) are clusters of a few hundred to a few thousand atoms that are only a few nanometres long. Because of their size, which is of the same order as the de Broglie wavelength associated with the valence electrons (following the wave-corpuscle duality principle, each particle can be described as a wave with wavelength λ), nanoparticles behave electronically as zero-dimensional quantum dots with discrete energy levels that can be tuned in a controlled way by synthesizing nanoparticles of different diameters.

In noble metals, nanostructures of smaller size than the de Broglie wavelength for electrons lead to an intense absorption in the visible/near-UV region that is absent in the spectrum of the bulk material. Fig. 1.1 Shows the sensing principle of LSPR sensors.

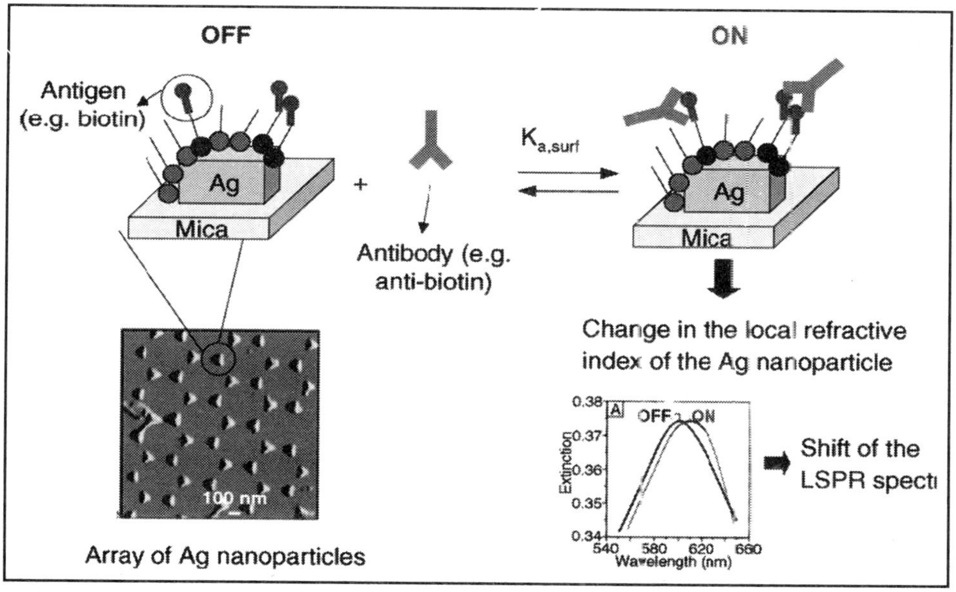

Fig. 1.1: Biosensing mechanism of silver pyramidal nanoparticle arrays using Localised Surface Plasmon Resonance to measure local changes in the refractive index of the Ag nanoparticles. (Riboh *et al.*, 2003)

The size-dependent properties of noble metal NPs have also been used for ion sensing. Liu *et al.* [2003] built a colorimetric nanosensor based on gold NPs functionalised with a Pb^{2+} dependent enzyme. The sensing principle is based on the change in colour from red to blue when gold NPs approach each other and aggregate. In the absence of Pb2+, the NPs assembled gradually. If the Pb^{2+} was present, the substrate was cleaved by the enzyme, thus inhibiting NP aggregation. Elghanian *et al.* [1997] had used the same principle for the colorimetric detection of polynucleotides.

The LSPR excitation of noble metal NPs also enhances local electromagnetic fields responsible for the intense signals observed in all surface-enhanced spectroscopies. For example, NPs made from silver and gold are known to enhance Raman light scattering by factors of up to 1014 [Fritzsche and Taton, 2003]. Cao *et al*. [2002] used surface enhancement Raman scattering (SERS) to tag DNA and RNA targets. This biosensor was based on 13 nm gold nanoparticles functionalised with both Raman-active dyes and oligonucleotides. The oligonucleotides attached to the NPs can be used to tag unlabelled complementary DNA and RNA targets. These tags can then be detected from the Raman scattering of the dye molecules. The authors were able to simultaneously distinguish six dissimilar DNA targets and two RNA targets. They reported that, because Raman spectral signals from the different dyes were so different, it was easy to image each dye bound to the same array separately. The detection limit of this sensor was 20 femtomolar. From the environmental point of view, this type of biosensor could be used to identify pathogens in water by functionalising the NPs with oligonucleotides that are complementary to the DNA sequences of the pathogens [Rodriguez-Mozaz *et al*., 2004].

SENSORS BASED ON NANOWIRES AND NANOTUBES

Carbon nanotubes (CNTs) are some of the most striking nanometric structures. These chemical compounds, whose structure is related to that of fullerenes, consist of concentric cylinders a few nanometres in diameter and up to hundreds of micrometres in length. These cylinders have interlinked hexagonal carbon rings. They were discovered in 1991 by the Japanese scientist Sumio Iijima [1991] in the soot resulting from an electrical discharge when using graphite electrodes in an argon atmosphere. One of commonest ways of producing carbon nanotubes is by means of hydrocarbon pyrolysis in the presence of a metallic catalyst (e.g. molybdenum, nickel or cobalt dust). This is known as chemical vapour deposition, or CVD. They can also be produced via the vaporisation of graphite in a furnace by laser in an argon atmosphere. These nanotubes may form bundles of strings of around 0.1mm in length or grow individually at catalytically selected points [Dresselhaus *et al*., 2001]. CNTs can be classified into single-walled carbon nanotubes (SWNT, for just one concentric cylinder) and multiple-walled carbon nanotubes (MWNT, for several concentric cylinders).

(a) Carbon nanotubes have a high length-to-radius ratio, which allows for greater control over the unidirectional properties of the materials produced.

(b) They can behave as metallic, semiconducting or insulating material depending on their diameter, their chirality, and any functionalisation or doping.

(c) They have a high degree of mechanical strength. In fact they have a greater mechanical strength and flexibility than carbon fibres.

(d) Their properties can be altered by encapsulating metals inside them to make electrical or magnetic nanocables or even gases, thus making them suitable for storing hydrogen or separating gases.

Murray *et al.* [2004] used silver mesowires prepared by electrochemical step edge decoration to investigate their behaviour as sensing devices in the presence of several gases. They found that the mesowires adequately detected qualitative amounts of NH3, that they can also be useful for detecting several amines (but with a slower response), and that their resistance does not change when they are exposed to CO, O_2, Ar, H_2O or hydrocarbons. Nanowires have also been synthesized from conducting polymers. Polyaniline/poly(ethylene oxide) (PANI/PEO) nanowires have also been used (deposited on lithographically defined microelectrodes) to design a NH_3 sensor. The similarity of the coordinative roles of nitrogen atoms in PANI and NH_3 gives rise to the affinity of the polymer for NH_3.

SENSORS BASED ON NANOSTRUCTURES EMBEDDED IN BULK MATERIAL

Several properties of nanoparticles are useful for applications in electrochemical sensors and biosensors but their catalytic behaviour is one of the most important. The high ratio of surface atoms with free valences to the total atoms has led to the catalytic activity of nanostructured material being used in electrochemical reactions. The catalytic properties of nanoparticles could decrease the overpotentials of electrochemical reactions and even provide reversibility of redox reactions, which are irreversible at bulk metal electrodes. Multilayers of conductive nanoparticles assembled on electrode surfaces produce a high porous surface with a controlled microenvironment. These structures could be thought of as assemblies of nanoelectrodes with controllable areas. latinum nanoparticles supported on materials such as porous arbon or noble metals such as gold are reported to be relevant in the design of gas diffusion electrodes [Hernandez-Santos *et al.*, 2002]. Fig. 1.2 shows the general method for constructing the multilayer Au-nanoparticle structures. The sensing mode of the devices based on modified nanoparticles is usually voltammetric.

Efficiency is therefore related to the concentration of the analyte at the surface of the electrode. Moreover, the sensors are limited to the redox-active analytes. The deposition of the nanoparticles linked to receptors on the ion-sensitive field effect transistors in away that is similar to that above for the NanoFETS and allows the detection of charged species. The exclusive properties of nanoparticles improve the performance of standard electrochemical methods. High current flows and sensitivities are attainable thanks to the conduction capacities combined with high surface areas.

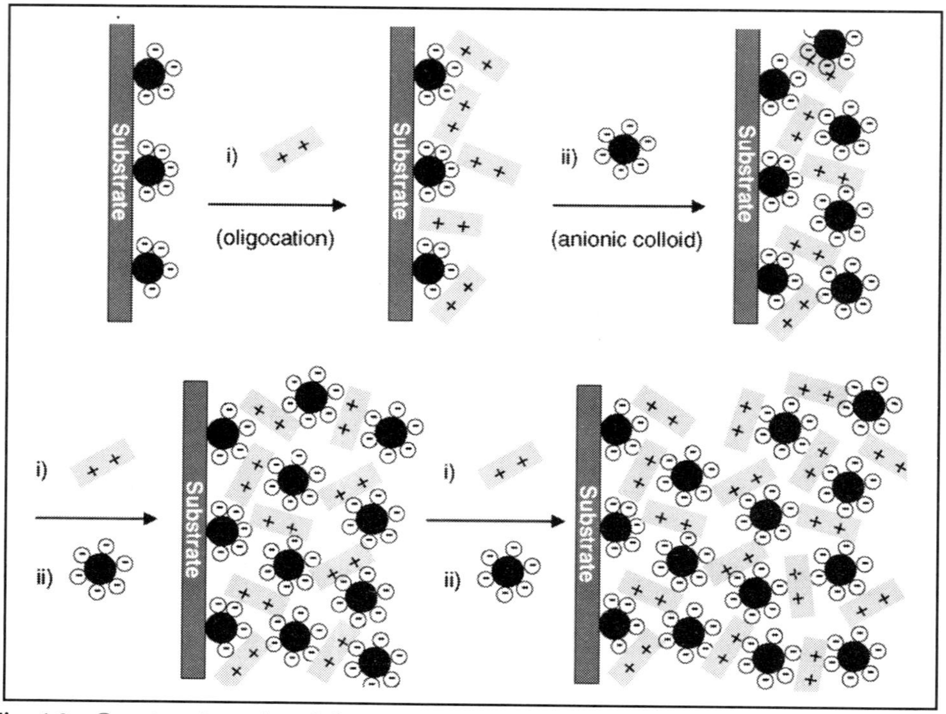

Fig. 1.2: Construction of multilayer Au-nanoparticle structures based on electrostatic interactions. The first layer of Au-nanoparticles is attached to the glass-siloxane surface. The various layers are then constructed using a positively charged cross-linker (step (i) in the upper figure). Cross-linkers may be anything from a small molecule (e.g. C60) to other nanoparticles, but they must bear multiple charges (Shipway *et al.*, 2000).

Simple Simple and highly-selective electroanalytical procedures can also be achieved by proper funtionalisation of nanoparticles. Finally, stable nanoparticles can substitute amplifying labels of limited stability, such as enzymes or liposomes, with equivalent or improved sensitivities [Katz *et al.*, 2004].

SENSORS BASED ON POROUS SILICON

When a silicon wafer is placed as the anode of an electrochemical cell and a current is passed through it in the presence of an ethanolic solution of fluorhydric acid, some Si atoms are dissolved and the remaining film material, similar to a sponge, is known as porous silicon. The porous material is a complicated network of silicon threads, each with a thickness in the 2-5 nm range. The dimensions of the pores range from a few nanometers to several microns. The result is a semiconductor material that displays an internal surface area-to-volume ratio of up to $500 m^2/cm^3$. The extremely tiny pores give the material a strong luminescence at room temperature. It is generally agreed that the light emission is due to quantum confinement effects, i.e. the spatial confinement of electron-hole pairs in nanometer-scale silicon particles that remain after etching [Vial *et al.*, 1992].

Steinem *et al.* [2004] reported the catalysed degradation of porous silicon by certain transition metal complexes is the basis for a new sensor principle in which the porous layer serves as matrix, transducer and signal amplification stage. Reflectance spectroscopy is used to monitor the degradation of the pores that takes place when the concentration of the metallic complex increases within the pore. To amplify the presence of the metal ions, receptors that recognize and bind to the metal-complexes are immobilized within the porous matrix. Contaminants, such as toxins or metallic ions in water samples, are detected by the blue shift in the Fabry-Perot fringe pattern and quick effective optical thickness decay.

NANOMECHANICAL SENSORS

Mass sensitive transducers are the basis of the different types of mechanical sensors such as quartz crystal microbalances and surface acoustic wave devices [Costello *et al.*, 1991]. The basic principle is that the resonance frequency changes when a mass is placed on the resonator. Although many applications are available, it is difficult to significantly improve their quality parameters at the macroscopic size. This can only be done when cantilever resonators are reduced to nanosize dimensions because the resonance frequency is proportional to the inverse of the linear dimension of the cantilever. Frequencies in the range of MHz are achieved in this way with cantilever sizes in the range of, μm and frequencies in the range of GHz can only be achieved at the nm scale. The change in the resonance frequency of the cantilever is proportional to the mass on the resonator. Nanosized cantilevers can therefore detect up to attograms, but the aim is to detect the mass of individual molecules.

As an example, Lavrik *et al.* [2003] obtained gold-coated silicon cantilevers that measured 2-6 _m long, 50-100 nm thick, and had resonance frequencies in the 1 to 6MHz range. A total mass of a few femtograms of 11-mercaptoundecanoic acid vapours that was chemisorbed on the surface of gold-coated cantilevers was monitored in air. Single-walled carbon nanotubes embedded in an epoxy resin have also been used as mechanical sensors because the position of the D* Raman band of SWNTs strongly depends on the strain transferred from the matrix to the SWNTs [Zhao *et al.*, 2002). This sensor was used to measure the stress field around an embedded glass fibre in a polymer matrix.

SELF-ASSEMBLED NANOSTRUCTURES

The nanostructures explained thus far have been developed following the top-down approach, i.e. starting with large-scale objects and gradually reducing its dimensions. Self-assembling tries to develop the nano and microstructures following the bottom-up procedure, i.e. from simple molecules to more complicated systems. Of the self-assembled structures, those using liposomes, polymerised lipid vesicles or pseudocellular membranes, are the most widely studied [Baeumner *et al.*, 2003]. In 1997 Cornell *et al.* [1997 and 1999] reported a bionanosensor that has been commercialised under the name of ion channel switch, ICSTM. This sensor is made up of a set of biomolecules that, mimicking nature very much, combine in such a way that the biochemical detection of an analyte is converted into an electrical signal. The biosensor is amperometric. An Au-coated support is the ionic conductor that is in contact with a reservoir to which sodium ions can only gain access through molecular channels made of gramicidin molecules. The gold electrode and the reservoir are isolated by a lipid bilayer membrane that contains gramicidin molecules. When the two dimers of the gramicidin coincide, the channel is activated and the sodium ions can flow through it, gain access to the reservoir and change the conductance of the sensor. The sensor works by relating the presence of the analyte to the alignment of the molecular channels and the presence of Na+ ions into the reservoir.

RECEPTOR-LIGAND NANOARRAYS

Nanoarrays are being developed based on the interaction between different types of receptors and ligands such as proteins or nucleic acids. Approximately 400 nanoarray spots can be placed in the same area as a traditional microarray spot. DNA biosensors are based on the immobilisation of a singlestranded nucleic acid sequence onto surface for hybridization ith an unknown target sequence. This DNA hybridisation typically occurs directly on the surface of an active signal transducer that produces a measurable signal, often in real time [Vercoutere and Akeson, 2002]. Depending on the transducer, DNA biosensors are grouped in evanescent or acoustic wave sensors, electrochemical sensors and optical sensors. Evanescent and acoustic wave sensors indirectly detect DNA hybridization by measuring physical properties changes such as the refractive index. Electrochemical biosensors measure current or resistance changes caused by the hybridisation of DNA probe molecules attached to an electrically active surface. Optic DNA biosensors measure fluorescence changes of DNA probes such as molecular beacons.

DNA biosensors have been applied in environmental analysis for the quantification of genes associated to numerous environmentally prominent pathogens, including *P. aerugniosa, Mycobacterium tuberculosis* and *Rhodococcus equi*. Molecular beacons have been also applied to pathogen detection but there is little literature published regarding with environmental applications. Harms et al. have recently applied molecular beacons to quantify nitrifying bacterial in a municipal wastewater treatment plant [Riu *et al.*, 2006].

CONCLUSION

We have discussed several types of existing nanosensors and their application in the field of environmental analysis, highlighting the relationship between the property monitored and the type of nanomaterial used. Although fundamental developments in the nanoscience field are still appearing, the well known effects arising only when the size of the structures is reduced are being applied to develop new sensing devices. Most of the reviewed nanostructures have successfully shown a great potential for being used in nanosensors, but the versatility and high applicability of nanoparticles and carbon nanotubes makes them clear candidates to be further used in nanosensors.

REFERENCES

A.J. Baeumner, R.N. Cohen, V. Miksic, J. Min, Biosens. Bioelectron , 18 (2003) 405.

Cao, Y.C., R. Jin, C.A. Mirkin, Science, 297 (2002): 1536.

Cornell, B., V. Braach-Maksvytis, L. King, P.D. Osman, B. Raguse, L.Wieczorek, R.D. Pace, Nature, 387 (1997): 580.

Cornell, B., V. Braach-Maksvytis, L. King, P.D. Osman, B. Raguse, L.Wieczorek, R.D. Pace, The Gramicidin-based Biosensor: A Functioning Nano-machine, in: D.J. Chadwick, G. Cardew (Eds.), Gramicidin and Related Ion Channel Forming Peptides, Wiley, London, 1999, p. 231.

Costello, B.J., S.W. Wenzel, R.M. White, Science, 251 (1991): 1372.

Dresselhaus, M.S., B. Dresselhaus, P.h. Avouris (Eds.), Carbon Nanctubes. Synthesis, Structure, Properties and Applications, Springer, Berlin, 2001.

Elghanian, R., J.J. Storhoff, R.C. Mucic, R.L. Letsinger, C.A. Mirkin, Science, 277 (1997): 1078.

Fritzsche, W., T.A. Taton, Nanotechnology, 14 (2003): 63.

Hernandez-Santos, D., M.B. Gonzalez-Garcia, A. Costa-Garcia, Electroanalysis, 14: (2002) 1225.

Iijima, S. Nature, 354 (1991); 56.

Katz, E., I. Willner, J. Wang, Electroanalysis, 16 (2004) 19.

Lavrik, N.V., P.G. Datskosa, Appl. Phys. Lett., 82 (2003): 2697.

Liu, J., Y. Lu, J. Am. Chem. Soc., 126 (2004): 12298.

Murray, B.J., E.C. Walter, R.M. Penner, Nano Lett., 4 (2004): 665.

Riboh, J.C., A.J. Haes, A.D. McFarland, C.R. Yonzon, R.P. Van Duyne, J. Phys. Chem., B 107 (2003): 1772.

Riu, J.,Maroto, A.F. Rius.X. Nanosensors in Environmental Analysis. Talanta, 69: (2006): 288.

Rodriguez-Mozaz, S., M.P. Marco, M.J. Lopez de Alda, D. Barcelo, Pure Appl. Chem., 76 (2004): 723.

Shipway, A.N., E. Katz, I. Willner, Chem. Phys. Chem. 1 (2000): 18.

Steinem, C., A. Janshoff, V.S. Lin, N.H. V¨olcker, M.R. Ghadiri, Tetrahedron, 60 (2004): 11259.

Vercoutere, W., M. Akeson, Chem. Biol., 6 (2002): 816.

Vial, J.C., A. Bsiesy, F. Gaspard, R. H´erino, M. Ligeon, F. Muller, R. Romestain, Phys. Rev., B 45 (1992): 14171.

Zhao, Q., M.D. Frogley, H.D. Wagner, Poym. Adv. Technol., 13 (2002): 759.

Pages: 10-46

AGRICULTURE, ENVIRONMENT AND NANO-SCIENCE

Edited by: Dr. Pawan Kumar 'Bharti'

ISBN: 978-93-5056-760-9

Edition: 2015

Published by: Discovery Publishing House Pvt. Ltd., New Delhi (India)

2

Bioprospecting of Extremophiles for Antimicrobials

E. Parameswari; V. Davamani; P. Kalaiselvi[1] and T. Anitha

ABSTRACT

Bioprospecting is the systematic search for valuable chemicals, genes and their products in living organisms. It is the intersection of biotechnological use and biodiversity conservation and comprehensive exploration of taxonomic space. Bioprospecting is nothing new, infact people have been bioprospecting since the dawn of civilization. Most of the potential bioprospecting is currently related to the study of microorganisms. Microorganisms can live almost every where and scientist expect that the study of microorganisms will lead to many new discoveries over the next few decades because they have realized that most of life on earth is microscopic. In fact there are more microorganisms by weight, by volume, by total number and by number of different species than all of the animals and plants put together. Current biological investigations have expanded our information into many habitats and among those are the

Horticultural College and Research Institute, Periyakulam,Tamilnadu, (India).

1 Department of Environmental Sciences, Tamil Nadu Agricultural University, Tamilnadu, (India).

extremophiles. Such microorganisms thrive in an endmost range of temperature levels, pH ranges, pressure, salinity, desiccation and other extreme conditions. Microorganisms from these severe environments may represent models for the origin of the first cells as well as a pattern for extra terrestrial life.

Only a small fraction of the chemicals made by microbes has been fully assessed for useful biological activity. It was argued that there was a real commercial value in retaining this unexplored biodiversity in order to preserve the valuable chemical diversity. The rate of discovery of novel metabolites from non-extreme, terrestrial microorganisms are decreasing and the emergence of multiple drug resistant bacterial infections creates a pressing need to develop new antimicrobial agents. Novel secondary metabolites including antibiotics from extremophiles are attracting the scientific attention in recent days.

INTRODUCTION

Bioprospecting is basically the search for commercially valuable biochemical and genetic resources in plants, animals and microorganisms. These resources may be used in food production, pest control, and the development of new drug and for other related biotechnological applications. Scientific research that looks for a useful application, process, or product in nature is called biodiversity prospecting, or bioprospecting. Biodiversity prospecting is nothing new. In fact, people have been bioprospecting since the dawn of civilization. Bioprospecting began when prehistoric people noticed that one plant root tasted better than another, or that some plants could be used as medicines. Later, scientists identified the active ingredients in these plants. People learned that the delicious plant root had higher sugar content, or they discovered that a plant used for medicine contained aspirin (salicylic acid).

Today, scientists continue to find useful applications for compounds from nature but their search methods have changed. Biochemists analyze plants, microorganisms, and other living things, but many of the things they work with are too small even to be seen with a microscope, so they use chemicals to perform experiments. Many of these new discoveries are enzymes, biological molecules that are like catalysts for chemical reactions.

Sometimes, the only way to obtain a useful organic compound is to harvest the organism that contains it. For instance, insulin is a hormone vital to human digestion. Many people with diabetes must take insulin as a medicine. Pharmaceutical manufacturers use genetic engineering techniques to produce insulin from microbial livestock. They use bacteria specially bred for lab use, much like a smaller version of the white lab mouse. Molecular biologists can also make compounds by identifying the gene in a wild organism that controls production of that compound. The compound-producing gene is inserted into lab bacteria and as the bacteria grow, they produce more of the compound, which humans can then use. Most of the potential bioprospecting is, currently related to the study of microorganisms. Microorganisms can live almost everywhere, including the bottom of the ocean, in Antarctica's ice, and in the boiling pools in Yellowstone National Park. Scientists expect that the study of microorganisms will lead to many new discoveries over the next few decades because they have realized that most life on Earth is microscopic. In fact, there are more microorganisms by weight, by volume, by total number and by number of different species than all of the animals and plants put together.

BIOPROSPECTING

The New Thrust Areas Under Bioprospecting

- Bioprospecting of novel genes, biomolecules and enzymes.

  Bioprospecting programme would focus on the entire bioresources including higher plants, microbes, fungi and lichens. The thrust could be on different agro climatic regions including Hot Spots, Temperate, coastal and Desert (both Arid and Cold) region. Priority areas identified for prospecting area are.
- Production of biomolecules for industrial and medicinal use.
- Novel genes/promoters to address biotic and abiotic stress.
- Genes for transcription factors.
- Metabolic Engineering pathways
- Nutritional Enhancement
  - Bioavailability of elements
  - Crop Improvement including proteins, fats and carbohydrates
- Microbial biodiversity

To study the community genomics and prospect for new enzymes and molecules.

Convention on Biological Diversity

The Convention on Biological Diversity (CBD) has three objectives: the conservation of biodiversity, the sustainable use of its components, and the fair and equitable sharing of the benefits from the use of genetic resources (UNEP 1992, Article 1). The CBD can, to a large extent, be seen as a result of a 'Coleman exchange' between countries of the North and the South as two actors controlling and having interests in opposite items. Bioprospecting has been defined as "the exploration of biodiversity for commercially valuable genetic and biochemical resources". The idea of bioprospecting was first presented by Thomas Eisner (1991) and then entitled 'chemical prospecting'. Bioprospecting is abbreviated from 'biodiversity prospecting'– a term widely dispersed by Reid *et al.* 1993. 'Pharmaceutical prospecting' and 'genetic prospecting' are related terms.

Brief History of Bioprospecting

To alleviate the loss of the flora and fauna of our planet, at the U.N. Earth Summit in Rio de Janeiro, Brazil, the Convention on Biological Diversity (CBD) was opened for signature on June 5, 1992. Objectives of the CBD are (*a*) the conservation of biodiversity, (*b*) the sustainable use of its components, and (*c*) the equitable sharing of the benefits resulting from the commercial use of genetic resources.Perhaps the most critical component of the CBD for biodiversity-rich countries is sovereignty over bioresources by nation states, as the treaty recognizes their right to regulate and charge outsiders for access to their biodiversity. No longer are biotic resources considered "common heritage," the pre-CBD paradigm that provided open access to bioresources. The "grand bargain" of the CBD is to balance how all interest groups involved can gain from the use of biodiversity by recognizing the economic, sociocultural, and environmental values of bioresources and the costs of preserving them. Since the CBD was introduced nine years ago, however, few of the 178 signatory nations have introduced legislation requiring benefit sharing for access to their national bioresources by outsiders with commercial interests.

At the same time, commercial users of bioresources voluntarily attempt to comply with convention provisions in order to gain access to the raw bioresources that can be developed into products. These arrangements to explore biological diversity for commercially valuable genetic and biochemical resources have come to be called biodiversity prospecting or bioprospecting. Although the unfortunate term suggests a new form of biocolonial appropriation, with all its attendant controversy, it has, nevertheless, become the most-used term for these transactions.

The commercial collecting of biological species is certainly not new, but their value has increased owing to the demand for genetic and biochemical raw materials for biotech products. Bioprospecting products include pharmaceuticals, botanical medicines, agribiotech, horticulture,cosmetics, and personal care products. Agribiotech is briefly reviewed here, but only in relationship to pharmaceuticals because it generates a different set of policy debates, such as biosafety and world food security.

Overview of Biological Prospecting Trends Elsewhere

General industry trends in bioprospecting and biotechnology provide some indication as to the likely future of biological prospecting activities.

General Industry Trends

Industry sectors involved in bioprospecting include biotechnology, agriculture, pharmaceuticals,and cosmetics. All of these sectors are increasingly using biotechnology to develop new products. Although every sector relies upon natural processes in different ways, some general observations are relevant. Development of commercial products from naturally occurring genetic resources or biochemical processes is typically a long, expensive,and uncertain process.

The accounting firm Ernst & Young publishes the most respected survey of the biotechnology sector annually. In its most recent survey, it concluded that the biotechnology industry continues to experience significant growth despite the downturn in global market. According to the report, the global biotech industry comprises 4,284 companies (622 public; 3,662 private) in 25 nations. In 2001, the 622 public companies generated revenues of $35 billion, spent $16 billion in R&D and employed more than 188,000 people. While seventy-two per cent of the public company revenues were generated by companies in the US, emerging biotech sectors in Europe, Canada, and the Asia/Pacific region have experienced significant growth in the number of companies as new technologies increasingly make their way from research labs into privately funded enterprises.

Quantifying the contribution that natural genetic resources make to this market is difficult for many reasons. Figures, for example, are often difficult to obtain due to the competitive nature of product development. Moreover, the contribution made by natural biochemical processes is frequently only one of many aspects leading to the final product. Nevertheless, the magnitude of the commercial use of biodiversity can be illustrated by considering some examples:

- Annual sales derived from traditional knowledge using genetic resources are US$ 3 billion for the cosmetic and personal care industry, US$ 20 billion for the botanical medicine sector, and US$ 75 billion for the pharmaceutical industry.
- Sixty–two per cent of cancer drugs approved by the US Food and Drug Administration are of natural origin or modelled on natural products.

Bioprospecting Stakeholders

During the decade since the CBD was introduced, the treaty has catalyzed new relationships. Biodiversity-rich countries, indigenous societies with their knowledge of the use of such bioresources as medicines, and companies that seek to discover new therapeutics through medicinal plants and indigenous knowledge now share common interests, and, often, conflicts.

Governments and their Agencies

Most biodiversity-rich countries are located in the tropics of the south, but technology- rich countries, with resources to develop biodiversity, are primarily in the temperate north. Most southern nations are burdened with poverty, oppressive external debt, impoverished university systems,and a dearth of scientists and technology. Few have been able to collect, identify, inventory, and screen their rich biological assets, let alone develop them into products. Thus, the CBD allows northern interests to access the biodiversity of southern countries through commitments to share the technology and benefits that arise from its commercial use. It is the responsibility of each CBD contracting party to devise a national biodiversity policy to document how this will work in their country, including a legal framework to implement it.Because many countries now have only a patchwork of legal provisions, such as collecting or export permits, the International Union for the Conservation of Nature, theWorld Conservation Union, recently published a guide (Glowka 1998). The United Nations Development Programme also offers CBD nations a guide, which includes case studies from the Democratic Republic of Congo, the Sultanate of Oman, the Republic of Niger, and the province of Quebec. Although the U.S. Senate has yet to ratify the CBD, the government is active in a multicountrybioprospecting programme in which conservation and development goals are linked to the bioprospecting process. Three federal agencies, the National Institutes of Health, the National Science Foundation, and the Department of Agriculture, support the programme, called the International Cooperative Biodiversity Groups (ICBG), in 12 developing countries, the United States and the United Kingdom.

BIOPROSPECTING AND BIOTECHNOLOGY

Bioprospecting, defined as the systematic search for valuable, molecules, genes and organisms in nature, has the potential to developing countries a means to use biodiversity without disrupting nature; to add value to their natural resources; to ensure that such resources are protected and used in a sustainable manner; and to build the necessary skills to apply biotechnology in improving quality of life. Today, important developments in biotechnology are rapidly generating new financial opportunities derived from the use of biological resources. However, such biotech opportunities that impact on managing the economy and the environment will in this century depend on how issues between biotechnology and biodiversity are treated and implemented within the principles of the Convention on Biological Diversity (CBD).Because of its nature, bioprospecting is at the intersection of biodiversity conservation and the use of biotechnology and thus has consequences in the areas of legal and regulatory frameworks; technology transfer and business development; intellectual property rights and facilitation of local, national and international collaborations.

Microbial Biodiversity

Microbes, including bacteria, archaea, and fungi, are the world's most genetically diverse organisms. Indeed, these prokaryotic domains and lower eukaryotes house the vast majority of phylogenetic and metabolic diversity and are found in every ecosystem. Through billions of years of natural selection in dissimilar environments, microbes have developed broader and more varied characteristics than those observed in plants or animals. The uniqueness of many of these microbes enables the existence and evolution of larger flora and fauna that have been traditionally preserved under biodiversity efforts. In addition to silently enabling and supporting life for larger plants and animals, microorganisms have already been proven to hold the keys to advances in human health, improvements in industrial processes, and a variety of other beneficial applications.Often the microorganisms found in extreme environments, extremophiles, provide the diversity required for these applications. The microbes are found in forbidding environments where little else lives, in such diverse and harsh environments as the thermal vents at the bottom of the Atlantic Ocean, the bellies of termites in Costa Rica, translucent stones in the dry desert valleys of Antarctica, and soils contaminated with polychlorinated biphenyls (PCBs) in Russia. Because of their ability to live in harsh environments,extremophiles are increasingly used in industrial processes.

Microbial Biodiversity and Technology

Recent advances in biotechnology allow target compounds from environmental samples to be identified much more rapidly. Traditionally, microorganisms are isolated and cultured in laboratories, a process that requires scientists to recreate the environments in which the target microbe lives. Partly because extreme environments are too difficult to replicate in the laboratory, many of these microorganisms remain unstudied. It is estimated that only approximately 1% of the world's billion plus microbial species have been studied (Marshall 2000).

Table 2.1: Microbial Challenge

Habitat	Cultured (%)
Seawater	0.001-0.1
Freshwater	0.25
Soil	0.3
Activated Sludge	1.0-15.0

Amann *et al.*, 1995

The genomic approach, in which DNA is isolated directly from environmental samples without culturing, holds the promise of accessing a larger percentage of microorganisms currently unavailable.it provide access to more microorganisms is possible than traditional approach.

Table 2.2: The Traditional vs. Genomic Approach

	Traditional Approach	Genomic Approach
Methodology	Culturing Direct	DNA Isolation
Characteristics	Slow and Limited	Fast and Novel
Results	104 Organisms	> 2 X 106 Genomes

Microbial Biodiversity as an Asset

Given the benefits provided by microbes known to us, if we speculate about the unlocked economic and scientific potential of the 99% of unstudied microbes, it is clear that this rich diversity has enormous value (even more value is created due to their constant and rapid evolution). Because of the vast potential that microbial biodiversity holds, its preservation and sustainable use seem a foregone conclusion. But in the case of biodiverse resources, "the absence of apparent value combined with absent or poorly defined property rights creates a problem of over exploitation and unregulated use" (OECD 2002).

Bioprospecting of Biodiversity

Bioprospecting is a targeted exploration and search for as yet undiscovered chemical compounds, genes and their products within wild species and biological organisms for a certain use with potential for commercial development. Bioprospecting is linked to conservation of biodiversity by sharing part of the benefits with the caretakers of the wild bio-resources.

Bioprospecting, often downstream screening, testing and development activities following discovery of a potentially useful substance, gene or organism.

Biotechprospecting of biodiversity for new medicines involves:

1. **Discovery:** Identification and collection of material by random, bio-rational and traditional (medicinal) approaches, followed by screening for particular bio-activities,and elucidation of novel molecular form.
2. **Intellectual property rights:** Protection of intellectual property through patenting of new genes and/or bioactive principles with novel antibiotic, insecticidal or anti-tumour properties.
3. **Process technology:** Isolation, synthesis and purification of new bioactive chemicals for laboratory, clinical and field trials to demonstrate and compare the effectiveness and bio safety of the newly discovered product with contemporary market products.
4. **Manufacturing and Marketing Strategies:** Development of techniques for larger scale industrial production of the final bioactive product and its market availability and accessibility to the public.

Bioprospecting – the hope

Pharmaceutical drugs currently have annual sales exceeding $200 billion. It has been estimated that over 25% of the drugs sold in the developed world and 75% in the less developed countries (LDCs) are based on chemicals made by organisms. These two facts have been given considerable emphasis by those seeking to put the case for conserving biodiversity. Noting that only a small fraction of the chemicals made by plants or microbes has been fully assessed for useful biological activity, it was argued that there was a real commercial value in retaining this unexplored biodiversity in order to preserve the valuable chemical diversity.

During the 1990s there was evidence of renewed interest in screening natural products. The pharmaceutical companies were not alone in renewing their interest in screening chemicals from the natural world. The National Cancer Institute (NCI) had screened 200000 extracts of organisms for anticancer activity in the period 1955-1980, with such limited success that they had turned their attention instead to 'rational drug design.' However, the introduction of improved screening methods (much higher throughputs, lower costs and targeting more specific biological targets) encouraged the NCI to begin screening biological samples again in 1986. By 1995 the NCI had produced 40000 extracts for screening and of the 18000 screened for anticancer activity about 1% showed some positive activity. The health-conscious, rich countries might be willing to pay the less developed countries for access to their biodiversity. Discussions about bioprospecting moved on to consider issues of equity.

Bioprospecting – the Reality

- Drug development is more than drug discovery
- Scientific drug discovery is essentially a reductionist extension of herbalism but with one crucial difference. Humans can make chemicals to supplement those that occur naturally.

Drug discovery at its initial phase is thus composed of two parts:

- obtaining chemical samples,
- testing the samples for a useful biological effect (often called 'screening').

However, the discovery of a potentially useful biological activity by screening is only the first step of a lengthy, expensive process. Each of the following questions must be addressed:

- Will the drug be safe to use? (e.g. are there adverse side effects due to the chemical having more than one effect?)
- Is the drug clinically useful? (e.g. does the effect found in the test tube translate into a positive outcome for the patient?)
- Can the chemical be extracted, synthesised or produced by fermentation on an industrial scale economically?
- Can the drug and its derivatives be adequately protected by patents?
- Is the market big enough to repay the typical. $500 million development costs for the drug?

Bioprospecting must thus be seen not as an independent process but as a contributor to a larger activity. The fact that so many large, successful pharmaceutical and agrochemical companies spend much more on making and screening synthetic chemicals than they do on isolating and testing natural products suggests that bioprospecting must bring with it disadvantages as well as advantages.

Bioprospecting – the Science

Why do some organisms make the kind of chemicals that, humans sometimes find useful as drugs ?

There are known to be hundreds of thousands of chemicals made by plants and microbes. Every species of plant or the microbe makes its own unique mix of such chemicals. This rich chemical diversity is apparent in the foods we eat daily. Secondary metabolites or natural products were being made because they possessed a biological activity that enhanced the fitness of the producer (Demain 1995). For example, a soil microbe making an antibiotic could have more exclusive access to resources for its growth if it could inhibit competing bacteria. Likewise, a plant making an insecticide could outperform its competitors if it was less susceptible to insect attack. The appealing concept of a 'chemical arms race' between organisms became the dominant paradigm. It followed from this concept that every plant or microbe would contain some potent biologically active substances. Consequently, plants and microbes should be excellent sources of potent biologically active substances that could have great value to humans. However, this paradigm is now being undermined by data that ironically come from the pharmaceutical and agrochemical industries.

Screening Programmes

After the discovery of penicillin, hundreds of thousands of microbial cultures were screened for their ability to produce antibiotics – the first era of large-scale bioprospecting had begun. The ready availability of soil samples, the ease of culturing at least some microbes from each sample and the simplicity of testing for antibiotic activity made such a large-scale screening viable, despite the very low success rate in finding useful biological activity. However, this huge effort yielded rather fewer antibiotics than predicted by the chemical arms race model.

METHODS OF BIOPROSPECTING

The biotechnological resource provided by extremophiles (e.g. antimicrobials, biopharmaceutins, agrichemicals, biocatalysts) is unique and far from being exhausted. Recent screening efforts focused on extremophiles have revealed many new chemical entities and bioactive metabolites (Fiedler et al., 2004) with a discovery rate that surpasses that of terrestrial microorganisms.The discovery of exploitable extremophile biology founded on culturedependent, culture-independent, or bioinformatics approaches (Bull 2004b). Our culture based strategy is summarised in Figure 2.1 the salient features of which are as follows:

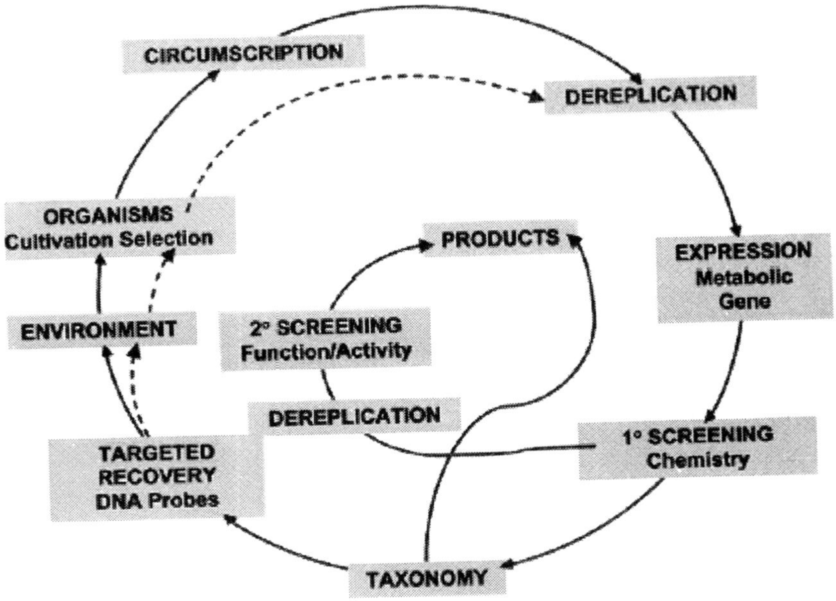

Fig. 2.1: A Culture-dependent Bioprospecting Strategy

(1) isolation from a wide compass of environments and geographic sites using taxon-selective media and sample retreatments; (2) preliminary circumscription of isolates based on macroscopic characters (e.g.spore colour grouping); (3) dereplication of the strain collections in order to avoid redundancy in screening; dereplication thresholds may be set in order to recover organisms of a prescribed taxonomic rank, (e.g intraspecific genetic diversity) using chemometric (e.g. PyMS, FT-IR) or molecular (e.g. SSCP, T-RFLP, rep-PCR) techniques; (4) expression/detection of the sought-after property in dereplicated strain libraries using fermentation protocols designed to maximize gene expression, or, gene probes; (5) primary screening of fermentation broths, for example, to define metabolite profiles (e.g. use of DAD-HPLC, Fiedler et al. 2004); (6) dereplication, if appropriate, by reference to chemical databases in order to identify metabolite novelty; and (7) secondary screening for sought-after activities using, for example, bioassay protocols. Our usual practice is to make full taxonomic characterisation (polyphasic taxonomy) only when an organism produces a successful 'hit', such characterisation then offers the option of designing specific DNA probes that can be used to identify related organisms that can be entered into the screening campaign.

Figure 2.2 depicts some of the opportunities afforded by a culture-independent approach to bioprospecting. The bioprospecting processes involves the following stages: (1) extraction of the total bacterial DNA from the environment; (2) clone into surrogate host systems; (3) primary detection of the target gene or gene cluster; (4) gene sequencing and replication by reference to appropriate sequence database(s); and (5) expression of the target gene/gene cluster and characterisation of the sought-after activity or other property. Optimisation of the latter stage might, for example, include co-expression of chaperonin genes as a means of enhancing production or the solubility of an expressed gene product. It may also be possible to identify the source of the target gene/gene cluster either by reference to databases, or by sequencing co-extracted 16S rRNA genes.

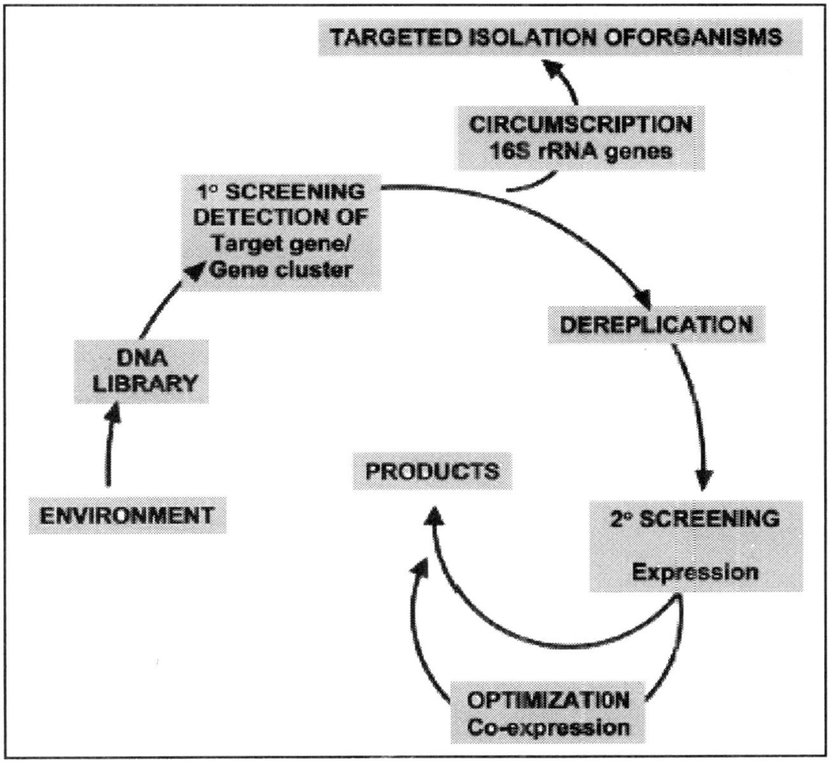

Fig. 2.2: A Culture-independent Bioprospecting Strategy

The challenge is to determine if and how chemical diversity and biodiversity are distributed at taxonomic levels (species, infraspecies) with the aim of establishing predictive rather than random search strategies. Ward and Good fellow caution that progress towards this goal is confounded by various factors: (1) the log-normal distribution of microbial diversity implies that most diversity will reside in rare organisms; (2) a very high proportion of microbial diversity currently is uncultivated; (3) microbial diversity is distributed heterogeneously in environments, space, and time; (4) microbial and chemical diversity may (to an unknown extent) be uncoupled due to lateral gene transfer; and (5) current procedures for eliciting gene expression are deficient. Nevertheless, these authors opine that improvements in taxonomic resolution and in procedures for detecting natural product diversity should lead to predictive patterns of biodiversity and chemo diversity and they illustrate the current position by reference to biomarkers and the taxonomic distribution of natural products in extremophiles.

Empirical routes to the discovery of novel microbial diversity (Bull 2004c), a bioinformatics approach is being developed in taxonomic space can be identified and subsequently explored. The argument for designing new ways to discover exploitable biology runs as follows: (1) big numbers and serendipity are insufficient to deliver new drugs and other products, therefore (2) greater emphasis needs to be placed on compound quality rather than compound quantity; and because (3) natural products present unrivalled chemical diversity; it follows that (4) novel natural chemistry is likely to be found in novel microorganisms. The extent of unexplored bacterial diversity in the environment is indisputable.

EXTREMOPHILES

An extremophile is an organism, usually unicellular, which thrives in or requires "extreme" conditions. The definition of "extreme" is anthropocentric; to the organism itself its environment is completely normal. Thus, strictly, "extremophilic" labels should be used to describe the environment that an organism thrives in, regardless of how "normal" or "extreme" they may seem to human beings. For example, human beings are classified as a mesophilicaerobe.When used in the context of describing organisms that thrive in environments that are extreme from human perspectives, most extremophiles are members of the Archaea family, although the terms are occasionally used interchangeably to describe the many extremophilic bacteria and eukarya. Not all extremophiles are unicellular. Examples of extremophilicmetazoa are the psychrophilic Grylloblattodea (insects) and antarctic krill (crustaceans).

Micro-organisms not only growing under but requiring unusual, thus extreme, environmental conditions for growth are grouped together under the term extremophiles. They come in all kinds of forms. Many of them cannot even survive under what we call, from an anthropogenic point of view, 'normal conditions', i.e. conditions conducive to the human physiology and for most of the micro-organisms associated with humans, which are mesophilicneutrophilic micro-organisms.

Nearly all presently known physiological types are represented among the extremophiles, e.g. phototrophs, organoheterotrophs, chemo-organotrophs and hemolithoautotrophs.With respect to microbial diversity, the word on what the prevalent microbial living conditions are is still undecided.This is because (i) we assume that we only know and can culture around 1-2% of the probably existing species and (ii) the diversity of microorganisms in the huge environments of the deep cold ocean or deep subsurface with oligotrophic growth conditions are very little explored. However, according to Whitman et al (1998) these servoirsharbour the highest numbers of microbial cells. The mesophiles associated with humans, animals and to some extent with plants have captured most of the attention in the past, despite the fact that some extremophiles have been used for decades in leather making, dye making and food-fermenting processes. Yet only during the last 10-15 years have various extremophiles, especially (hyper) thermopiles, entered more into mainstream research in microbiology and biochemistry.

Most extremophiles are microorganisms that thrive under conditions that from a human perspective are clearly extreme. RD MacElroy first coined the term 'extremophile', in a 1974 paper entitled 'Some comments on the evolution of extremophiles'. From the mid 1970s, increasing numbers of these novel microorganisms have been isolated as researchers have acknowledged that extreme environments are capable of sustaining biological life. Studies on extremophiles have progressed to the extent that there are now regular international extremophile symposia, as well as dedicated scientific journals: Extremophiles and Archaea.

The importance of extremophile research to biology should not be underestimated. It is only through the search for and elucidation of extremophilic microorganisms that we have the universal phylogenetic tree proposed by Woese in 1996 (Figure 2.3). Molecular studies of RNA sequences from the extremophilic Archaea (formerly Archaebacteria) showed that these microorganisms were distinct from bacteria, giving rise to the three domains of life that exist today: Bacteria, Archaea and Eucarya. Ground breaking research on extremophiles continues to this day, with the recently discovered 22nd genetically encoded amino acid – pyrrolysine – from the archaeon, *Methanosarcinabarkeri.*

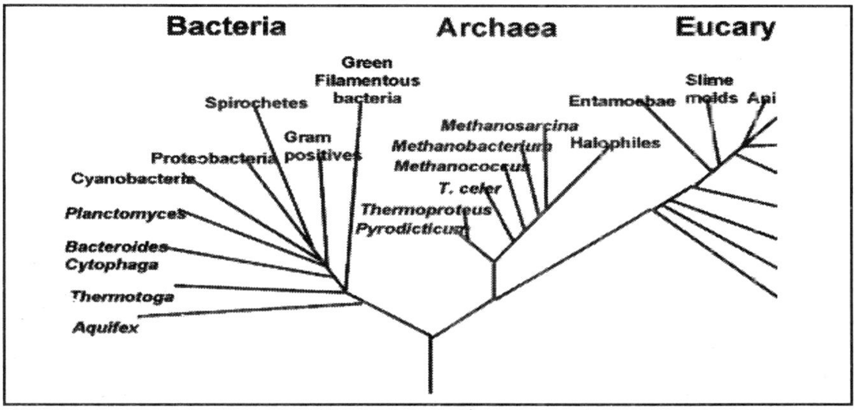

Fig. 2.3: The Universal Phylogenetic Tree Proposed by Woese in 1996

What is an extremophile?

Extremophiles thrive in extreme environments where no other microorganisms are found, including high temperature, pH, pressure and salt concentration; or low temperature, pH, nutrient conceration, or water availability. Some extremophiles can tolerate extremely high levels of radiation or toxic compounds.

A vast number of extremophiles belong to a newly defined domain of life, the Archaea, and the term 'extremophile' is often used synonymously with them. Some Archaea live near rift vents in the deep sea at temperatures well over 100°C. Others live in hot springs, or in extremely alkaline or acid waters. More recently, scientists have also found bacteria in these extreme environments. Indeed, the ratio of thermophilic bacteria to Archaea was 50 to 1 in a range of samples taken from Yellowstone Park's Obsidian Pool, which is high in hydrogen sulphide, iron, hydrogen and carbon dioxide.

Obsidian's Pool, Yellowstone Park

TYPES OF EXTREMOPHILES

There are many different classes of extremophiles; each corresponding to the way its chosen environment differs from what is considered "normal" by other organisms. These classifications are not exclusive. Many extremophiles fall under multiple categories. For example, organisms living inside hot rocks deep under Earth's surface are both thermophilic and barophilic.

Acidophile: An organism with an optimum pH level at or below pH 3.

Aerobe: requires O_2 to survive.

Alkaliphile: An organism with optimal growth at pH levels of 9 or above.

Anaerobic: does not need O_2 to survive.

Endolith: An organism that lives inside rocks.

Halophile: An organism requiring at least 0.2M of NaCl for growth.

Hypolith: An organism that lives inside rocks in cold deserts.

Mesophile: An organism that thrives in temperatures between 15-60 °C.

Metalotolerant: capable of tolerating high levels of heavy metals, such as copper, cadmium, arsenic, and zinc.

Microaerophilic: requires levels of O_2 that are lower than atmospheric levels.

Oligotroph: An organism capable of growth in nutritionally limited environments.

Piezophile: An organism that lives optimally at high hydrostatic pressure.

Psychrophile: An organism that can thrive at temperatures of 15 °C or lower.

Radioresistant: resistant to high levels of ionizing radiation.

Thermophile: An organism that can thrive at temperatures between 60-80 °C.

Xerotolerant: requires very little water to survive.

Important Extremophiles

- **Thermophile:** An organism having a growth temperature optimum of 50°C or higher. In the case of hyperthermophiles the optimum may between 80°C and 110°C.
- **Halophile:** An organism requiring at least 0.2 M (3-30%) salt for growth.
- **Psychrophile:** An organism having a growth temperature optimum of 15°C or lower, (some can survive at –10°C), and are unable to grow above 20°C.
- **Alkaliphile:** An organism with optimal growth at pH values above 10.
- **Acidophile:** An organism with a pH optimum for growth at, or below, pH 2.
- **Piezophile:** (previously termed barophile) an organism that lives optimally at high hydrostatic pressure.

Also micro-organisms growing at high concentrations of heavy metal ions, under high doses of Gammaand UV radiation, high solvent concentrations or very low-water-activity conditions, i.e. dry-resistant microorganisms from the desert, are regarded as extremophiles. We maintain furthermore that bacteria that can grow extremely fast with doubling times below 15 min ('hyperauxanophiles' i.e. significantly faster than *Escherichia coli*) should be regarded also as extremophiles. Examples include some of the alkalithermophiles with doubling times around 10 min or the neutrophilic marine mesophile *Vibrio natriegans* with doubling times below 10 min. In other words what is 'normal' for *E. coli* and similar micro-organisms is extreme for the extremophiles and vice versa. Thus mesophilic and neutrophilic conditions and atmospheric pressure are just physicochemical parameters in the 'middle of the road'.

Extremophiles in Space

By definition, most of the habitats on Earth are not extreme. Extremophiles are the exception, rather than the rule. And yet when we search the solar system for biology, we expect that if there are alien life-forms nearby, they will most likely be analogs to Earth's extremophiles. This is simply because, whether you're talking about aquifers beneath the cold, ultraviolet-stung sands of Mars, or the deep, salty seas of Europa, you're describing environments as brutal as Green Bay's defensive line. Most of your local flora and fauna would perish straight-away in these nasty niches. But Earth's extremophiles some of them could be transplanted to such otherworldly habitats and never look back.The question is less whether *survival* in the hypothesized ecological recesses of Mars and a few of Jupiter and Saturn's moons is possible – that seems more than likely – but whether it could arise in the first place. The fact that extremophiles may be our oldest living relatives here on Earth suggests that these highly specialized organisms can appear quickly, and do so in the hellish environments that would exist on many young solar system worlds.

It is, in fact, currently fashionable to argue that life on Earth may have begun, not in Charles Darwin's "warm little pond," but in a seething, scalding and turbulent sub-ocean geyser, where chemical reactions run fast and hard. This, of course, is a habitat that thermophiles are pleased to call home. In the 1970s, DNA studies revealed that thermophiles branched off early from the tree of life, and that they are as old as any creatures we know. This is obviously compatible with the view that they were the first sort of life to arise. After all, although naturally boiling water is confined to only a few places on Earth today, there was a time, more than 3-1/2 billion years ago, when our planet was laced with seething, sizzling caldrons. The earliest life might well have had to be capable of hanging tough in a tough and sweaty world. Thermophiles might have paved the way for today's millions of species.

Thermophiles

Microbes that reproduce and grow in the temperature range 40 to 70°C (104 to 158°F). A key thermophilic adaptation of an organism is the presence of heat stable proteins. These proteins are more densely packed to exclude internal water, are more hydrophobic, have more salt bridges, and have more saturated and longer chained fatty acids. Thermophilicarchaea have ether-linked, branched chain fatty acids that are more hydrophobic still. Capable of thriving at even higher temperatures than thermophiles are hyperthermophiles.

Table 2.3: Microbes, Temperature Ranges

Four categories of microbes are recognized according to the temperature range in which they can reproduce and grow:

Type of Microbe	Minimum. °C (°F)	Maximum. °C (°F)
Psychrophile	-10 (14)	20 (68)
Mesophile	10 (50)	50 (122)
Thermophile	40 (104)	70 (158)
Hyperthermophile	60 (140)	115 (239)

Prokaryotic Thermophiles

Microbes that reproduce and grow at very high temperatures, in the range 60 to 113°C (140 to 235°F). The first to be identified, *Sulfolobusacidocaldarius*, which is both a hyperthermophile and an acidophile, was found in the late 1960s in a hot, acidic spring in Yellowstone National Park, Wyoming. Since then, more than 50 hyperthermophiles have been isolated. The majority are archaea, although some cyanobacteria and anaerobic photosynthetic bacteria grow well at 70 to 75°C (158 to 167°F). The most heat-resistant of all known hyperthermophiles are the anaerobic archaea, including members of the genuses *Pyrolobus*, *Pyrodictium*, and *Pyrococcus*. For example, *Pyrolobusfumarii*, of the Crenarchaeota, a nitrate-reducing chemolithotroph (an organism that derives energy from minerals), grows on the walls of marine hydrothermal vents ("smokers"). It multiplies best at about 105°C (221°F), can reproduce at up to 113°C (235°F) and stops growing in "cooler" environments below 90°C (194°F).

Eukaryaotic Thermophiles

The best studied high-temperature eukaryote is the acidophilic phototroph *Cyanidium caldarium*. Its exact taxonomic affiliations are still unclear, but it is generally grouped with the "red algae" (rhodophytes) since its chloroplasts possess chlorophyll-a and C-phycocyanin. The growth and ecology of this organism and determined its optimal growth temperature was 45°C and the maximum temperature at which growth occurred was 57°C. Earlier reports of growth at much higher temperatures, Brock and his colleagues to either the measurement of temperature away from the organisms themselves, or to the temperature having increased and the organisms being observed in the process of dying. It is interesting to note that Brock isolated numerous strains of *Cyanidium caldarium* growing at various temperatures and found that they all had the same optimum growth temperature: that is, they do not seem to have formed strains adapted to growth at higher temperatures. It is also interesting to note that the niche occupied by *Cyanidium*, of hot acid conditions, does not seem to have any competition for the available resources in that thermophilic cyanobacteria require alkaline conditions for growth.

Psychrophiles

Microbes that reproduce and grow best at low temperatures, in the range -10 to 20°C (14 to 68°F). Psychrophiles, a form of extremophile, thrive in the Arctic and Antarctic oceans, which remain frozen for much of the year. Typically, they have enzymes that are adapted to function at lower temperatures and are denatured at moderate temperatures. They also exhibit polyunsaturated fatty acids in their lipids. *Psychrotolerant* organisms, by contrast, are mesophiles that can survive at low temperatures but grow more slowly.

Prokaryotic Psychrophiles

Cold environments are actually more common than hot ones. The oceans,which maintain an average temperature of one to three degrees C (34 to 38 degrees F), make up over half the earth's surface. And vast land areas of the Arctic and Antarctic are permanently frozen or are unfrozen for only a few weeks in summer. Surprisingly, the most frigid places,like the hottest, support life, this time in the form of psychrophiles (cold lovers). James T. Staley and his colleagues at the University of Washington have shown, for example, that microbial communities populate Antarctic sea ice-ocean water that remains frozen for much of the year. These communities include photosynthetic eukarya, notably algae and diatoms, as well as a variety of bacteria. One bacterium obtained by Staley's group, *Polaromonasvacuolata,* is a prime representative of a psychrophile,its optimal temperature for growth is four degrees C, and it finds temperatures above 12 degrees C too warm for reproduction.

While sperm banks and bacterial culture collections rely on the preservation of live samples in liquid nitrogen at -196°C, the lowest recorded temperature for active microbial communities and animals is much higher at -18°C.Freezing of water located within a cell is almost invariably lethal. The only exception to this rule known from nature is the nematode *Panagrolaimusdavidi,* which can withstand freezing of all of its body water.

Eukaryaotic Psychrophiles

Water is the solvent for life and must be present in a liquid state for growth to occur. This sets a practical lower limit for growth slightly below 0°C. Colouring of snow can be caused by a variety of photosynthetic eukaryotes such as *Chlamydomonasnivalis, Chloromonas (Scotiella), Ankistrodesmus, Raphionema, Mycanthococcus* and certain dinoflagellates and represents a well-known illustration of cold-adaptation. One adaptation to life in the cold has been studied in *Heteromitaglobosa*, which is a heterotrophic flagellate growing in Antarctic fell fields whose physical environment is characterised by highly variable moisture and temperature regimens, including short-term freeze-thaw cycles and diurnal temperature fluctuations of up to 20°C (occasionally up to 40°C). At least 24 species of protist and some fruticose lichens and mosses grow in these conditions in addition to bacteria).

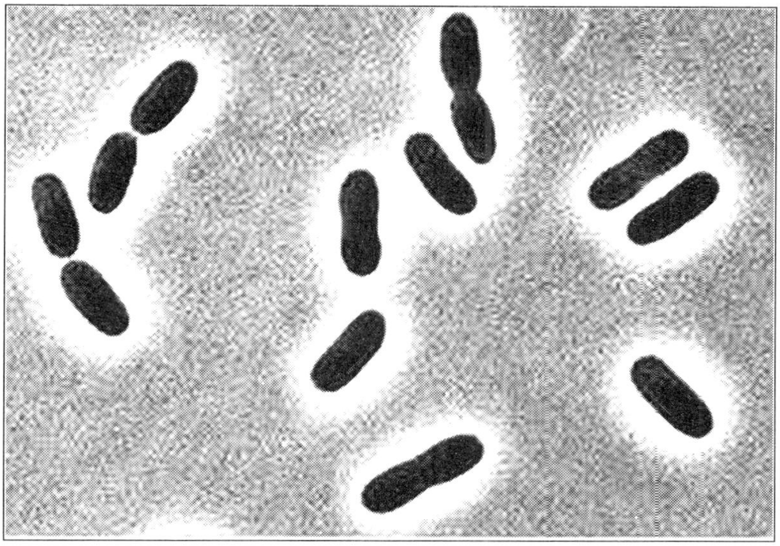

Desulfofrigus Oceanense

Halophiles

Halophiles—make its home in intensely saline environments, especially natural salt lakes and solar salt evaporation ponds. The latter are human-made pools where seawater collects and evaporates, leaving behind dense concentrations of salt that can be harvested for such purposes as melting ice. Some saline environments are also extremely alkaline because weathering of sodium carbonate and certain other salts can release ions that produce alkalinity. Not surprisingly, microbes in those environments are adapted to both high alkalinity and high salinity. Halophiles are able to live in salty conditions through a fascinating adaptation. Because water tends to flow from areas of high solute concentration to areas of lower concentration, a cell suspended in a very salty solution will lose water and become dehydrated unless its cytoplasm contains a higher concentration of salt (or some other solute) than its environment. Halophiles contend with this problem by producing large amounts of an internal solute or by retaining a solute extracted from outside.

Salt flats at Lake Magadi, Kenya. The flats are red due tothe proliferation of halobacteria.

Eukaryaotic Halophiles

Hypersaline conditions support a wide variety of eukaryotic microbes, including diatoms. There are many salt-adapted flagellates, including numerous heterotrophs. The African soda-lakes are also hypersaline (Lake Nakuru was reported being 8% Na; see above under alkalophiles), and as discussed above can support a very diverse microbial population if there is a ample energy input. Halophilic and halotolerant algae have been reviewed by and although Grant (1991) reports that there are no eukaryotes among the extreme halophiles, this view must depend on an exact definition of "extreme" since *Dunaniellasalina* grows up to saline saturation.

Prokaryoytic Halophiles

Archaean, *Halobacteriumsalinarum* concentrates potassium chloride in its interior. As might be expected, the enzymes in its cytoplasm will function only if a high concentration of potassium chloride is present. But proteins in *H. salinarum* cell structures that are in contact with the environment require a high concentration of sodium chloride.

Alkaliphiles

Microbes, including some bacteria and archaea which thrive in highly alkaline environments, such as soda lakes and carbonate-rich soils, where the pH values range from about 9 to 11. Alkaliphiles maintain a mildly alkaline intracellular pH of about 8 amid surroundings of much higher pH by continuously pumping hydrogen ions across their cell membranes into their cytoplasm. Alkaliphiles live in soils laden with carbonate and in so-called soda lakes,such as those found in Egypt, the Rift Valley of Africa and the western U.S. Above a pH of eight or so, certain molecules,notably those made of RNA, break down. Consequently, alkaliphiles, like acidophiles, maintain neutrality in their interior, and their extremozymes are located on or near the cell surface and in external secretions. Detergent makers in the U.S. and abroad are particularly excited by alkaliphilic enzymes.

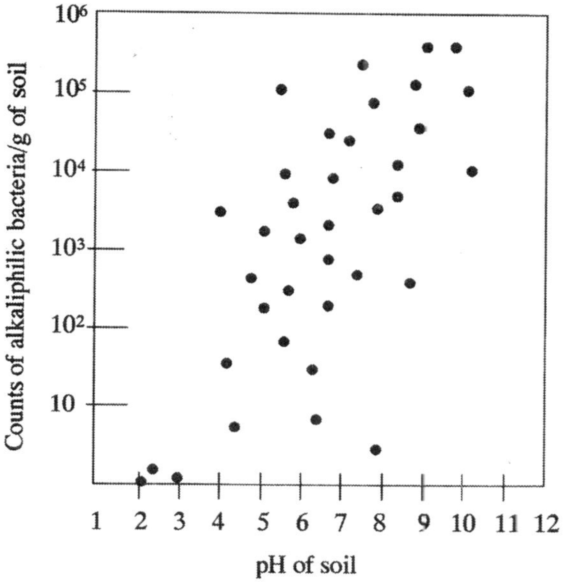

Fig. 2.4: Distribution of Alkaliphilic Microorganisms in Environments at Various pHs

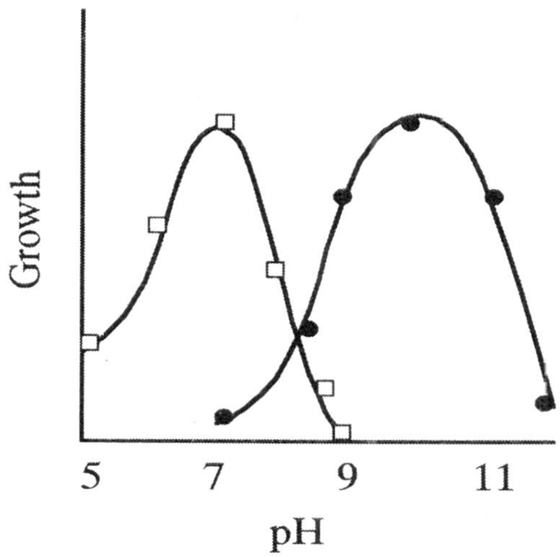

Fig. 2.5: pH Dependency of Alkaliphilic Microorganisms

Prokaryotic Alkaliphiles

The typical pH dependency of the growth of neutrophilic and alkaliphilic bacteria is shown by open squares and solid circles, respectively.

The first brief report on anaerobic alkaliphiles was communicated in 1987, although no taxonomic details were reported. Subsequently, many anaerobic spore-forming alkaliphiles were isolated by conventional procedures, and a few applications have been studied. Podkovyrov and Zeikus recorded the isolation and purification of a cyclomaltodextring lucano transferase from *Clostridium thermohydrosulfuricum* 39E (Podkovyrov, 1992). Wiegel and colleagues have isolated and characterized a range of thermophilic anaerobic alkaliphiles.

Eukaryaotic Alkaliphiles

Two African soda lakes, with a pH of about 10, have been studied for their microbial populations: Lake Nakuru and Lake Simbi. The former lake supports a very high population of flamingos, counted in millions, feeding largely on cyanobacteria dominated by *Spirulina*, growing in the lake. The flamingos have been calculated to return about 15.6 tonnes dry weight of faecal and urinary matter to the lake each day, which resulted in a standing crop of non-cyanobacterial prokaryotes in the region of 3×10^8 cells/ml. In this rich environment, there were at least 20 different heterotrophic species of protest, and three species of rotifers. Lake Simbi, on the other hand, was stratified with an extensive hypolimnion and there were far fewer flamingos, fewer than 20 individuals during the study period.

Acidophiles

Microbes, including certain types of bacteria and archaea, which thrive in acidic environmentssuch as sulfuric pools, where the pH values are in the range 1 to 5. Because high intracellular acidity levels would destroy essential molecules, such as DNA acidophiles have evolved the ability to pump hydrogen ions out of their cells at a constantly high rate. The result is a mildly acidic internal pH of about 6.5 compared with a typical external pH of about 2. Highly acidic environments can result naturally from geochemical activities (such as the production of sulfurous gases in hydrothermal vents and some hot springs) and from the metabolic activities of certain acidophiles themselves. Acidophiles are also found in the debris left over from coal mining. Interestingly, acid-loving extremophiles cannot tolerate great acidity inside their cells, where it would destroy such important molecules as DNA. They survive by keeping the acid out. But the defensive molecules that provide this protection, as well as others that come into contact with the environment, must be able to operate in extreme acidity. Indeed, extremozymes that are able to work at a pH below one more acidic than even vinegar or stomach fluids have been isolated from the cell wall and underlying cell membrane of some acidophiles.

Prokaryoytic Acidophiles

Acido-thermophilic archaea include *sulfolobus*, a chemoautotroph in hot springs as well as thermoplasma, a hetrotroph in hot coal tailings, both thrive in hot acid habitats. the hyper thermophilic archaea pyrolobusfumari (maximum growth at 113°c) lives at ph ranges of 4 to 6.5 (Madigan & Oran, 1999).

Eukaryaoticacidophiles

Until recently only four organisms, all eukaryotes,were known to grow near pH 0: *Cyanidium caldarium*, and three fungi, *Acontiumcylatium*, *Cephalosporium spp.*, and *Trichosporoncerebriae* (Schleper *et al.*, 1995). It has been observed that *Cyanidium* maintains its internal milieu at close to neutral pH, and the means to do that is presumably a primary adaptation to this niche. Another species, *Ferroplasmaacidarmanus*, has been found growing at pH 0 in acid mine drainage in Iron Mountain in California.

Barophiles

Organisms, both macroscopic and microscopic, that thrives in environments where the pressure is unusually high, for example, deep in the ocean or far underground. Three categories of microbes found in high-pressure environments can be distinguished. *Barotolerant* microbes are found in the ocean to depths of 4 km (about 400 atmospheres) but grow better at 1 atmosphere. *Barophilic* species occur at 5 to 6 km and grow better at high pressure (500-600 atmospheres) than low. *Extreme barophiles* live at great depths where the pressure is at least 700 atmos and will not grow at all at 1 atmosphere.

Eukaryaoticbarophiles

High pressure is used as a means of sterilising drugs and foodstuffs. The mechanisms by which pressure affects cellular physiology are many and varied (Markley *et al.*, 1996). Ciliates can certainly withstand rapid, repeated cycling (up and down in unit minutes) from 0.1 to 0.3 MPa without ill effects (Roberts, unpublished data). The fungus *Magnaporthegrisea* is capable of producing an internal pressure of 8 MPa during the process of mechanical penetration of its host plant by the synthesis of glycerol. There are abundant eukaryotic communities on the continental shelf (up to 20 MPa).

Endoliths

Organisms that live inside rock, or the tiny pores between interlocking mineral grains. Thousands of different species are known, including representatives of bacteria, archaea, and fungi. Endoliths have been found inhabiting the Earth's crust at depths up to nearly 3 km (2 miles). Many are autotrophs which manufacture their own organic compounds from inorganic chemicals in the rock. Other varieties of endolith feed on the organics produced by the autotrophs, giving rise to microscopic underground communities known as SliMEs. Subsurface Lithotrophic Microscopic Environments). The extreme depth at which endoliths can exist has yet to be established. The main problem that organisms face at increasing depth is not so much the very high pressure but the rising temperature.

Xerophiles

The driest regions can support eukaryotic life, for instance lichens which grow on stones, even in the Negev Desert (Palmer & Friedmann, 1990). However, the ability to grow in conditions out of liquid water seems to be restricted in the microbes to the fungi. It is an everyday observation in food spoilage that the first colonisers are normally fungi, especially of foods with reduced water activity as a means of preservation (jams, marmalades and similar conserves). The fungi are also able to utilize the filamentous habit to grow through regions unsuitable for growth including bridging air spaces in the search for suitable habitats. The capacity to distribute nutrients through the filamentous colony is clearly an important adaptation for this niche as the capacity to withstand desiccation while growing out of water.

Other Extreme Environments

Microorganisms are now accepted as being the product of symbiotic events, which are normally thought of as between a eukaryote and a prokaryote (as in the mitochondrion or plastid, for instance). Many eukaryotes are themselves involved in a variety of intimate associations and there is some evidence that this close relationship is stressful, or in this context extreme (Douglas, 1996). There are many highly evolved groups of parasites, which have adapted to these stresses and now cannot grow outside their hosts and thus can be considered, to be living in an extreme habitat.

Examples of Interesting Extremophiles

Bacillus infernus - the 'bacillus from hell' – was identified as the first anaerobic member of he bacterial genus *Bacillus* in 1995. Obtained from depths of approximately 2700 m below the land surface, this extremophile was found to be thermophilic (60°C), halotolerant (salt concentrations 0.6 M) and slightly alkaliphilic (pH 7.8). *Methanococcusjannaschii* was the very first archaeon to have its genome sequenced in 1996. It was isolated in 1983 from the sea floor surface of a Pacific thermal vent – 'white smoker' – off the coast of Baja, California. It is methanogenic (methane producer), thermophilic, strictly anaerobic and autotrophic (uses CO_2 as the sole source of cell carbon), and normally lives at about 2400 m below sea level, where the pressure is approximately 230 atmospheres (Bult *et al.*, 1996).

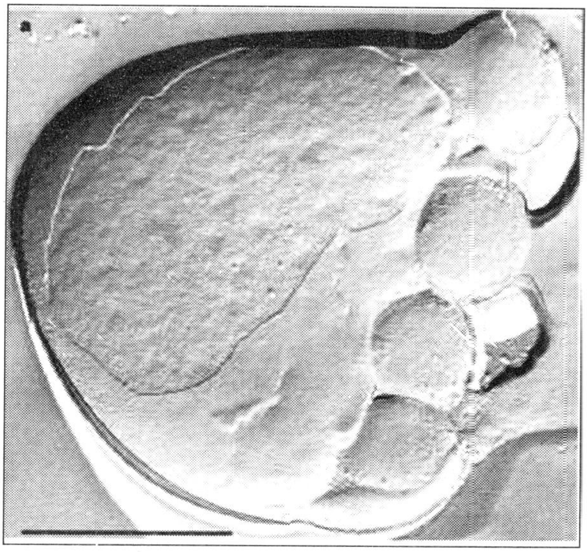

Nanoarchaeum equitans

BIOTECHNOLOGY OF EXTREMOPHILES

Without doubt, the major impetus driving extremophile research is the biotechnological potential associated with them. Indeed, the application of extremophiles in industrial processes has opened a new era in biotechnology. Each group has unique features that can be exploited to provide biomolecules with a wide variety of applications, as illustrated in Table 2.6.

Billions of dollars have been spent worldwide in the development of industrial as well as biomedical applications (Cavicchioli and Thomas, 2000). Applications range from the production of sweeteners and detergents to the diagnosis of infectious and genetic disease.

From a commercial perspective, enzymes from extremophiles – extremozymes – have made the most impact so far. As an example, alkaline proteases, derived from alkaliphilic species, constitute an important group of enzymes that find applications primarily as protein-degrading additives in detergents. Given the robust nature of alkaliphiles, these enzymes can be subjected to harsh environments, including elevated temperature, high pH, surfactants, bleach chemicals, and chelating agents, where applications of many other enzymes are limited because of their low activity or stability. Enzyme production for detergents is a huge market – constituting approximately 30% of the total enzymes produced worldwide and is worth hundreds of millions of dollars.

Table 2.6: Extremophiles and Some Examples of Their Biotechnological Products and Applications

Thermophiles and Hyperthermophiles	**Applications**
DNA polymerases	DNA amplification by PCR
Lipases, pullulanases and proteases	Detergents
Amylases	Baking and brewing
Xylanases	Paper bleaching
Halophiles	**Applications**
Bacteriorhodopsin	Optical switches and photocurrent generators
Lipids	Liposomes for drug delivery and cosmetics
Compatible solutese.g. Ectoin	Protein, DNA and cell protectants
g-Linoleic acid, b-carotene and cell extracts, *e.g. Spirulina* and *Dunaliella*	Health foods, dietary supplements, food colouring and feedstock
Psychrophiles	**Applications**
Alkaline phosphatase	Molecular biology
Proteases, lipases, cellulases and amylases	Detergents
Polyunsaturated fatty acids	Food additives, dietary supplements
Ice nucleating proteins	Artificial snow, food industry e.g. ice cream
Alkaliphiles and Acidophiles	**Applications**
Proteases, cellulases, lipases and pullulanases	Detergents
Elastases, keritinases	Hide de-hairing
Cyclodextrins	Foodstuffs, chemicals and pharmaceuticals
Acidophiles	Fine papers, waste treatment and de-gumming
Sulphur oxidizing acidophiles	Recovery of metals and de-sulphurication of coal
Acidophiles	Organic acids and solvents

Table 2.7: Thermostable DNA Polymerases and their Sources

DNA Polymerase	Source
Taq	Thermusaquaticus
Amplitaq®	Thermusaquaticus
Hot Tub™	Thermusflavis
Pyrostase™	Thermusflavis
Vent™	Thermococcuslitoralis
Deep Vent™	Pyrococcus GB-D
Tth	Thermusthermophilus
Pfu	Pyrococcusfuriosus
ULTma™	Thermotogamaritima

There is certainly an urgent need for new antimicrobial agents, given the increase in drug resistance in many common bacterial pathogens and changes in the spectrum of pathogens, together with the emergence of new diseases. The 'Golden Age' of antibiotic research lasted from the 1940s to the late 1960s, such that by the late 1970s, the medical world proclaimed that the battle against infectious agents had been won. Unfortunately, the proclamations were all too premature as serious antibiotic resistance gradually emerged in pathogens such as *Staphylocoocus aureus, Streptococcus pneumoniae* and *Enterococcus faecalis*.

ANTIMICROBIALS

The discovery, development and clinical use of antibiotics during the 20th century have decreased substantially the morbidity and mortality from bacterial infections. The antibiotic era began with the therapeutic application of sulfonamide drugs in the 1930s, followed by a "golden" period of discovery from approximately 1945 to 1970, when a number of structurally diverse, highly effective agents were discovered and developed. However, since the 1980s the introduction of new agents for clinical use has declined, reflecting both the challenge of identifying new drug classes and a declining commitment to antibacterial drug discovery by the pharmaceutical industry.

History of Antimicrobials

Ancient records show that the Egyptians, Chinese and Persians practiced preservation, drinking water sanitation, antisepsis for wounds and injuries, and both physical and chemical methods for mummification. A recurring theme in history was the belief that epidemic diseases were spread by something in the air. A prime example of this idea is the record that Hippocrates attempted to drive the plague from Athens by lighting fires of aromatic wood in the streets. In the 19th century, Louis Pasteur was credited with dispelling the belief in spontaneous generation. John Tyndall, in the late 1800s, showed that spores were resistant to boiling and, if given time, could germinate. Their vegetative offspring could be killed by repetitive heating. This technique became known as Tyndallisation Nicholas Appert (1810) demonstrated methods for preserving food during long sea voyages by sealing vegetables and fruit in glass jars and heating them. In England in 1842, Chadwick proposed that filth led to disease which in turn led to loss of income and consequent poverty. Following this lead, Snow showed that cholera was transmitted by a contaminated water supply in 1855. Budd (1856) demonstrated that typhoid fever was not caused by bad odors but rather by an agent carried through sewage to the drinking water and milk.

Pasteur (1857), who developed the process known as "pasteurization" to control microorganisms, showed that souring of milk was due to microorganisms. In 1886 he helped solve spoilage problems in the wine industry. Semmelweiss proved that puerperal fever could be prevented if physicians washed their hands after performing autopsies and prior to assisting in childbirth. William Henry published studies in the 1830s on the "disinfection power of increased temperatures with a view for the suggestion of a substitute for quarantine." Based on the first published results regarding the use of sterilizers, Pasteur, Koch and Wolffhugel developed scientifically based procedures for both dry heat and steam sterilization in the late 1800s. Many disinfectants have been in use for 150-200 years and have stood the test of time. Chemicals such as pitch, wine, copper and silver were the earliest disinfectants. Mercury had been known since the fourth century. Mercuric chloride was used by Arab physicians as an antiseptic and a wood preservative. Coal, tar and wood tar were some of the first compounds to be used as disinfectants in the distilling industries and were used to preserve ship timber in the early 1700s. Chlorine and formaldehyde were discovered in 1744 and 1859 respectively.

Chlorine was introduced for water treatment in 1843 and is still used for this purpose today. Copper sulfate, zinc chloride and sodium permanganate, acids, alkalis, sulfurs and alcohols were disinfectants introduced in the mid-1800s.

NEEDS FOR NEW MEDICINES AND AGROCHEMICAL AGENTS

There is a general call for new antibiotics, chemotherapeutic agents, and agrochemicals that are highly effective, possess low toxicity, and have a minor environmental impact. This search is driven by the development of resistance in infectious microorganisms (e.g., species of *Staphylococcus*, *Mycobacterium*, and *Streptococcus*) to existing compounds. The majority of the report discusses the rationale, presence of naturally resistant organisms. The ingress to the human population of new diseases such as AIDS and severe acute respiratory syndrome requires the discovery and development of new drugs to combat them. Not only do diseases such as AIDS require drugs that target them specifically, but so do new therapies for treating ancillary infections which are a consequence of a weakened immune system. Furthermore, others who are immuno compromised (e.g., cancer and organ transplant patients) are at risk for opportunistic pathogens, such as *Aspergillus*spp., *Cryptococcus* spp., and *Candida* spp., that normally are not major problems in the human population. In addition, more drugs are needed to efficiently treat parasitic protozoan and nematodal infections, such as malaria,leishmaniasis, trypanomiasis, and filariasis. Malaria alone is more effective in claiming lives each year than any other single infectious agent with the exception of the AIDS virus and *Mycobacterium tuberculosis* (National Institutes of Health, 2001). Finally, because of safety and environmental problems, many synthetic agricultural agents have been and currently are being targeted for removal from the market, which creates a need to find alternative ways to control farm pests and pathogens (Demain, 2000.) Novel natural products and the organisms that make them offer opportunities for innovation in drug and agrochemical discovery.

Reevaluation of Older, Unexploited Agents

The discovery and successful development of the antibiotics currently used for chemotherapy led to termination of interest in other antibiotic classes discovered during the 1960s and 1970s. These underexploited agents include the everninomycins, avilamycins, kirromycins, lankacidins, sideromycins, pleuromutilins, and indolymycin, as well as several antimicrobial peptides.

A number of these agents appear to have structures and modes of action that are distinct from those of the antibiotics in current use, suggesting that cross-resistance with agents already in use may be minimal. Therefore, reevaluation of these older agents with a view to developing them for use against organisms resistant to current agents may be worthwhile (Zahner et al., 1995). Nevertheless, the development of the avilamycins and pleuromutilins for human use could be contraindicated because they have already been utilized for animal husbandry and veterinary medicine. Use of these agents in animals may have led to the selection of resistant environmental isolates that could serve as a source of resistance determinants in human pathogens, thereby potentially compromising the therapeutic potential of new avilamycin or pleuromutilin analogs in humans.

Natural Products and Traditional Approaches in Medicine

Natural products are naturally derived metabolites and/or by-products from microorganisms, plants, or animals (Baker *et al.*, 2000). These products have been exploited for human use for thousands of years, and it has been the chief source of compounds used for medicine.

Pasteur discovered that fermentation is caused by living cells that people seriously began to investigate microbes as a source for bioactive natural products. Then, scientific serendipity and the power of observation provided the impetus to Fleming to usher in the antibiotic era via the discovery of penicillin from the fungus *Penicilliumnotatum*. Since then, people have been engaged in the discovery and application of microbial metabolites with activity against both plant and human pathogens. Furthermore, the discovery of a plethora of microbes for applications that span a broad spectrum of utility in medicine (e.g., anticancer and immuno suppressant functions), agriculture and industry is now practical because of the development of novel and sophisticated screening processes in both medicine and agriculture. These processes use individual organisms, cells, enzymes, and site-directed techniques, many times in automated arrays, resulting in the rapid detection of promising leads for product development.

Even with untold centuries of human experience behind us and a movement into a modern era of chemistry and automation, natural-product-based compounds have had an immense impact on modern medicine since about 40% of prescription drugs are based on them. Furthermore, 49% of the new chemical products registered by the U.S. Food and Drug Administration are natural products or derivatives 60% of approved drugs and pre-new drug application candidates were of natural origin.From 1983 to 1994, over 60% of all approved cancer drugs and cancer drugs at the pre-new drug application stage were of natural origin, as were 78% of all newly approved antibacterial agents.

Natural-product research efforts have lost popularity in many major drug companies and, in some cases, have been replaced entirely by combinatorial chemistry,which is the automated synthesis of structurally related small molecules. In addition, many drug companies have developed interests in making products that have a larger potential profit base than anti-infectious drugs. These include compounds that provide social benefits, that reduce the symptoms of allergies and arthritis, or that can soothe the stomach. It appears that this loss of interest can be attributed to the enormous effort and expense that is required to pick and choose a biological source and then to isolate active natural products,decipher their structures, and begin the long road to product development.

Manipulating Microbial Physiology to Activate Microbial Natural Product Machinery

In order to exploit the true potential of microorganisms the physiology growth conditions used for generating extracts need to be diversified, the physiology of secondary metabolism has been neglected. Very few of the regulatory features of secondary metabolism have been elucidated, the global physiological regulation situation is very complex due to the variety of microbes,the variety of biosynthetic pathways, and the variety of controls. Environmental conditions remain, however, a key element in the discovery and production of secondary metabolites. Strategies that exploit the full metabolic potentional of each microorganism have to be developed in order to maximize chemical diversity. Biochemical pathways,induction and regulation of secondaty metabolism by internal molecules (such as autoregulators).

There are usually differences between the optimal carbon sources and those that are good for secondary metabolism.For example glucose is an excellent carbon source for growth in most cases but depresses the production of a series of secondary metabolites such as actinomycin, cephalosporine, ergotalkaloids, andtylosin. However, glucose does not interfere with the production of aflatoxin, aminoglycosides or chloramphenical and the production of anticapsine by *streptomycesgriseoplanus* is maximal at a concentration of glucose as high as 100 g/l. Secondary metabolic pathways are often negatively affected by nitrogen sources favourable to rapid growth, for example, ammonium salts inhibit the production of cephamycin, fusidine, and rifamycin. However, other biosynthetic pathways, such as production of pyrroindomycins by *Streptomyces rugosporus*, are not affected.

Phylsiological Exploitation of Talented Strains

Some microorganisms are able to produce a variety of compounds from different chemical families and are termed "metabolically talented" most recently described microbial compounds are produced by actinomyces, mostly *strrepytomyces* strains, and by saprophytic fungi. One metabolically talented microorganisms *Strrepytomycesp.* Strain Go.40/10, synthesis at least 30 different Secondary metabolites, many of which are new compounds. Some strains can synthesize more than 50 compounds, which can be detected only by classical chemical methods. Myxobacteria and fungi are also considered talented microbes.

Genetically Modifying Strains for Unnatural Microbial Natural Products

- **Cloning the metagenome**

Culturable organisms provide only a finite pool of secondary metabolites. One approach to maximize the diversity of natural product extract libraries has been to access the DNA can be isolated directly from an environmental sample digested in to large fragments with restriction enzymes and cloned into an artificial vector. The vector is then transformed into a surrogate host. Environmental DNA libraries can be prepared with large fragments of DNA from a wider range of uncultivated bacteria with in an environmental sample (Courtosis *et al.*, 2003).

- **Gene shuffling**

Microbial genes can be engineered to produce enzymes with novel catabolic activities. Novel compounds were produced by gene transfer between strains producing the isochromanquinone antibiotics actinorhodin, granaticin, and medermycin.

Identification of New Bacterial Targets and New Antimicrobial Agents

An alternative approach to the problem of emerging resistance to current antibiotics is to seek structurally novel antibiotics that inhibit new molecular targets. Such agents are unlikely to be susceptible to existing mechanisms of resistance because of their structural novelty and unique mode of action. New molecular targets for antibiotic action are discussed in the following sections.

New Molecular Targets Involved in Bacterial Growth

Nucleic acid, protein, and cell wall syntheses are already the targets of existing antibacterial agents. Nevertheless, the complexities of these processes provide a rationale for continuing to screen for inhibitors acting on new molecular targets within these pathways. Indeed, this position is supported by the discovery and current development of the oxazolidinones (Jones *et al.*, 1996), which inhibit bacterial protein synthesis by a novel mechanism. The antibiotic mupirocin inhibits bacterial isoleucyl-tRNA synthetase, which charges its cognate tRNA species with isoleucine. Mupirocin inhibits the formation of isoleucyladenylate, the first step of this aminoacylation reaction, leading to depletion of charged tRNA. The resulting amino acid starvation not only leads to inhibition of protein synthesis but also has widespread effects on cellular metabolism through induction of the stringent response.

New Molecular Targets Involved in Bacterial Infection

Recent interest in the mechanisms by which pathogenic bacteria cause disease has raised the possibility of designing new agents that act against gene products expressed primarily or exclusively during infection. An anticipated advantage of developing such agents will be the likely absence of preexisting resistance mechanisms. The search for new microbial targets associated with infection will be substantially assisted by new techniques designed to detect bacterial genes expressed selectively in vivo. However, even before the introduction of these techniques, other approaches had already identified a number of gene products that are involved in infection and that offer good candidates for new intervention strategies.

EXTREMOPHILES AND FOR NOVEL ANTIMICROBIALS

It is well known that terrestrial microorganisms, in particular the Streptomycetes, as well as Gram-positive soil bacteria of the order, Actinomycetales are the major source of antimicrobial agents. These are produced as complex secondary metabolites and net billions of US dollars per year in sales. The soil-dwelling filamentous *Streptomyces coelicolor* is responsible for over half the naturally-derived antibiotics in current use today.

In recent years extremophiles have been recognized as valuable sources of novel bioproducts and this may well include antimicrobials (Horikoshis, 1995), although it is not so clear whether extremophiles can actually produce antibiotics. If one believes the theory that microorganisms have evolved to produce antimicrobials in response to external stimuli and stresses, such as other microbial competitors, it is difficult to believe that extremophiles will produce them, as in their extreme environments they are likely to have few competitors. However, this argument may not hold true as microorganisms produce a huge range of chemicals for which there is no obvious role, and any large collection of chemicals will, by chance, contain molecules with high biological activity. Indeed, the ability to produce and retain a rich chemical diversity surely enhances the chances of a microorganism to produce the very rare compound that gives it enhanced fitness.

This means that many microorganisms will make chemicals with potent antibiotic properties, but only some of these chemicals will give the maker increased fitness because of that antimicrobial activity. It has been proposed that secondary metabolism will have evolved so that traits that optimise the production and retention of chemical diversity at minimum cost, will have been selected.Extremophile research worldwide has generated some evidence to suggest that extremophiles do produce antibiotics.

APPLICATION OF EXTRMOPHILES: CASE STUDY

- In Japan, several research groups have attempted to exploit alkaliphiles and piezophiles. In the case of alkaliphiles – although many compounds have been screened – many of the antibiotic compounds have proved to be unstable during cultivation (Horikoshi, 1999). Evidence from piezophiles is limited – although piezophilic mutants of antibiotic-producing Actinomyces species have been shown to produce novel antibiotics when grown under high-pressure.
- Sincealkaliphiles were rediscovered, many Japanese pharmaceutical companies have tried using alkaline media to isolate new microorganisms producing new antibiotics. Although several have been found and reported. The first report was published in 1980, where they recorded the isolation of *Paecilomyceslilacinus* 1907 from soil by using an alkaline medium (pH 10.5). New antibiotics were produced only under alkaline conditions (pH 9 to 10.5). *P. lilacinus*1907 produced a major product, 1907-II, and a minor product, 1907-VIII, which had antibacterial and antifungal activities. Subsequently, an alkaliphilic *Nocardiopsis dassonvillei* strain, OPC-15, that produced phenazine antibiotics under alkaline culture conditions was isolated, Strain OPC-15 grew well at pH 10 and accumulated two phenazine antibiotics in the mycelia, 1, 6-dihydroxyphenazine (I) and 1, 6-dihydroxyphenazine 3, 5-dioxide (III), at different growth temperatures. (Bahn, 1998).
- Some researchers believe that the salt-loving halophiles provide the most potential as they are more easily manipulated 'cell factories' compared with other extremophiles (Das Sarma and Arora, 2001).

Evidently, the haloarchaea *Haloferaxmediterranii* and *Haloferaxgibbonsii* are known to produce halocins, which, like bacteriocins, inhibit growth of closely related species.

- Interestingly, a recent paper has highlighted extremophiles as an 'unexplored source of antifungal compounds'. A novel thermophilic *Pseudomonas* species was demonstrated to synthesize an iron-binding compound– pyochelin – that has activity against several species of Candida and *Aspergillus fumigatus* (Phoebe Jr *et al*., 2001).
- A heat-labile b-lactamase has been purified from the cold-adapted psychrophile: *Psychrobacter immobilis*. The kinetic parameters of this enzyme for the hydrolysis of some b-lactam antibiotics are comparable to those observed for the highly specialized cephalosporinases from pathogenic mesophilic bacteria (Feller *et al*., 1997).
- Researchers have additionally isolated a cold-active lysozyme – chlamysin – with antimicrobial activity, from the viscera of the marine bivalve *Chlamysislandica*. Chlamysin appears to be a rather robust enzyme and can inhibit the growth of a number of Gram-positive and Gram-negative bacteria (Nilsen *et al*., 1999). Given the findings of Russell Hill and his team, it is possible that it is derived from a symbiotic psychrophilic marine microorganism.
- Under fermenter controlled growth conditions in a glutamate salts medium revealed that biosynthesis of the polyketide-derived antibiotic granaticion by this *streptomyceteoccurred* at temperature up to 50°C but optimally at 45°C (James, 1991).

The *streptomycete* also secretes large amounts of protein coincident with antibiotic efflux from the mycelium. Protease activity has been identified as a component of this secreted protein.The effects of temperature on growth and production of extra cellular products by *Streptomyces thermoviolaceus* are complex. Synthesis and secretion of the antibiotic granaticin is accompanied by that of protein, a component of which is protease activity.

Table 2.8: Antimicrobials from *Bacillus* spp. (Schallmey, 2004)

Class	Antimicrobial Products	Function	Species
Cyclic loigopeptides	Bacitracin	Inhibit cell wall synthesis	*B.licheniformis*
Linear or cyclic ligopeptides	Gramicidines and Tyrocidines	Interfere with membrane function, Polymixins Colistins circulins	*Brevibacillus brevis* *B. polymyxa* *B. colistinus* *B. circulans*
Basic peptides	Edeines	Inhibit formation of the initiation complex on the small ribosome sub unit	*Brevibacillus brevis*
Amino glycoside antibiotics	Butirosin	Affect ribosome function	*B.circulans*

REFERENCES

Amann, R., W. Ludwig and K-H Schleifer. 1995. Phylogenetic Identification and *in situ* Detection of Individual Microbial Cells without Cultivation. *Microbiol. Rev.*, 59: 143-169

Bahn, Y.S., J.M. Park, D.H. Bai, S. Takase, and J.H. Yu. 1998. YUA001, a Novel Aldose Reductase Inhibitor Isolated from Alkalophilic *Corynebacterium* sp. YUA25. I. Taxonomy, Fermentation, Isolation and Characterization, J. Antibiot., 51: 902-907.

Baker, D., U. Mocek, and C. Garr. 2000. Natural Products vs. Combinatorials: A Case Study, *In* S.K. Wrigley, M.A. Hayes, R. Thomas, E.J.T. Chrystal, and N. Nicholson (ed.), Biodiversity: New Leads for Pharmaceutical and Agrochemical Industries. The Royal Society of Chemistry, Cambridge, United Kingdom. 66-72.

Bull, A.T. 2004b. The Paradigm Shift in Microbial Prospecting. In: Bull A.T. (ed.), Microbial Diversity and Bioprospecting. ASM Press, Washington, DC, 241-249.

Bull, A.T. 2004c. Microbial Ecology – The Key to Discovery. How Look, Where to Look. In: Bull A.T. (ed.), Microbial Diversity and Bioprospecting. ASM Press, Washington, DC, 71-79.

Bult, C.J, O. White, G.J. Olsen, L. Zhou, R.D. Fleischmann, G.G. Sutton. J.A. Blake, L.M. Fitz Gerald, R.A. Clayton, J.D. Gocayne, A.R. Kerlavage, B.A. Dougherty. J.F.Tomb, M.D. Adams, C.I. Reich, R. Overbeek, E.F. Kirkness, K.G. Weinstock, J.M. Merrick, A. Glodek, J.L. Scott, N.S. Geoghagen, and J.C. Venter 1996. Complete Genome Sequence of the Methanogenic Archaeon, *Methanococcusjannaschii. Science.*, 273: 1058-1C.

Cavicchioli, R. and T.Thomas. 2000. Extremophiles In *Encyclopaedia of Microbiology*. Editors Lederberg J *et al.*, Academic Press Inc: San Diego. 2: 317-337.

Courtosis et al., (2003) Recombinant Environmental Libraries Provide Access to Microbial Diversity for Drug Discovery from Natural Products. Appl. Environ Microbiol., 69: 49-55.

Das Sarma S & Arora P (2001). Halophiles In: *Encyclopedia of Life Sciences,*. Nature Publishing Group: London. 1-9.

Demain A.L. 1995. Why do Microorganisms Produce Antimicrobials? In: Hunter P.A., Darby G.K. and Russell N.J. (eds), 50 Years of Antimicrobials. Society for General Microbiology Symposium, Vol. 53.Cambridge University Press, Cambridge, UK. 205-228.

Demain, A.L. 2000. Microbial Natural Products: A Past with a Future, *In* S.K. Wrigley, M.A. Hayes, R. Thomas, E.J.T. Chrystal, and N. Nicholson (ed.), Biodiversity: New Leads for Pharmaceutical and Agrochemical Industries. The Royal Society of Chemistry, Cambridge, United Kingdom, Development of Food Plants Used as Medicines. 3-16.

Douglas, A.E. (1996). Microorganisms in Symbiosis: Adaptation and Specialization. In *Evolution of Microbial Life* (Eds D.M. Roberts, P. Sharp, G. Alderson & M.A. Collins), J Gen Microbiol., 225-242.

Feller G, Zekhnini Z, Lamotte-Brasseur J & Gerday C (1997). Enzymes from Cold-adapted Microorganisms. The Class C ß-lactamase from the antarcticpsychrophile *Psychrobacterimmobilis* A5. *Euro J Biochem.,* 244: 186-191.

Fiedler H.P., Bruntner C., Bull A.T., Ward A.C., Good Fellow M., Potterat O., Puder C. and Mihm G. 2004. Marine Actinomycetes as a Source of Novel Secondary Metabolites.

Glowka L. 1998. *A Guide to Designing Legal Frameworks to Determine Access to Enetic Resources.* Gland, Switzerland: Int. Union Conserv. Nat., World Conserv. Union.

Horikoshi K (1995). Discovering Novel Bacteria with an Eye to Biotechnological Applications. *Curr Opin Biotechnol.,* 6: 292-297.

James PDA, Iqbal M, Edwards C, and Miller PGG (1991) Extracellular Protease Activity in Antibiotic – Producing *Streptomyces Thermoviolaceus*. Currmicrobiol., 22: 377-382.

Jones, R.N., D.M. Johnson, and M.E. Erwin. 1996. *In vitro* Antimicrobial Activities and Spectra of U-100592 and U-100766, Two Novel Fluorinated Oxazolidinones. Antimicrob. Agents Chemother. 40: 720-726. Resistance, 2nd ed. Ellis Horwood, New York, N.Y.

Madigan, M.T., & Oren, A. 1999, curr. opin Microbiol., 2: 265-274.

Markley, J.L., Northrop, D.B. & Royer, C.A. (Eds) (1996). *High-pressure Effects in Molecular Biophysics and Enzymology*. Oxford University Press, New York. 211-214.

Marshall C. 2000. Bioprospectors Mine Nature for Genetic Gold. May 29.

Nilsen IW, Overbo K, Sandsdalen E, Sandaker E, Sletten K & Myrnes B (1999). Protein Purification and Gene Isolation of Chlamysin, a Cold-active Lysozyme-like Enzyme with Antibacterial Activity. *FEBS Lett.*, 464: 153-158.

Palmer, R. J & Friedmann, E.I. (1990). Water Relations and Photosynthesis in the Cryptoendolithic Microbial Habitat of Hot and Cold Deserts. *Microbiol Ecol.*, 19: 111-118.

Phoebe CH Jr Combie J, Albert FG, Van Tran K, Cabrera J, Correira HJ, Guo Y, Lindermuth J, Rauert N, Galbraith W & Selitrennikoff CP (2001). Extremophilic Organisms as an Unexplored Source for Antifungal Compounds. *J Antibiot.*,54: 56-65.

Podkovyrov, S.M., and J.G. Zeikus. 1992. Structure of the Gene Encoding Cyclomaltodextrinase from *Clostridium thermohydrosulfuricum*-39E and Characterization of the Enzyme Purified from *Escherichia coli*. J. Bacteriol.,174: 5400-5405.

Reid W,V, Laird SA, Meyer CA, Gamez R, Sittenfeld A, (1993). *Biodiversity Prospecting: Using Genetic Resources for Sustainable Development*. Washington, DC: World Resourc. Instit. 173-178.

Schallmey M, A Sibgh, O P Ward, (2004), Developments in the Use of *Bacillus* Species for Industrial Production, Can J. Microbial., 50: 1-17.

Schleper C, Puehler G, Holz I, Gambacorta A, Janekovic D, Santarius U, Klenk HP & Zillig W (1995). *Picrophilus* gen. Nov., fam. Nov.: A Novel Aerobic, Heterotrophic, Thermoacidophilic Genus and Family Comprising Archaea Capable of Growth Around pH 0. *J Bacteriol.*, 177: 7050-7059.

Woese CR (1996). Whither Microbiology? Phylogenetic Trees. *Currt Biol.*, 6: 1060-1063.

Pages: 47-80

AGRICULTURE, ENVIRONMENT AND NANO-SCIENCE
Edited by: Dr. Pawan Kumar 'Bharti'
ISBN: 978-93-5056-760-9
Edition: 2015
Published by: Discovery Publishing House Pvt. Ltd., New Delhi (India)

3

Bioremediation
A Solution for Environmental Clean Up

Aakansha Goswami[1]; Rizuta Tripathi[2] and B. Singh[3]

INTRODUCTION

Industrialization and extraction of natural resources have resulted in large scale environmental contamination and pollution. Contamination of soils, groundwater, sediments, surface water, and air with hazardous and toxic chemicals is one of the major problems facing the industrialized world today. Indiscriminate and uncontrolled discharge of industrial and urban wastes into the environmental sink has become an issue of major global concern (Hernandez *et al.*, 1998; Gupta and Mahapatra, 2003; Strong and Burgess, 2008). Excess loading of hazardous waste has led to scarcity of clean water and disturbances of soil this limiting crop production (Kamaludeen *et al.*, 2003). The need to remediate these natural resources (soil, water and air)

1 Department of Horticulture, Sardar Vallabhbhai Patel University of Agriculture and Technology, Meerut - 250 110 (UP), (India).

2 Department of Agriculture Biotechnology, Sardar Vallabhbhai Patel University of Agriculture & Technology, Meerut - 250 110 (UP), (India).

3 Department of Horticulture, Sardar Vallabhbhai Patel University of Agriculture and Technology, Meerut - 250 110, (India).

has led to the development of new technologies that emphasize the destruction of the pollutants rather than the conventional approach of disposal. Bioremediation is the use of biological interventions of biodiversity for mitigation (and wherever possible, complete elimination) of the noxious effects caused by environmental pollutants in a given site. The term bioremediation has been introduced to describe the process of using biological agents to remove toxic waste from environment.

Bioremediation can be defined as a natural or managed biological degradation of environmental pollution. The indigenous microorganisms normally carry out bioremediation and their activity can be enhanced by a more suitable supply of nutrients and/or by enhancing their population. Therefore, this process exploits such microorganisms and their enzymatic activities to effectively remove contaminants from contaminated sites. This process is a cost effective means of cleanup of hydrocarbon spills from contaminated sites as it involves simple procedures only and it is an environmentally friendly technology which optimizes microbial degradation activity via control of the pH, nutrient balance, aeration and mixing (Desai and Banat 1997). Also, bioremediation is a versatile alternative to physicochemical treatments (Atlas 1991a, Bartha 1986) and produces non-toxic end products such as CO2, water and methane from petroleum hydrocarbons (PHCs) (Walter *et al*. 1997). Bioremediation is often considered a cost effective and environmental friendly method and is gradually making inroads for environmental clean-up applications. Bioremediation relies on improved detoxification and degradation of toxic pollutants either through intracellular accumulation or via enzymatic transformation to less or non-toxic compounds [2]. Many microorganisms naturally possess the ability to degrade, transform, or chelate various toxic chemicals. Bioremediation process involves biotransformation and biodegradation by transforming contaminants to non–hazardous or less hazardous chemicals. Often, the micro-organisms metabolize the chemicals to produce carbon dioxide or methane, water and biomass. Biotransformation is any alteration of the molecule or structure of a compound by micro-organisms. Biodegradation is the breaking down of organic or bioaccumulation and biotransformation of inorganic compounds into environmental friendly compounds.

Principle of Bioremediation

Since the late 1980s, after the chemical and mechanical treatments of lands and water bodies and thermal treatment (incineration) of hazardous wastes proved economically and environmentally unsustainable, focus shifted towards the biological methods which are cost-effective as well as environmentally sustainable and also socially acceptable. The rapid expansion and increasing sophistication of the chemical industries in the last century has meant that there has been increasing levels of complex toxic effluents being released into the environment and contaminating the natural resources and it is bioremediation that can remove pollutants from the environment thus restoring the original natural surroundings and preventing further pollution. Bioremediation is a process that uses naturally occurring microorganisms to transform harmful substances to nontoxic compounds (Lal *et al.*, 1996). It is defined as the process whereby organic wastes are biologically degraded under controlled conditions to an innocuous state, or to levels below concentration limits established by regulatory authorities (Mueller, 1996). Often the microorganisms metabolize the chemicals to produce carbon dioxide or methane, water and biomass. For bioremediation to be effective, microorganisms must enzymatically attack the pollutants and convert them to harmless products (Vidali, 2001). Most bioremediation systems are run under aerobic conditions, but running a system under anaerobic conditions (Colberg and Young, 1995) may permit microbial organisms to degrade otherwise recalcitrant molecules. Most important parameters for bioremediation are (i) the nature of pollutants; (ii) the soil structure, pH, Moisture contents and hydrogeology; (iii) the nutritional state, microbial diversity of the site; and (iv) Temperature and oxidation-reduction (redox- Potential) (Dua *et al.*, 2002). In bioremediation processes, microorganisms use the contaminants as nutrient or energy sources (Tang *et al.*, 2007). Bioremediation activity through microbe is stimulated by supplementing nutrients (nitrogen and phosphorus), electron acceptors (oxygen), and substrates (methane, phenol, and toluene), or by introducing microorganisms with desired catalytic capabilities (Ma *et al.*, 2007; Baldwin *et al.*, 2008). Bioremediation techniques are typically more economical than traditional methods such as incineration, and some pollutants can be treated on site, thus reducing exposure risks for clean-up personnel, or potentially wider exposure as a result of transportation accidents. Since bioremediation is based on natural attenuation the public considers it more acceptable than other technologies. Most bioremediation systems are run under aerobic conditions, but running a system under anaerobic conditions may permit microbial organisms to degrade otherwise recalcitrant molecules [3].

Microbial Populations for Bioremediation Processes

Microorganisms can be isolated from almost any environmental conditions. Microbes can adapt and grow at subzero temperatures, as well as extreme heat, desert conditions, in water, with an excess of oxygen and in anaerobic conditions, with the presence of hazardous compounds or on any waste stream. The main requirements are an energy source and a carbon source (Vidali 2001). Because of the adaptability of microbes and other biological systems, these can be used to degrade or remediate environmental hazards. Natural organisms, either indigenous or extraneous (introduced), are the prime agents used for bioremediation (Prescott et al., 2002). The organisms that are utilized vary, depending on the chemical nature of the polluting agents, and are to be selected carefully as they only survive within a limited range of chemical contaminants (Prescott et al., 2002~ Dubey, 2004). Since numerous types of pollutants are to be encountered in a contaminated site, diverse types of microorganisms are likely to be required for effective mediation. The first patent for a biological remediation agent was registered in 1974, being a strain of *Pseudomonas putida* (Prescott et al., 2002) that was able to degrade petroleum. In 1991, about 70 microbial genera were reported to degrade petroleum compounds (U.S Congress, 1991) and almost an equal number has been added to the list in the successive two decades (Glazer and Nikaido, 2007).

Essential Factors for Microbial Bioremediation

Factor	Desired Conditions
Microbial Population	Suitable kinds of organisms that can be biodegrade all of the contaminants
Oxygen	Enough to support aerobic biodegradation (about 2 oxygen in the gas phase or 0.4 mg./litre in the soil water
Water	Soil moisture should be from 50-70% of the water holding capacity of the soil
Nutrients	Nitrogen, phosphorus, sulfur and other nutrients to support good microbial growth
Temperature	Appropriate temperatures for microbial growth (D-4D C)
pH	Best range is from 6.5 to 7.5

Some Groups of Microbes

1. **Aerobic:** Examples of aerobic bacteria recognized for their degradative abilities are *Pseudomonas, Alcaligenes, Sphingomonas, Rhodococcus,* and *Mycobacterium*. These microbes have often been reported to degrade pesticides and hydrocarbons, both alkanes and polyaromatic compounds. Many of these bacteria use the contaminant as the sole source of carbon and energy.
2. **Anaerobic:** Anaerobic bacteria are not as frequently used as aerobic bacteria. There is an increasing interest in anaerobic bacteria used for bioremediation of polychlorinated biphenyls (PCBs) in river sediments, dechlorination of the solvent trichloroethylene (TCE) and chloroform.
3. **Ligninolytic fungi:** Fungi such as the white rot fungus *Phanaerochaete chrysosporium* have the ability to degrade an extremely diverse range of persistent or toxic environmental pollutants. Common substrates used include straw, saw dust, or corn cobs.
4. **Methylotrophs:** Aerobic bacteria that grow utilizing methane for carbon and energy. The initial enzyme in the pathway for aerobic degradation,

methane monooxygenase, has a broad substrate range and is active against a wide range of compounds, including the chlorinated aliphatic trichloroethylene and 1, 2dichloroethane.

Metabolic Processes

Primary metabolism of an organic compound has been defned as the use of the substrate as a source of carbon and energy. This substrate serves as an electron donor resulting in microbial growth. Application of cometabolism to site-remediation of xenobiotics is required when the compound cannot serve as a source of carbon and energy by nature of the molecular structure, which does not induce the required catabolic enzymes. The term co-metabolism has been defined as the metabolism of a compound that does not serve as a source of carbon and energy or as an essential nutrient which can be achieved only in the presence of a primary (enzyme inducing) substrate.

Aerobic processes are characterized by metabolic activities involving oxygen as a reactant. Dioxygenases and monooxygenases are two of the primary enzymes employed by aerobic organisms during transformation and mineralization of xenobiotics. Anaerobic microbes take advantage of a range of electron acceptors, which, depending on their availability and the prevailing redox conditions, include nitrate, iron, manganese, sulfate, and carbon dioxide.

Scientific factors affecting bioremediation:

1. **Energy sources:** One of the primary variables affecting the activity of bacteria is the ability and availability of reduced organic materials to serve as energy sources. Whether a contaminant will serve as an effective energy source for an aerobic heterotrophic organism is a function of the average oxidation state of the carbon in the material. In general, higher oxidation states correspond to lowerenergy yields which thus provide less energetic incentive for microorganism degradation. The outcome of each degradation process depends on microbial (biomass concentration, population diversity, enzyme activities), substrate (physico-chemical characteristics, molecular structure, and concentration), and a range of environmental factors (pH, temperature, moisture content, Eh, availability of electron acceptors and carbon and energy sources). These parameters affect the acclimation period of the microbes to the substrate. The molecular structure and contaminant concentration have been shown to strongly affect the feasibility of bioremediation and the type of microbial transformation occurring, and whether the compound will serve as a primary, secondary or co-metabolic substrate.
2. **Bioavailability:** The rate at which microbial cells can convert contaminants during bioremediation depends on the rate of contaminant

uptake and metabolism and the rate of transfe: to the cell (mass transfer). Increased microbial conversion capacities do not lead to higher biotransformation rates when mass transfer is a limiting factor (Boopathy and Manning, 1998). This appears to be the case in most contaminated soils and sediments. For example, the contaminating explosives in soil did not undergo biodegradation process even after 50 years. Treatments involving rigorous mixing of the soil and breaking up of the larger soil particles stimulated biodegradation drastically (Manning et al., 1995). The bioavailability of a contaminant is controlled by a number of physico-chemical processes such as sorption and desorption, diffusion, and dissolution. A reduced bioavailability of contaminants in soil is caused by the slow mass transfer to the degrading microbes. Contaminants become unavailable when the rate of mass transfer is 0. The decrease of the bioavailability in the course of time is often referred to as aging or weathering.

It may result from:

1. chemical oxidation reactions incorporating contaminants into natural organic matter;
2. slow diffusion into very small pores and absorption into organic matter; and
3. the formation of semi-rigid ®lms around non-aqueous- phase liquids (NAPL) with a high resistance toward NAPL-water mass transfer. These bioavailability problems can be overcome by the use of food-grade surfactants (Boopathy and Manning, 1999), which increase the avilability of contaminants for microbial degradation.

3. **Bioactivity and biochemistry:** The term bioactivity is used to indicate the operating state of microbiological processes. Improving bioactivity implies that system conditions are adjusted to optimize biodegradation (Blackburn and Hafker, 1993). For example, if the use of bioremediation requires meeting a certain minimum rate, adjustment of conditions to improve biodegradation activity becomes important and a bioremediation configuration that makes this control possible has an advantage over one that does not. In nature, the ability of organisms to transfer contaminants to both simpler and more complex molecules is very diverse. In light of our current limited ability to measure and control biochemical pathways in complex environments, favorable or unfavorable biochemical conversions are evaluated in terms of whether individual or groups of parent compounds are removed, whether increased toxicity is a result of the bioremediation process, and sometimes whether the elements in the parent compound are converted to measurable metabolites. These biochemical activities can be controlled in an in situ operation when one can control and optimize the conditions to achieve a desirable result.

Types of Bioremediation

On the basis of removal and transportation of wastes for treatment there are basically two methods:

1. In situ bioremediation
2. Ex situ bioremediation

In Situ Bioremediation

1. Intrinsic bioremediation

This approach deals with stimulation of indigenous or naturally occurring microbial populations by feeding them nutrients and oxygen to increase their metabolic activity.

2. Engineered in situ bioremediation

The second approach involves the introduction of certain microorganisms to the site of contamination. When site conditions are not suitable, engineered systems have to be introduced to that particular site. Engineered in situ bioremediation accelerates the degradation process by enhancing the physicochemical conditions to encourage the growth of microorganisms. Oxygen, electron acceptors and nutrients (nitrogen and phosphorus) promote microbial growth.

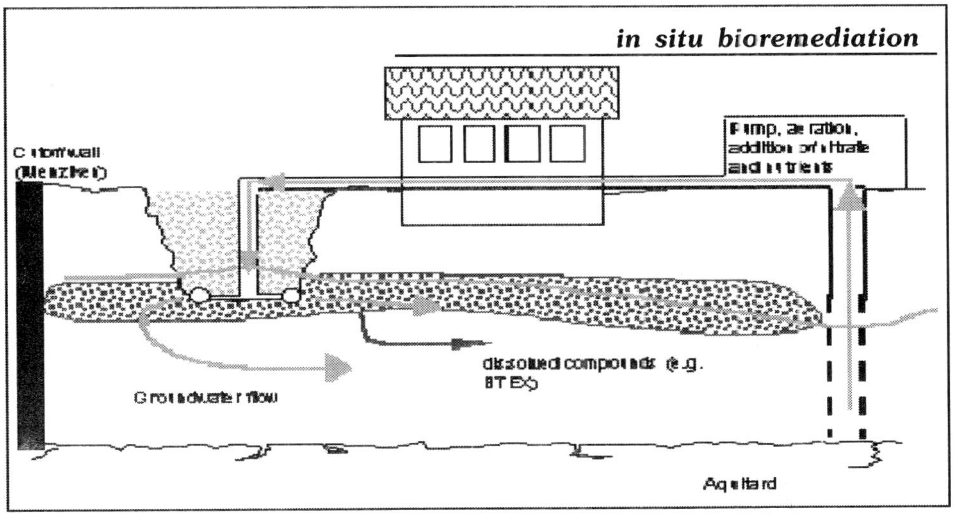

Advantage and Disadvantage of in situ Bioremediation

This method have many potential advantages as it does not require excavation of the contaminated soil and hence proves to be cost effective, there is minimal site disruption, so the amount of dust created is less and simultaneous treatment of soil and groundwater is possible. It poses some disadvantages also as the method is time consuming compared to the other remedial methods, seasonal variation of the microbial activity due to direct exposure to changes in environmental factors that cannot be controlled and problematic application of treatment additives. Microorganisms act well only when the waste materials present allow them to produce nutrients and energy for the development of more cells. When these conditions are not favorable then their capacity to degrade is reduced. In such cases genetically engineered microorganisms have to be used, although stimulating indigenous microorganisms is preferred.

Ex Situ Bioremediation

This process requires excavation of contaminated soil or pumping of groundwater to facilitate microbial degradation. This technique has more disadvantages than advantages. Ex situ bioremediation techniques involve the excavation or removal of contaminated soil from ground.

Depending on the state of the contaminant to be removed, ex situ bioremediation is classified as:

1. Solid phase system (including land treatment and soil piles).
2. Slurry phase systems (including solidliquid suspensions in bioreactors).

Solid Phase Treatment

It includes organic wastes (leaves, animal manures and agricultural wastes) and problematic wastes e.g. domestic and industrial wastes, sewage sludge and municipal solid wastes. Solid phase soil treatment processes include landfarming, soil biopiles, and composting.

1. **Land farming:** Land farming, also known as land treatment, is a bioremediation technique that involves the excavation of the contaminated soil and spreading it on a thin surface. Biodegradation of pollutants is stimulated aerobically by tilling or plowing the soil. Nutrients and minerals are also added to promote the growth of the indigenous species. According to The Unites States Environmental Protection Agency (EPA) report on underground storage tanks (EPA, 2003), before the remediation takes place the site must be prepared by clearing and grading the soil, by installing leach ate collection and treatment systems, and also building vapor treatment facilities. Also, the report states that if a contaminated soil is less than three feet then there is no need for excavation. Soil moisture is controlled by periodically sprinkling soil with water, building barriers or terraces around the contaminated soil controls erosion. Sprinkling with water also minimizes the dust created while tilling the soil to promote aeration (Rubinos *et al.*, 2007).
2. **Composting:** It involves mixing the contaminated soil with a bulking agent such as straw, hay, or corncobs to make it easier to

deliver the optimum levels of air and water to the microorganisms. The most common designs are static pile composting, mechanically agitated composting, and window composting. In static pile composting the contaminated soil is placed into piles and aerated with blowers or vacuum pumps. Mechanically agitated composting involves the placement of the contaminated soil in treatment vessels where it is mixed to achieve aeration. In window composting, the soil is placed in long piles knows as windows and periodically mixed by tractors (Cunningham, 2000). As stated before, the contaminated soil is mixed with a bulking agent or compost to enhance bacterial growth. A typical ratio of soil to compost is 75% contaminated soil to 25% compost. This ratio is changeable depending on the soil type, contaminants level and characteristics. After mixing, the soil is covered to protect it from erosion and to maintain the proper moisture and temperature necessary for bacterial growth. Compost remediation is known to have faster cleanup results since cleanup can be estimated in terms of weeks instead of months.

3. **Slurry Phase Bioremediation:** Slurry phase bioremediation is a relatively more rapid process compared to the other treatment processes. Contaminated soil is combined with water and other additives in a large tank called a bioreactor and mixed to keep the microorganisms, which are already present in the soil, in contact with the contaminants in the soil. Nutrients and oxygen are added and conditions in the bioreactor are controlled to create the optimum environment for the microorganisms to degrade the contaminants. When the treatment is completed, the water is removed from the solids, which are disposed of or treated further if they still contain pollutants.

1. **Bioreactors:** Slurry reactors or aqueous reactors are used for ex situ treatment of contaminated soil and water pumped up from a contaminated plume. Bioremediation in reactors involves the processing of contaminated solid material e.g. soil, sediment, sludge or water through an engineered containment system. A slurry bioreactor may be defined as a containment vessel and apparatus used to create a three phase e.g. solid, liquid, and gas, mixing condition to increase the bioremediation rate of soil bound and water soluble pollutants as a water slurry of the contaminated soil and biomass capable of degrading target contaminants. In general, the rate and extent of biodegradation are greater in a bioreactor system than in situ or in solid phase systems because the contained environment is more manageable and hence more controllable and predictable. Despite the advantages of reactor systems, there are some disadvantages. The contaminated soil requires pre treatment or alternatively the contaminant can be stripped from the

soil via soil washing or physical extraction before being placed in a bioreactor (U.S. EPA Handbook).

2. **Bioventing:** It is the most common in situ treatment and involves supplying air and nutrients through wells to contaminated soil to stimulate the indigenous bacteria. Bioventing employs low air flow rates and provides only the amount of oxygen necessary for the biodegradation while minimizing volatilization and release of contaminants to the atmosphere. It works for simple hydrocarbons and can be used where the contamination is deep under the surface.
3. **Biosparging:** Biosparging involves the injection of air under pressure below the water table to increase groundwater oxygen concentrations and enhance the rate of biological degradation of contaminants by naturally occurring bacteria. Biosparging increases the mixing in the saturated zone and thereby increases the contact between soil and groundwater. The ease and low cost of installing small diameter air injection points allows considerable flexibility in the design and construction of the system.
4. **Bioaugmentation:** Bioremediation frequently involves the addition of microorganisms indigenous or exogenous to the contaminated sites. Two factors limit the use of added microbial cultures in a land treatment unit: no indigenous cultures rarely compete well enough with an indigenous population to develop and sustain useful population levels and most soils with longterm exposure to biodegradable waste have indigenous microorganisms that are effective degrades if the land treatment unit is well managed.

Ex Situ Treatment

(A) Composting

Solid-phase treatment carried out after extraction. A process that treats soils in above-ground treatment areas equipped with collection systems to prevent any contaminant from escaping the treatment.

This involves mixing contaminated materials with compost containing bioremediation organisms. The mixture incubates under aerobic and warm conditions. The resultant compost can be used as a soil augmentation or be placed in a sanitary landfill.

- Moisture, heat, nutrients, or oxygen are controlled to enhance biodegradation for the application of this treatment.
- Are relatively simple to operate and maintain, require a large amount of space, and cleanups require more time to complete than with slurry-phase processes.
- Contaminated soil + Straw; bark; wood chips $\twoheadrightarrow$ pile into heaps (Windrow process).

- Increase temperature to 65 °C, as a result of microbial activity.
- More expensive than land farming, but mare rapid.

(B) Land farming

The use of farming tilling and soil amendment techniques to encourage the growth of bioremediation organisms in a contaminated area. It has been used successfully to remove large petroleum spills in soil. Contaminated soils are excavated and spread on a pad with a built-in system to collect any contaminated liquids that seep out of contaminant soaked soil.

The soils are periodically turned over to mix air into the waste. Moisture and nutrients are controlled to enhance bioremediation.

- Regular tilling to increase aeration.
- Fertilization to encourage microbial population.
- Moisture and nutrients are controlled to enhance bioremediation.
- The area to be treated is lined & dammed to retain any contaminants that leak out.
- Rate of degradation depends on:
    1. Microbial population
    2. Type of contamination
    3. Level of contamination
    4. Soil type

Ex. ½ life for degradation of diesel fuel & heavy oils is 54 day with this type of system.

(C) Soil Biopiles

Contaminated soil is piled in heaps within a lined area (to prevent leaching) several meters high over an air distribution system. Aeration is provided by pulling air through the heap with a vacuum pump. Moisture and nutrient levels are maintained at levels that maximize bioremediation. The soil heaps can be placed in enclosures. Volatile contaminants are easily controlled since they are usually part of the air stream being pulled through the pile.

The Process

- *Oxygen, nitrate acid sulfate:* An electron acceptor is required for breakdown of hydrocarbons.
- *Moisture:* Moisture levels in the range of 20% to 80% of saturation generally allow suitable biodegradation in soils
- *Temperature:* In general, most mesophilic bacteria perform best at about 35° C.
- *pH:* Appropriate monitoring and adjustments should be made to keep such systems in the 7.0 to 7.5 pH range.

(D) Bioreactors

- The treatment of a contaminated substance in a large tank containing organisms or enzymes.
- Bioreactors are commonly used to remove toxic pollutants from solid waste and soil.
- Soil is extracted from a contaminated site can be treated as bioreactors of various designs with controlled parameters as temperature, pH, mixing, O2 supply.

(E) Biofilters

- The removal of organic gases by passing air through compost or soil containing microorganisms capable of degrading the gases.
- It has been used to remove volatile organic compounds (VOC's) from air.
- Biofilter is a reactor containing inert support packing with a high surface area which supports an active microbial film. This film can be maintained by continuous supply of nutrients & high humidity.

In Situ Treatments

(A) Bioventing

This process combines an increased oxygen supply with vapour extraction. A vacuum is applied at some depth in the contaminated soil which draws air down into the soil from holes drilled around the site and sweeps out any volatile organic compounds. The development and application of venting and bioventing for *in situ* removal of petroleum from soil have been shown to remediate approximately 800 kg of hydrocarbons by venting, and approximately 572 kg by biodegradation (van Eyk 1994).

- This is similar to biostimulation. It is not suitable for removing halogenated gases that contribute to ozone layer damage.
- May not work well in clays or in highly layered subsurface environments because O2 cannot be evenly distributed throughout the treatment area.

(B) Biosparging

This is used to increase the biological activity in soil by increasing the O_2 supply via sparging air or oxygen into the soil. In some instances air injections are replaced by pure oxygen to increase the degradation rates. However, in view of the high costs of this treatment in addition to the limitations in the amount of dissolved oxygen available for microorganisms, hydrogen peroxide (H_2O_2) was introduced as an alternative, and it was used on a number of sites to supply more oxygen. Each liter of commercially available H2O2 (30%) would produce more than 100 L of O2 (Schlegel 1977), and was more efficient in enhancing microbial activity during the bioremediation of contaminated soils and groundwaters (Brown and Norris

1994, Flathman *et al.* 1991, Lee *et al.* 1988, Lu 1994, Lu and Hwang 1992, Pardieck *et al.* 1992). The H2O2 put into the soil would supply ~ 0.5 mg/L of oxygen from each mg/L of H2O2 added, but a disadvantage comes from its dangerous toxicity to microorganisms even at low concentrations (Brown and Norris 1994, Scragg 1999).

(C) Bioaugmentation

This process involves the introduction of preselected organisms to the site for the purpose of increasing the rate or extent, or both, of biodegradation of contaminants. It is usually done in conjunction with the development and monitoring of an ideal growth environment, in which the selected bacteria can live and work. The selected microorganisms must be carefully matched to the waste contamination present as well as the metabolites formed. Effective seed organisms are characterized by their ability to degrade most petroleum components, genetic stability, viability during storage, rapid growth following storage, a high degree of enzymatic activity and growth in the environment, ability to compete with indigenous microorganisms, nonpathogenicity and inability to produce toxic metabolites (Atlas 1991b). Mixed cultures have been most commonly used as inocula for seeding because of the relative ease with which microorganisms with different and complementary biodegradative capabilities can be isolated (Atlas 1977). Different commercial cultures were reported to degrade petroleum hydrocarbons (Compeau *et al.* 1991, Leavitt and Brown 1994, Chhatre *et al.* 1996, Mangan 1990, Mishra *et al.* 2001, Vasudevan and Rajaram 2001). Compeau *et al.* (1991) compared two different commercial cultures to indigenous microorganisms with respect to their ability to degrade petroleum oil in soil. Neither of the cultures was capable of degrading the oil.

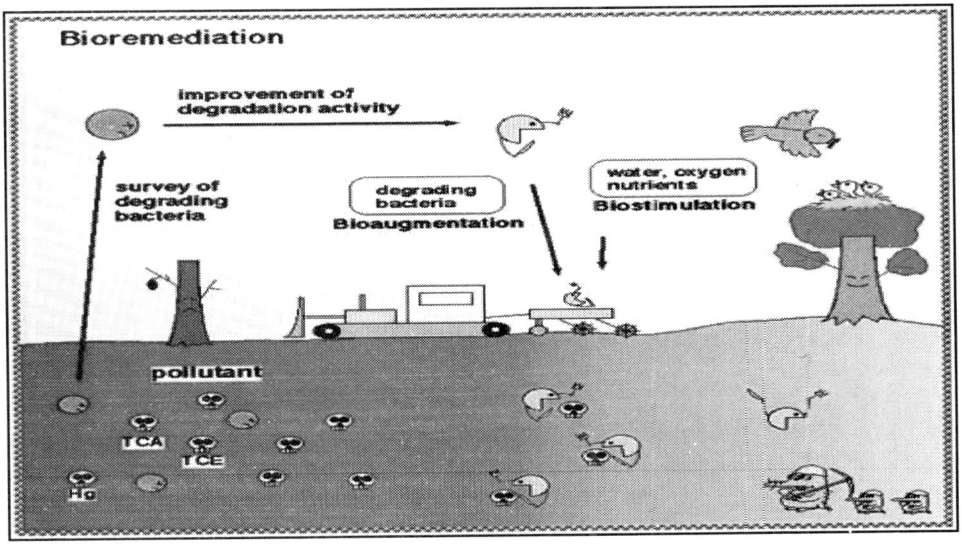

The case studies of Leavitt and Brown (1994) evaluated the benefits of adding such bacterial cultures in terms of cost and performance to bioremediation systems. The potential of a bacterial consortium for degradation of Gulf and Bombay High crude oil was reported by Chhatre *et al.* (1996). They showed that some members of the consortium were able to enzymatically degrade 70% of the crude oil, while others effectively degraded crude oil by production of biosurfactant and rhamnolipid. The wide range of hydrocarbonclastic capabilities of the selected members of the bacterial consortium led to the degradation of both aromatic and aliphatic fractions of crude oil in 72 hours. In study by Ruberto *et al.* (2003) on the bioremediation of a hydrocarbon contaminated Antarctic soil demonstrated a 75% removal of the hydrocarbon when the contaminated soil was bioaugmented with a psychrotolerant strain (B-2-2) and that bioaugmentation improved the bioremediation efficiency. Fungi have also been used. Lestan and Lamar (1996) used a number of fungal inocula to bioaugment soils contaminated with pentachlorophenol (PCP) which resulted in the removal of 80-90% within four weeks. A high rate trichloroethylene (TCE) transformant strain of *Methylosinus trichosporium* was selected and used in a field study to degrade TCE efficiently (Erb *et al.* 1997). Two white rot fungal species, *Irpex lacteus* and *Pleurotus ostreatus,* were used as inoculum for bioremediation of petroleum hydrocarbon-contaminated soil from a manufactured-gas-plant-area. The two fungal species were able to remove PAHs from the contaminated soil where the concentrations of phenanthrene, anthracene, fluorranthene and pyrene decreased up to 66% after a 10-week treatment (Sasek *et al.* 2003).

However, some degradative pathways can produce intermediates, which are trapped in deadend pathways, or transform the pollutants into toxic compounds. Such situation can be improved by the addition of a seed culture of selected or genetically engineered microoorganisms. The use of these genetically manipulated organisms to degrade a variety of pollutants has been suggested as a way to increase the rate or extent of biodegradation of pollutants. The genes encoding the enzymes of biodegradative pathways often reside onplasmids (Chakrabarty 1974, Chakrabarty *et al.* 1973). The best studied plasmid-based pathway is the toluene degradation by *Pseudomonas putida* mt-2 and the plasmid TOL (Glazer and Nikaido 1994). Kostal *et al.* (1998) reported that the ability of *Pseudomonas* C12B to utilize n-alkanes (C9-C12) and n-alkenes (C10 and C12) of medium chain length is plasmid-encoded. These plasmids are usually transferred to other microorganisms by conjugation by which homologous regions of DNA will recombine to generate a fusion plasmid carrying the enzymes for more than one degradative pathway. For example, Chakrabarty (1974) transferred a camphor-degrading plasmid (CAM plasmid) into a bacterium carrying a plasmid with the genes for degrading octane (OCT plasmid). As a result of their homologous regions, the CAM and OCT plasmids recombined to form a fusion plasmid that encoded enzymes for both pathways. Subsequent mating with other strains can generate a bacterium that can degrade a variety of different types of hydrocarbons.

Chakrabarty and his colleagues generated the first engineered microorganisms with degradative properties in the 1970s. Chakrabarty obtained the first U.S. patent for a genetically engineered hydrocarbon-degrading pseudomonad. The engineered organism was capable of degrading a number of low molecular weight aromatic hydrocarbons, but did not degrade the higher molecular weight persistent polynuclear aromatics, and thus has not been used in the bioremediation of oil spills.

(D) Biostimulation

This process involves the stimulation of indigenous microorganisms to degrade the contaminant. The microbial degradation of many pollutants in aquatic and soil environments is limited primarily by the availability of nutrients, such as nitrogen, phosphorus, and oxygen availability. The addition of nitrogen- and phosphorus-containing substrates has been shown to stimulate the indigenous microbial populations. Zucchi *et al.* (2003), while studying the hydrocarbon-degrading bacterial community in laboratory soil columns during a 72-day biostimulation treatment with a mineral nutrient and surfactant solution of an aged contamination of crude oil-polluted soil, found a 39.5% decrease of the total hydrocarbon content. The concentrations of available nitrogen and phosphorus in seawater have been reported to be severely limiting to microbial hydrocarbon degradation (Atlas and Bartha 1972, Leahy and Colwell 1990). The problem of nutrient limitations has been overcome by applying fertilizers (Atlas 1977, Dibble and Bartha 1979, Jamison *et al.* 1975, Jobson *et al.* 1974, Margesin 2000, Verstraete *et al.* 1976) which, range from soluble and slow release agricultural fertilizers of varying formulations to specialized oleophilic nitrogen-and phosphorus-containing fertilizers for use in treating oil spills.

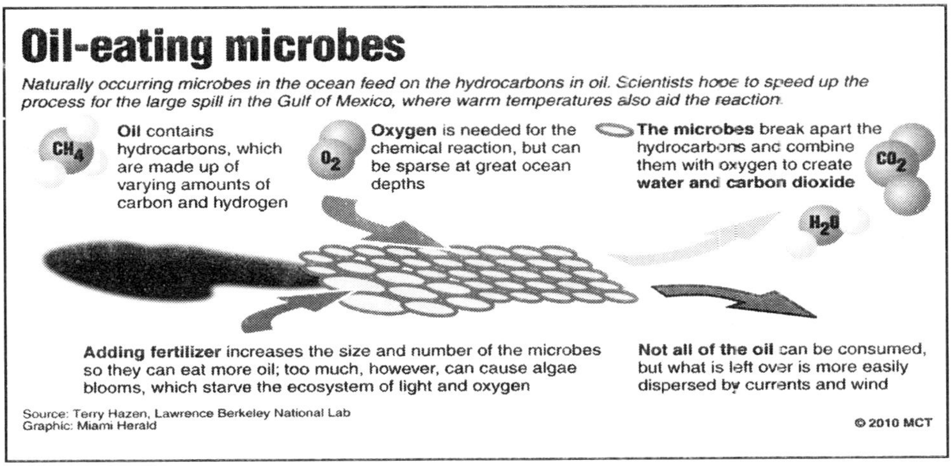

The cost of fertilizer and the potential for groundwater contamination encourage more conservative application rates. Most agricultural fertilizers contain excessive phosphorus and potassium. Urea and ammonium compounds are added to such fertilizers to bring up the nitrogen levels. Laboratory experiments by Dibble and Bartha (1979) showed a C:N ratio of 60:1 and a C:P ratio of 800:1 to be optimum. Another course of action is the addition of a second carbon source to stimulate *cometabolism* (Semprini 1997). Cometabolism occurs when an organism is using one compound for growth and gratuitously oxidizes a second compound that is resistant to being utilized as a nutrient and energy source by the primary organism, but the oxidation products are available for use by other microbial populations (Atlas and Bartha 1993). This cooxidation process was noted by Leadbetter and Foster (1958) when they observed the oxidation of ethane, propane and butane by *Pseudomonas methanica* growing on methane, the only hydrocarbon supporting growth. Beam and Perry (1974) described this phenomenon when *Mycobacterium vaccae* cometabolized cyclohexane while growing on propane. The cyclohexane is oxidized to cyclohexanol, which other bacterial populations (*Pseudomonas*) can then utilize. Therefore, such cometabolism transformation in a mixed culture or in the environment may lead to the recycling of relatively recalcitrant compounds, that do not support the growth of any microbial culture (Atlas and Bartha 1993). The study of Burback and Perry (1993) demonstrated that *M. vaccae* can catabolize a number of major groundwater pollutants to more water-soluble compounds. When toluene and benzene were present concomitantly, toluene was catabolized and benzene oxidation was delayed (Burback and Perry 1993).

Phytoremediation

Phytoremediation is the use of higher plants to bio remediates contamination in soil, water, or sediments. Variations of phytoremediation that have been used in the past include wetlands to treat municipal sewage or neutralize acidic mine drainage.

Types

Phytodegradation

Specifically, phytodegradation, also called "phytotransformation," refers to the uptake of contaminants with the subsequent breakdown, mineralization, or metabolization by the plant itself through various internal enzymatic reactions and metabolic processes.

Depending on factors such as the concentration and composition, plant species, and soil conditions, contaminants may be able to pass through the rhizosphere only partially or negligibly impeded by phytosequestration and/or rhizodegradation.

In this case, the contaminant may then be subject to biological processes occurring within the plant itself, assuming it is dissolved in the transpiration stream and can be phytoextracted.

Phytovolatilization

Phytovolatilization is the volatilization of contaminants from the plant either from the leaf stomata or from plant stems (Anonymous, 2009). Chemical characteristics such as the, Henry s constant, and vapor pressure dictate the ability of organic contaminants to volatilize. In some cases, a breakdown product derived from the rhizodegradation and/or phytodegradation of the parent contaminant along the transpiration pathway may be the phytovolatilized constituent. This effect was studied for the uptake and phytovolatilization of trichloroethene (TCE) or its breakdown products in poplars (Anonymous, 2009). Similarly, certain inorganic constituents such as mercury may be volatilized as well. Specifically, tobacco plants have been modified to be able to take up the highly toxic methyl-mercury, alter the chemical speciation, and phytovolatilize relatively safe levels of the less toxic elemental mercury into the atmosphere (Anonymous, 2009). Once volatilized, many chemicals that are recalcitrant in the subsurface environment react rapidly in the atmosphere with hydroxyl radicals, an oxidant formed during the photochemical cycle.

Phytostabilization

Phytostabilization refers to the holding of contaminated soils and sediments in place by vegetation, and to immobilizing toxic contaminants in soils. Establishment of rooted vegetation prevents windblown dust, an important pathway for human exposure at hazardous waste sites. Hydraulic control is possible, in some cases, due to the large volume of water that is transpired through plants which prevents migration of leach ate towards groundwater or receiving waters. Phytostabilization is especially applicable for metal contaminants at waste sites where the best alternative is often to hold contaminants in place. Metals do not ultimately degrade, so capturing them *in situ is the best alternative at sites with low* contamination levels (below risk thresholds) or vast contaminated areas where a large-scale removal action or other *in situ remediation is not feasible.*

Phytoextraction

This process has been tried more often for extracting heavy metals than for organics, We can find five types of phytoremediation techniques, classified based on the contaminant fate: phytoextraction, phytotransformation, phytostabilization, phytodegradation, rhizofiltration, even if a combination of these can be found in natureThe main advantage of phytoextraction is environmental friendly. The traditional methods those are used for cleaning up the heavy metal contaminated soil are responsible for disruption of soil structure and reduce soil productivity, whereas phytoextraction can clean up the soil without causing any kind of harm to the soil quality. Another benefit of phytoextraction is less expensive than any other cleanup process. As this process is controlled by plant, so it takes more time than any traditional soil cleanup process. *Phytoextraction* or *phytoaccumulation* is the process used by the plants to accumulate contaminants into the roots and aboveground shoots or leaves. This technique saves tremendous remediation cost by accumulating low levels of contaminants from a widespread area. Unlike the degradation mechanisms, this process produces a mass of plants and contaminants (usually metals) that can be transported for disposal or recycling.

Phytotransformation or phytodegradation

It refers to the uptake of organic contaminants from soil, sediments, or water and, subsequently, their transformation to more stable, less toxic, or less mobile form. Metal chromium can be reduced from hexavalent to trivalent chromium, which is a less mobile and noncarcinogenic form. *Phytostabilization* is a technique in which plants reduce the mobility and migration of contaminated soil. Leachable constituents are adsorbed and bound into the plant structure so that they form a stable mass of plant from which the contaminants will not reenter the environment. *Phytodegradation* or *rhizodegradation* is the breakdown of contaminants through the activity existing in the rhizosphere. This activity is due to the presence of proteins and enzymes produced by the plants or by soil organisms such as bacteria, yeast, and fungi. Rhizodegradation is a symbiotic relationship that has evolved between plants and microbes. Plants provide nutrients necessary for the microbes to thrive, while microbes provide a healthier soil environment.

Rhizofiltration

Rhizofiltration can be defined as the use of plant roots to absorb, concentrate, and/or precipitate hazardous compounds, particularly heavy metals or radionuclides, from aqueous solutions. Rhizofiltration is effective in cases where wetlands can be created and all of the contaminated water is allowed to come in contact with roots. Contaminants should be those that sorb strongly to roots, such as lead, chromium (III), uranium, and arsenic (V). Roots of plants are capable of sorbing large quantities of lead and chromium from soil water or from water that is passed through the root zone of densely growing vegetation.

Role of Biotechnology

Biotechnological processes for the bioremediation of chemical pollutants offer the possibility of in situ treatments and are mostly based on the natural activities of microorganisms. Biotechnological processes to destroy hazardous wastes offer many advantages over physicochemical processes. When successfully operated, biotechnological processes may achieve complete destruction of organic wastes. However, an important factor limiting the bioremediation of sites contaminated with certain hazardous compounds is the slow rate of degradation (Iwamoto and Nasu 2001). This slow degradation rate often limits the practicality of using microorganisms in remediating contaminated sites. This is an area where genetic engineering can make a marked improvement. Molecular techniques can be used to increase the level of a particular protein or enzyme or series of enzymes in bacteria with an increase in the reaction rate (Chakrabarty 1986). The easiest way to create an appropriate genetically engineered strain is to begin with an organism that already possesses much of the necessary degradative enzymatic machinery. Genetically engineered microorganisms Advances in genetic and protein engineering techniques have opened up new avenues to move towards the goal of genetically engineered microorganisms (GEMs) to function as "designer biocatalysts", in which certain desirable biodegradation pathways or enzymes from different organisms are brought together in a single host with the aim of performing specific reactions. A number of opportunities for improving degradation performance using GEMs have been described (Timmis and Piper 1999). The enzyme 2, 3-dihydroxybiphenyl 1, 2-dioxygenase from *Rhodococcus* RDC1 (*etbC*-encoded) grown on ethylbenzene contains the broadest substrate specificity of any *meta*-cleavage dioxygenase identified in *Rhodococcus* strains (Masai et al. 1995). The co-expression of two 2, 3-dihydroxybiphenyl 1, 2-dioxygenases encoded by *bphC* and *etbC* genes in *Rhodococcus* strain RHA1 grown either on biphenyl or ethylbenzene has been found to increase the spectrum of PCB substrates (Hauschild et al. 1996). A gene encoding *s*-triazine hydrolase (for dechlorination and deamination of de ethylatrazine and de-isopropylatrazine) was transferred from *R. corallinus* to *Rhodococcus* TE1 (Chen and Mulchandani 1998). This resulted in the complete degradation of atrazine to cyanuric acid by the recombinant *Rhodococcus*. Recombinant *Escherichia coli* harboring and expressing the phenol hydroxylase gene from *Pseudomonas putida* BH could efficiently degrade trichloroethylene (TCE; Fujita et al. 1995). A *P. fluorescens* strain expressing the toluene *o*-monooxygenase genes from *Burkholderia cepacia* PR1 could very efficiently degrade TCE from contaminated soil (Yee et al. 1998). The genes for phenol hydroxylase and catechol 2, 3-dioxygenase activities were also cloned and expressed independently and constitutively under various conditions in *Alcaligenes eutrophus* JMP134 (Hauschild et al. 1996). The expression of the gene(s) encoding phenol hydroxylase activity was found to affect the oxidative removal of TCE. Cloning of the *tod* gene encoding toluene dioxygenase into *Deinococcus radiodurans* enabled the bacterium to oxidize toluene, chlorobenzene, 3, 4-dichloro-1-butene and indole. The engineered *D. radiodurans* was successfully applied to the bioremediation of mixed wastes containing both radionuclides and organic solvents (Lange et al. 1998). Erb and Wagner-Dobber (1993) demonstrated the enhanced degradation of a mixture of phenols, using a genetically engineered pseudomonad in a laboratory-scale sewage plant fed with a mixture of chlorophenols and 4-methylphenol. They also showed that the microbiota can be protected from the lethal effects of the pollutants and thereby assure maintenance of the waste-treatment process. Researchers from the University of Tennessee, in collaboration with Oak Ridge National Laboratory, recently conducted bioremediation field tests, using a genetically modified strain of *P. fluorescens* strain HK44 (Sayler et al. 1999; Ripp et al. 2000). Strain HK44 was designed for the purpose of sensing an environmental contaminant and responding to it through bioluminescence signaling, to be used as an online tool for in situ monitoring of the bioremediation process (Sayler and Ripp 2000). The possibilities of using genetic engineering for improvement of bioremediation process had an early boost in the late 1980's. Recombinant DNA techniques have been studied intensively to improve the degradation of hazardous waste under laboratory condition. The genetically engineered microorganisms have higher degradative capacity and have been demonstrated successfully for the degradation of various pollutants under defined conditions. Genetic modification technology has resulted often in a wide variety of current and potential applications for use in the process of bioremediation. Bioremediation explores gene diversity and metabolic versatility of microorganisms (Fulekar, 2009). The genetic architecture of these organisms makes them valuable in biodegradation, biotransformation, biosorption and bioaccumulation. The necessary blue print of gene encoding for biodegradative enzymes is present in chromosomal and extra-chromosomal DNA of such microbes. Recombinant DNA techniques facilitate to evolve the ability of an organism to metabolize a xenobiotic by detection of such degradative genes and transforming them into appropriate host via suitable vector under the tight control of appropriate promoters. It depends on susceptibility to alteration and exchange of genetic information. The recombinant DNA technology explores PCR, anti-sense RNA technique, site directed mutagenesis, electroporation and particle bombardment techniques. The biotechnology armed with recombinant DNA technology is now fine tuning the bioremediation technology by improving pollutant degrading microbes through strain improvement and genetic modification of specific regulatory and metabolic genes that are crucial in developing effective, safe and economical techniques for bioremediation. Bioremediation is not effective only for the degradation of pollutants but it can also be used to clean unwanted substances from air, soil, water and raw materials form industrial waste.

Genetic engineering also permits the combination of several degradative activities within a single host organism. If a single strain is constructed to perform several related or unrelated metabolic activities, the efficiency and predictability of the process may be significantly enhanced. Such recombinant strains may be useful for the bioremediation of recalcitrant compounds (Brenner et al. 1994). Requirements for the design of bacteria with multiple pathways for use in bioremediation have been described in recent articles (Lau and Lorenzo 1999; Gibson and Parales 2000). The catabolic pathway for the total degradation of PCBs is encoded by two different sets of genes that are not normally found in the same organism. As the catecholic intermediates of both pathways are frequently inhibitory to each other, incompatibilities result. Therefore, hybrid strains have been constructed that can metabolize simple chlorobiphenyls through complementary pathways by comprising the biphenyl, benzoate and chlorocatechol genes of the parental strains. By creating recombinant strains between *P. pseudoalcaligenes* KF707 and *B. cepacia* LB400 *bph* genes, not only was an enhanced degradation of PCBs demonstrated, but also the simultaneous degradation was shown of single aromatic hydrocarbons, such as benzene and toluene, which are otherwise poor substrates for the original biphenyl dioxygenases (Kumamaru et al. 1998).

P. aeruginosa 142, isolated from a PCB-degrading consortium, was shown to be able to grow on chlorobenzoates (Romanov and Hausinger 1994). However, the presence of a broad substrate specificity and high-regiospecificity oxidative dehalogenation pathway involving an *ortho*-halobenzoate 1, 2-dioxygenase provided the bacterium with the ability to utilize mixtures of chlorobenzoates and PCBs. After inoculating *P. aeruginosa* JB2, a chlorobenzoate degrader, into soil having indigenous biphenyl degraders, two recombinant strains, *P. aeruginosa* JB2-3 and JB2-M, were isolated after some time (Foght et al. 1996). These strains were able to degrade both biphenyls and chlorobenzoates. Genetic analysis indicated that the *bph* genes were transferred to the original *P. aeruginosa* JB2 from the indigenous biphenyl degraders. The construction of hybrid *Pseudomonas* strains, JR1A::ipb and CBS-3::ipb, was achieved by inserting an *ibp* module (for degradation of isopropylbenzene) into the genomes of different *Pseudomonas* strains. The hybrid strains could effectively degrade TCE along with isopropyl benzene (Berendes et al. 1998).

Recently, Timmis and Piper (1999) suggested a strategy for designing organisms with novel pathways and the creation of a bank of genetic modules encoding broad specificity enzymes or pathway segments that can be combined at will to generate new or improved activities. The use of appropriate regulatory circuits can enhance substrate flux through these designed pathways; and rationally engineering the pathway branch-points can avoid or reduce substrate misrouting. Using genes encoding the biosynthetic pathway of biosurfactants can enhance biodegradation rates by improving the bioavailability of the substrates; and genes encoding resistance to critical stress factors may enhance both the survival and the performance of designed catalysts, Pathway engineering for enhanced bioremediation.

Achievements of Bioremediation Technology

Many research laboratories and companies are engaged to develop bioremediation products. These operate on very thin profit margins and few have a primary focus. Only few research laboratories and companies exploiting the genetic engineering for bioremediation commercially. Nonetheless, there continues to be significant research development in the genetics and molecular biology of biodegradative systems in bioremediation.

Bioremediation of petroleum oil contaminated sites has become possible in India. Recently, Tata Energy Research Institute (TERI, New Delhi) developed TERI'S Oilzapper. It is a crude oil degrading bacterial system that has been developed to reclaim contaminated sites. TERI has stocks of bacteria that isolated from the natural environment and have capacity to eat up the harmful compounds in oil spill sites. These bacteria are cultivated in the laboratory. Then mixed with specific carrier material and packed in poly-bags for easily transportation to petroleum contaminates sites. "Oilzapper" name has been given these carrier-based bacteria by TERI. This Oilzapper was applied at the Mathura refinery over a field (a larger area, covering about three acres of land) on an experimental basis and encouraging results were obtained. A similar activity has also been undertaken at the Barauni oil refinery. Only a very few nutrient additives have been developed and available in markets as commercial bioremediation agents for oil spill cleanup. Bioremediation agents are the microbiological cultures, enzyme additives, or nutrient additives that significantly increase the rate of biodegradation to mitigate the effects of the discharge (Nichols, 2001). Bioremediation agents are classified as bioaugmentation agents and biostimulation agents based on the two main approaches to oil spill bioremediation. In the early 1990s, bioremediation was popularized as the ultimate solution to oil spills (Hoff, 1993). Most of the common fertilizers are economical, readily available, and have been shown effective if used appropriately. However common fertilizers have some limitations e.g. beingrapidly washed out due to tide and wave action. Therefore several organic nutrient products, such as oleophilic nutrient products, have recently been evaluated and marketed as bioremediation agents. Four agents, namely, Inipol EAP22, Oil Spill Eater II (OSE II), BIOREN 1 and BIOREN 2, listed on the NCP Product schedule. Inipol EAP22 (Societe, CECA S.A., France) is listed on the NCP Product schedule as a nutrient additive. It is probably the most well known bioremediation agent for oil spill cleanup because it was used in the cleanup of the oil tanker Exxon Valdez oil spill in Prince William Sound and the Gulf of Alaska. This nutrient product is a microemulsion containing urea as a nitrogen source, sodium laureth phosphate as a phosphorus source, 2-butoxy-1- ethanol as a surfactant, and oleic acid to give the material its hydrophobicity. The claimed advantages of Inipol EAP22 include (1) preventing the formation of water-in-oil emulsions by reducing the oil viscosity and interfacial tension; (2) providing controlled release of nitrogen and phosphorus for oil biodegradation; and (3) exhibiting no toxicity to flora and fauna. One good quality of this is biodegradability (Ladousse and Tramier, 1991). Oil Spill Eater II (Oil Spill Eater International, Corp.) is another nutrient product listed on the NCP schedule. This product is listed as a nutrient/enzyme additive and consists of nitrogen, phosphorus, readily available carbon, and vitamins for quick colonization of naturally occurring bacteria. A field demonstration was carried out at a bioventing site in a Marine Corps Air Ground Combat Center (MCAGCC) in California to investigate the efficacy of OSEII (Oil Spill Eater II) for enhancing hydrocarbon biodegradation in a fuel-contaminated vadose zone and it showed positive results (Zwick et al., 1997). A field trial in an estuary environment was conducted by researchers from European EUREKA BIOREN to evaluate the effectiveness of two bioremediation products (BIOREN 1 and 2). These two products were derived from fish meals in a granular form with urea as nitrogen source, super phosphate as a phosphorus sources and proteinaceous material as the carbon source. The major difference between the two formulations was that BIOREN 1 contained a bio-surfactant. The results showed that the presence of bio-surfactant in BIOREN 1 was the most active ingredient which contributed to the increase in oil degradation rates whereas BIOREN 2 (without bio-surfactant) was not effective in that respect. The biosurfactant could have contributed to greater bioavailability of hydrocarbons to microbial attack (Le Floch et al., 1997; 1999). The success of bioremediation efforts in the cleanup of the oil tanker Exxon Valdez oil spill of 1989 in Prince William Sound and the Gulf of Alaska created tremendous interest in the potential of biodegradation and bioremediation technology (Atlas and Bartha, 1998). The majority of the studies have intense on determination of the factors affecting oil bioremediation and testing the methods in laboratory studies (Mearns, 1997). Only limited numbers of pilot scale and field trials have provided the most convincing demonstrations of this technology which have been reported in the peer-reviewed literature (Prince, 1993; Swannell et al., 1996; Venosa et al., 1996; 2002). The scope of petroleum hydrocarbons bioremediation is also restricted because most of these field studies reviews have been given on the evaluation large-scale oil spills on marine shorelines (Das and Chandran, 2011). By the present review, it may be concluded that biodegradation can be considered as a key component in the cleanup strategy for petroleum hydrocarbon remediation. However, data shows that bioremediation process may be successful in the laboratory but significantly less in the field conditions (Ladousse and Tramier, 1991; Mearns, 1997; Venosa et al., 1996; 2002). This is because laboratory studies cannot contain real environmental conditions suchas spatial heterogeneity, biological competitions, climatic conditions, and nutrient availability. Therefore, field tests are the ultimate way to demonstration of the efficiency of bioremediation technology.

Microbial Bioremediation of Heavy Metals

Metals play important role in the life processes of microbes. Some metals such as chromium (Cr), calcium (Ca), magnesium (Mg), manganese (Mn), copper (Cu), sodium (Na), nickel (Ni) and zinc (Zn) are essential as micronutrients for various metabolic functions and for redox functions. Other metals have no biological role e.g. cadmium (Cd), lead (Pb), mercury (Hg), aluminum (Al), gold (Au) and silver (Ag). They are non-essential and potentially toxic to soil microbes. Some of them e.g. Cd2+, Ag2+, Hg2+ tend to bind the SH groups of enzymes and inhibit their activity (Turpeinen, 2002). Soil micro-organisms have been shown to bio-accumulate metals in tissues in concentrations up to 50 times higher than the surrounding soil. *Oscillatoria* spp. (a blue-green algae), *Chlorella vulgaris* & *Chlamydomonas* spp. (green algae), *Arthrobacter, Agrobacter, Enterobacter* & *Pseudomonas aeruginosa* are some metal reducing microbes (Ramasamy *et al.*, 2006). Degradation of dyes is also brought about by some anaerobic bacteria and fungi (Colberg, 1995).

Microbial Remediation of Toxic Metals Occurs in Two Ways: (1) Direct reduction by the activity of the bacterial enzyme „metal reductase. It is applied for groundwater decontamination, using bioreactors (pump & treat) and also for soils after excavation (pulping or heaping and inoculation with appropriate microbial consortium). These techniques are *ex-situ* methods, and very expensive and has low metal extraction efficiencies. (2). Indirect reduction by biologically produced hydrogen sulfide (H2S) by sulfate reducing bacteria to reduce and precipitate the metals. This is an *in-situ* method, and an environmentally sound & inexpensive alternative to pump & treat (for contaminated groundwater) or excavate & treat (for contaminated soils). Microbial growth is induced in sub-surface zones by injecting substrates. The migrating metals are intercepted and immobilized by precipitation with biologically produced H2S. Toxic metals readily binds to sulfhydryl group of proteins (Nies, 1999; Sandrin and Hoffman, 2006). In-situ bioremediation of uranium contaminated sites have been conducted successfully with *Desulfosphorosinus* spp. and *Closteridium* spp. (Bruschi and Goulhen, 2006).

1. Bioremediation of pesticide in surface soil treatment unit using microbial consortia

The manufacturing and use of pesticides has been rising tremendously in India. The waste generated by the pesticide industry has become an environmental problem due to the present insufficient and ineffective waste treatment technology involving physico-chemical and biological treatment. The available data indicates that pesticide residues remain in surface soil, leading to toxicity in the soil-water environment. The recent advances in bioremediation technology using microbial consortium has been found effective for treatment of pesticides in soil. In the present study, a Surface

Soil Treatment Unit has been designed wherein bioremediation of commonly used pesticides namely chlorpyrifos, cypermethrin, fenvalerate, and trichlopyr butoxyethyl ester at varying concentration viz. 25, 50 and 100 mg/kg have been carried out using cow-dung microbial consortia under simulated environmental conditions. The bioremediation conditions have been monitored and maintained during the study. The investigation has been extended till the parent compound was converted into intermediates and/or less harmful compounds. These then will further mineralize, from part of the microbial food chain and/or become integrated into the humic fractions. The results presented here highlight the potential of cow-dung slurry consortia for bioremediation of soil contaminated with pesticides in surface soil treatment unit (Geetha and Fulekar, 2008).

2. Bioremediation of pesticides using scale up process bioreactors

To assess the bioremediation potential of *Pseudomonas aeruginosa* (NCIM, 2074) by improving its adaptability to increasing concentration of chlorpyrifos using scale up process. *Pseudomonas aeruginosa* isolate NCIM 2074 was adapted by subjecting to varying concentrations of chlorpyrifos, i.e. 10, 20, 50, 75 and 100 mg/l in incubator shaker at 37°C and 150 rpm. An initial 10 mg/l concentration of chlorpyrifos was supplied in minimal salt medium (MSM) under controlled environmental conditions for 14 days. The culture was subsequently scaled up to higher concentrations of chlorpyrifos by transferring one milliliter from the medium with 10mg/L to 25 mg/l of the compound. After every 14 days this process was repeated, each time using medium with higher chlorpyrifos concentration. The entire scale up process continued for a period of 70 days. *Pseudomonas aeruginosa* (NCIM 2074) was adapted to increasing chlorpyrifos up to 50 mg/l, but 75 and 100 mg/l was inhibitory to the organism. The biodegradation of chlorpyrifos, as assessed by GC-MS, showed that chlorpyrifos at 10, 25, 50 mg/l degraded completely over a period of 1, 5 and 7 days, respectively. The intermediate 3, 5, 6 trichloro-2-pyridion, 2, 4-bis (1, 1 dimethyiethyl) phenol and 1, 2 zenedicarboxylic acid persisted during bioremediation, but in the long run these convert to CO2, biomass and nutrients. *Pseudomonas aeruginosa* (NCIM 2074) has been of potential use in bioremediation of chlorpyrifos at concentrations up to 50 mg/l, but the organism is inhibited by higher concentrations (Fulekar and Geetha, 2008).

3. Bioremediation of benzene using a designed and developed partitioning bioreactor

A bioreactor has been designed and developed for partitioning of aqueous and organic phases with a provision for aeration and stirring, a cooling system and a sampling port. The potential of a cow dung microbial consortium has been assessed for bioremediation of phenol in a single-phase bioreactor and a two-phase partitioning bioreactor. The advantages of the two-phase partitioning bioreactor are discussed. The *Pseudomonas putida* IFO 14671 has been isolated, cultured and identified from the cow dung microbial consortium as a high-potential phenol degrader. The methods developed in this study present an advance in bioremediation techniques for the biodegradation of organic compound such as phenol using a bioreactor. We have also demonstrated the potential of microorganisms from cow dung as a source of biomass (Singh and Fulekar, 2009).

4. Bioremediation of benzene using cow dung microflora in two phase partitioning bioreactor

Bioremediation of benzene has been carried out using cow dung microflora in a bioreactor. The bioremediation of benzene under the influence of cow dung microflora was found to be 100% and 67.5%, at initial concentrations of 100 mg/l and 250 mg/l within 72 h and 168 h respectively; whereas at higher concentration (500 mg/l), benzene was found to be inhibitory. Hence the two phase partitioning bioreactor (TPPB) has been designed and developed to carryout biodegradation at higher concentration. In TPPB the contaminant found to be biodegraded at 5000 mg/l concentration up to 50.17% over a period Q1 of 168 h. Further the *Pseudomonas putida* MHF 7109 was isolated from cow dung microflora as potential benzene degrader and its ability to degrade benzene at various concentrations was evaluated. The data indicates 100%, 81% and 65% degradation at the concentrations of 50 mg/l, 100 mg/l, 250 mg/l within the time period of 24 h, 96 h and 168 h respectively. The GC-MS data also shows the presence of catechol and 2-hydroxymuconic semialdehyde, which confirms the established pathway of benzene biodegradation. The present research proves the potential of cow dung microflora as a source of biomass for benzene biodegradation in TPPB (Singh and Fulekar, 2009).

5. Bioremediation of pesticide chlorpyrifos in mycorrhizosphere ecological remediation Unit using ryegrass

The potential of ryegrass for rhizosphere bioremediation of chlorpyrifos in mycorrhizal soil was investigated by the green house pot culture experiments. The pot cultured soil amended at initial chlorpyrifos concentration of 10 mg/kg was observed to be degraded completely within 7 days where the rest amended concentrations (25-100 mg/kg) decreased rapidly under the influence of ryegrass mycorrhizosphere as the incubation progressed till 28 days. This bioremediation of chlorpyrifos in soil is attributed to the microorganisms associated with the roots in the ryegrass rhizosphere, therefore the microorganisms surviving in the rhizospheric soil spiked at highest concentration (100 mg/kg) was assessed and used for isolation of chlorpyrifos degrading microorganisms. The potential degrader identified by 16S rDNA analysis using BLAST technique was *Pseudomonas nitroreducens* PS-2. Further, bio-augmentation for the enhanced chlorpyrifos biodegradation was performed using PS-2 as an inoculum in the experimental set up similar to the earlier. The heterotrophic bacteria and fungi were also enumerated from the inoculated and non-inoculatedrhizospheric soils. In bio-augmentation experiments, the percentage dissipation of chlorpyrifos was 100% in the inoculated rhizospheric soil as compared to 76.24, 90.36 and 90.80% in the non-inoculated soil for initial concentrations of 25, 50 and 100 mg/kg at the 14th, 21st and 28th day intervals respectively (Korade and Fulekar, 2009).

6. Biodegradation of petroleum hydrocarbon compounds toluene and o-xylene (BTX) by *Pseudomonas putida* strain MHF 7109

Pseudomonas putida MHF 7109 has been isolated and identified from cow dung microbial consortium for biodegradation of selected petroleum hydrocarbon compounds – benzene, toluene, and o-xylene (BTX). Each compound was applied separately at concentrations of 50, 100, 250, and 500mgL-1 in minimal salt medium to evaluate degradation activity of the identified microbial strain. The results indicated that the strain used has high potential to degrade BTX at a concentration of 50mgL-1 within a period of 48, 96, and 168 h, respectively; whereas the concentration of 100mgL-1 of benzene and toluene was found to be completely degraded within 120 and 168 h, respectively. Sixty-two percent of o-xylene was degraded within 168 h at the 100mgL-1 concentration level. The maximum degradation rates for BTX were 1.35, 1.04, and 0.51mgL-1 h-1, respectively. At higher concentrations (250 and 500mgL-1) BTX inhibited the activity of microorganisms. The mass spectrometry analysis identified the intermediates as catechol, 2-hydroxymuconic semialdehyde, 3- methylcatechol, cis-2- hydroxypenta-2,4-dienoate, 2-methylbenzyl alcohol, and 1,2-dihydroxy-6-methylcyclohexa- 3,5-dienecarboxylate, for BTX, respectively. *P. putida* MHF 7109 has been found to havehigh potential for biodegradation of volatile petroleum hydrocarbons (Singh and Fulekar, 2010).

Special Features of Bioremediation

- It is a natural process; it takes a little time, as an acceptable waste treatment process for contaminated material such as soil. Microbes able to degrade the contaminant increase in numbers when the contaminant is present; when the contaminant is degraded, the biodegradative population declines. The residues for the treatment are usually harmless products.
- Bioremediation also requires a very less effort and can often be carried out on site, often without causing a major disruption of normal activities. This also eliminates the need to transport quantities of waste off site and the potential threats to human health and the environment that can arise during transportation.
- Bioremediation is also a cost effective process as it lost less than the other conventional methods that are used for clean-up of hazardous waste.

- It also helps in complete destruction of the pollutants, many of the hazardous compounds can be transformed to harmless products, this feature also eliminates the chance of future liability associated with treatment and disposal of contaminated material.
- It does not use any dangerous chemicals. The nutrients added to make microbes grow are fertilizers commonly used on lawns and gardens. Because bioremediation changes the harmful chemicals into water and harmless gases, the harmful chemicals are completely destroyed.

Limitations of Bioremediation:

- Bioremediation is limited to those compounds that are biodegradable. Not all compounds are susceptible to rapid and complete degradation.
- There are some concerns that the products of biodegradation may be more persistent or toxic than the parent compound. Biological processes are often highly specific. Important site factors required for success include the presence of metabolically capable microbial populations, suitable environmental growth conditions, and appropriate levels of nutrients and contaminants.
- It is difficult to extrapolate from bench and pilot-scale studies to full-scale field operations.
- Research is needed to develop and engineer bioremediation technologies that are appropriate for sites with complex mixtures of contaminants that are not evenly dispersed in the environment. Contaminants may be present as solids, liquids, and gases.
- Bioremediation often takes longer than other treatment options, such as excavation and removal of soil or incineration.
- Regulatory uncertainty remains regarding acceptable performance criteria for bioremediation. There is no accepted definition of "clean", evaluating performance of bioremediation is difficult.

CONCLUSION

Various molecular, genetic, and metabolic engineering tools have accelerated the progress toward bioremediation and have led to specifically designed microorganism for various bio-based clean-up processes. The ever expanding knowledge base about biodegradation pathways, structural and functional knowledge of key enzymes, and extensive molecular characterization of naturally detoxifying microorganisms will further our progress to cleverly designed pathways toward a new era of bioremediation. Although a wide range of new microorganisms have been discovered that are able to degrade highly stable, toxic organic xenobiotics, still many pollutants persist in the environment. A number of reasons have been identified as challenges posed to the microorganisms working in contaminated sites. Such potential limitations to biological treatments include:

poor bioavailability of chemicals, presence of other toxic compounds, inadequate supply of nutrients and insufficient biochemical potential for effective biodegradation. A wide range of bioremediation strategies have been developed for the treatment of contaminated soils using natural and modified microorganisms.

Selecting the most appropriate strategy to treat a specific site can be guided by considering three basic principles: the amenability of the pollutant to biological transformation to less toxic products, the bioavailability of the contaminant to microorganisms and the opportunity for bioprocess optimization. With the help of advances in bioinformatics, biotechnology holds a bright future for developing bioprocesses for environmental applications. There is no doubt that bioremediation is in the process of paving a way to greener pastures. Regardless of which aspect of bioremediation that is used, this technology offers an efficient and cost effective way to treat contaminated ground water and soil. Its advantages generally outweigh the disadvantages, which is evident by the number of sites that choose to use this technology and its increasing popularity. Once again thanks to the bioremediation technology to clean up the polluted environment and therefore may be used as management tool.

REFERENCES

1. Al-Hasan, R., N., Sorkhoh, and S. Radwan. 1992. Self-cleaning the Gulf. Nature. 359: 109.
2. Al-Lihaibi, S.S. and L. Al-Omran. 1995. Petroleum Hydrocarbons in Offshore Sediments from the Gulf. *Mar. Poll. Bull.* 32: 65-69.
3. Al-Muzaini, S and P.G. Jacob. 1996. An Assessment of Toxic Metals Content in the Marine Sediments of the Shuiba Industrial Area, Kuwait, After the Oil Spill during the Gulf War. *Water Sci. Technol.* 34: 203-210.
4. Al-Zarban, S. and C. Obuekwe. 1998. Bioremediation of Crude Oil Pollution in the Kuwait Desert: The Role of Adherent Microorganisms. *Environ. Int.* 24: 823-834.
5. Atlas R.M. 1981. Microbial Degradation of Petroleum Hydrocarbons: An Environmental Perspective, Microbiology Reviews, 45, pp. 180-209.
6. Atlas, R.M. 1977. Stimulated Petroleum Biodegradation. *Crit. Rev. Microbiol.* 5: 371-386.
7. Atlas, R.M. 1991a. Microbial Hydrocarbon Degradation-bioremediation of Oil Spills. *J. Chem. Technol. Biotechnol.* 52: 149-156.
8. Atlas, R.M. 1991b. Bioremediation: Using Nature's Helpers-Microbes and Enzymes-to remedy Mankind's Pollutants. pp. 255-264 in *Biotechnology in the Feed Industry: Proceedings of Alltech's Thirteenth Annual Symposium*, Lyons, T.P. and K.A Jacques, eds., Alltech Technical Publications, Nicholasville, Kentucky.
9. Atlas, R.M. and R. Bartha. 1972. Degradation and Mineralization of Petroleum in Sea Water: Limitation by Nitrogen and Phosphorus. *Biotech. Bioeng.* 14: 309-317.
10. Atlas, R.M. and R. Bartha. 1972. Degradation and Mineralization of Petroleum in Sea Water: Limitation by Nitrogen and Phosphorus. *Biotech. Bioeng.* 14: 309-317.

11. Atlas, R.M. and R. Bartha. 1993. *Microbial Ecology, Fundamentals and Applications*. The Benjamin/Cummings Publishing Company, Inc., San Francisco, California.
12. Atlas, R.M. and R. Bartha. 1993. *Microbial Ecology, Fundamentals and Applications*. The Benjamin/Cummings Publishing Company, Inc., San Francisco, California.
13. Berendes FN, Sabarth B, Averhoff G, Gottschalk G (1998) Construction and Use of an *ipb* DNA Module to Generate *Pseudomonas* Strains with Constitutive Trichloroethene and Isopropylbenzene Oxidation Activity. Appl Environ Microbiol 64: 2454-2462.
14. Blackburn, J.W., Hafker, W.R., 1993. The Impact of Biochemistry, Bioavilability, and Bioactivity on the Selection of Bioremediation Technologies. TIB Tech. 11, 328-333.
15. Boopathy, R., Manning, J., 1999. Surfactant-enhanced Bioremediation of Soil Contaminated with 2, 4, 6-trinitrotoluene in Soil Slurry Reactors. Water Environ. Res. 71, 119-124.
16. Bossert, I.D. and G.C. Compeau. 1995. Cleanup of Petroleum Hydrocarbon Contaminating in Soil. pp. 77-128 in *Microbial Transformation and Degradation of Toxic Organic Chemicals*, L.Y. Young and C.E. Cerniglia, eds., Wiley-Liss, New York, and John Wiley & Sons, Chichester, UK.
17. Brar SK, Verma M, Surampalli RY, Misra K, Tyagi RD, Meunier N, Blais JF: Bioremediation of Hazardous Wastes: A Review. Pract Periodical Hazard, Toxic Radioactive Waste Manag 2006, 10: 59-72.
18. Brenner V, Arensdorf JJ, Foght DD (1994) Genetic Construction of PCB Degraders. Biodegradation 5: 359-377.
19. Brown, R.A and R.D. Norris. 1994. The Evolution of a Technology: Hydrogen Peroxide in *in situ* Bioremediation. pp. 148-162 in *Hydrocarbon Bioremediation*, R.E. Hinchee, B.C. Alleman, R.E. Hoeppel, and R.N. Miller eds., CRC Press, Boca Raton, Florida.
20. Burback, B.L. and J.J. Perry. 1993. Biodegradation and Biotransformation of Groundwater Pollutant Mixtures by *Mycobacterium vaccae*. *Appl. Environ. Microbiol.* 59: 1025-1029.
21. Chakrabarty AM (1982) Genetic Mechanisms in the Dissimilation of Chlorinated Compounds. In: Chakrabarty AM (ed) Biodegradation and Detoxification of Environmental Pollutants. CRC, Boca Raton, pp. 127-139.
22. Chakrabarty, A.M. 1974. Microorganisms having Multiple Compatible Degradative Energy Generating Plasmids and Preparation Thereof. *Off Gaz. US Patent Office* 922: 1224.
23. Chakrabarty, A.M., G. Chou and I.C. Gunsalus. 1973. Genetic Regulation of Octane Dissimilation Plasmid in *Pseudomonas*. *Proc. Nat. Acad. Sci.* USA, 70: 1137-1140.
24. Chhatre, S., H. Purohit, R. Shanker and P. Khanna. 1996. Bacterial Consortia for Crude Oil Spill Remediation. *Water. Sci. Technol.* 34: 187-193.
25. Chianelli, R.R., T. Aczel, R.E. Bare, G.N. George, M.W. Genowitz, M.J. Grossman, C.E. Haith, F.J. Kaiser, R.R. Lessard, R. Liotta, R.L. Mastracchio, V. Minak-Bern-ero, R.C. Prince, W.K. Robbins, E.I. Stiefel, J.B. Wilkinson, S.M. Hinton, J.R. Bragg, S.J. McMillan, and R.M. Atlas. 1991. Bioremediation Technology Development and Application to the Alaskan Spill. pp. 549-558 in *Proceedings of the 1991 International Oil Spill Conference*. American Petroleum Institute, Washington, D.C.
26. Cohen, Y. 2002. Bioremediation of Oil by Marine Microbial Mats. *Int. Microbiol.* 5: 189-193.
27. Colberg PJS and Young LY (1995). Anaerobic Degradation of No Halogenated Homocyclic Aromatic Compounds Coupled with Nitrate, Iron, or Sulfate Reduction. In: *Microbial Transformation and Degradation of Toxic Organic Chemicals*, Wiley Liss, New York 307-330.

28. Compeau, G.C., W.D. Mahaffey, and L. Patras. 1991. Full-scale Bioremediation of a Contaminated Soil and Water. pp. 91-110. in *Environmental Biotechnology for Waste Treatment*, G.S. Sayler, R. Fox and J.W. Blackburn, eds., Plenum Press, New York.

29. Das N. and Chandran P. (2011), Microbial Degradation of Petroleum Hydrocarbon Contaminants: An Overview. Biotechnology Research International, 2011, pp. 1-13.

30. Dibble, J.T., and R. Bartha. 1979. Effect of Environmental Parameters on the Biodegradation of Oil Sludge. *Appl. Environ. Microbiol.* 37: 729-739.

31. Dua M, Sethunathan N and Johri AK (2002). Biotechnology Bioremediation Success and Limitations. *Applied Microbiology and Biotechnology* 59: 143-152.

32. Erb RW, Wagner-Dobber I (1993) Detection of Polychlorinated Biphenyl Degradation Genes in Polluted Sediments by Direct DNA Extraction and Polymerase Chain Reaction. Appl Environ Microbiol 59: 4065-4073.

33. Erb, R.W., C.A. Eichner, I. Wangler-Dobler and K.N. Timmis. 1997. Bioprotection of Microbial Communities from Toxic Phenol Mixtures by Genetically Designed Pseudomonad. *Nature Biotechnol.* 15: 378-382.

34. Flathman, P.E., J.H. Carson, Jr., S.J. Whitenhead, K.A. Khan, D.M. Barnes and J.S. Evans. 1991. Laboratory Evaluation of the Utilization of Hydrogen Peroxide for Enhanced Biological Treatment of Petroleum Hydrocarbon Contaminants in Soil.

35. Fowler, S.W. 1988. Coastal Baseline Studies of Pollutants in Bahrain, UAE and Oman. pp. 155-180 in *Proceedings of Symposium on Regional Marine Pollution Monitoring and Research Programms*, ROPME IGC-412. Regional Organization for the Protection of the Marine Environment, Kuwait.

36. Fox, J.E. 1991. Confronting Doubtful Oil Cleanup Data. *Biotechnology* 9 14.

37. Geetha M, Fulekar MH. 2008. Bioremediation of Pesticides in Surface Soil Treatment Unit Using Microbial Consortia. African Journal of Environmental Science & Technology, 2(2): 36-45.

38. Glazer AN, Nikaido H (1995) Microbial Biotechnology: Fundamentals of Applied Microbiology. Freeman, New York.

39. Glazer, A.N., and H. Nikaido. 1994. *Microbial Biotechnology*. Freeman, New York. Kostal, J., M. Suchaneck, H. Klierova, K. Demnerova, B. Kralova and D.L. McBeth. 1998.

40. Hauschild JE, Masai E, Sugiyama K, Hatta T, Kimbara K, Fukuda M, Yano K (1996) Identification of an Alternative 2, 3- dihydroxybiphenyl 1, 2-dioxygenase in *Rhodococcus* sp. Strain RHA1 and Cloning of the Gene. Appl Environ Microbiol 62: 2940-2946.

41. Hinchee, R.E., B.C. Alleman, R.E. Hoeppel and R.N. Miller, eds., CRC Press, Inc., Boca Raton, Florida, Lestan, D. and R.T. Lamar. 1996. Development of Fungal Inocula for Bioaugmentation of Contaminated Soils. *Appl. Environ. Microbiol.* 62: 2045-2052.

42. Hoff R. (1993), Bioremediation: An Overview of its Development and Use for Oil Spill Cleanup, Marine Pollution Bulletin, 26, 9, pp. 476-481.

43. Iwamoto T, Nasu M (2001) Current Bioremediation Practice and Perspective. J Biosci Bioeng 92: 1-8.

44. Jamison, V.M., R.L. Raymond, and J.O. Hudson, Jr. 1975. Biodegradation of High-octane Gasoline in Groundwater. *Dev. Ind. Microbiol.* 16: 305-312.

45. Jobson, A., M. McLaughlin, F.D. Cook, and D.W.S. Westlake. 1974. Effect of Amendments on the Microbial Utilization of Oil Applied to Soil. *Appl. Microbiol.* 27: 166-171.

46. Korade D, Fulekar MH. 2009. Rhizosphere Remediation of Chlorpyrifos in Mycorhizospheric Soil Using Ryegrass. Journal of Hazardous Material, 172: 1344-1350

47. Kumamaru T, Suenaga H, Mitsuoka M, Watanabe T, Furukawa H (1998) Enhanced Degradation of Polychlorinated Biphenyls by Directed Evolution of Biphenyl Dioxygenase. Nat Biotechnol 16: 663-666.

48. Ladousse A. and Tramier B. (1991), Results of 12 Years of Research in Spilled Oil Bioremediation: Inipol EAP 22. Proceedings of the International Oil Spill Conference, March 4-7, 1991, San Diego, California, pp. 577-581.

49. LaDousse, A. and B. Tramier. 1991. Results of 12 Years of Research in Spilled Oil Bioremediation: Inipol EAP 22. pp. 577-581 in *Proceedings of the 1991 International Oil Spill Conference*. American Petroleum Institute, Washington, D.C.

50. Lal B and Khanna S (1996). Degradation of Crude Oil by Acinetobacter Calcoaceticus and Alcaligenes Odorans. *Journal of Applied Bacteriology* 81: 355-362.

51. Lange CC, Wackett LP, Minton KW, Daly MJ (1998) Engineering a Recombinant *Deinococcus radiodurans* for Organopollutant Degradation in Radioactive Mixed Waste Environments. Nat Biotechnol 16: 929-933.

52. Lau PCK, Lorenzo VDE (1999) Genetic Engineering: The Frontier of Bioremediation. Environ Sci Technol 4: 124A-128A.

53. Le Floch S., Merlin F.X. and Guillerme M. (1997), Bioren: Recent Experiment on Oil Polluted Shoreline in Temperate Climate. In: *In-Situ* and On-Site Bioremediation, Alleman, B.C. and Leeson A. (Eds.). Battelle Press, Columbus, pp. 411-417.

54. Leadbetter, E.R. and J.W. Foster. 1958. Studies of Some Methane Utilizing Bacteria. *Arch. Microbiol.* 30: 91-118.

55. Leahy, J.G., and R.R. Colwell. 1990. Microbial Degradation of Hydrocarbons in the Environment. *Microbiol. Rev.* 54: 305-315.

56. Lee, M.D., J.M. Thomas, R.C. Borden, P.B. Bedient and C.H. Ward. 1988. Biorestoration of Aquifers Contaminated with Organic Compounds. *CRC Crit. Rev. Environ. Control* 18: 29-89.

57. Lu, C.J. 1994. Effects of Hydrogen Peroxide on the *in situ* Biodegradation of Organic Chemicals in a Simulated Groundwater System. pp. 140-147 in *Hydrocarbon Bioremediation*, Hinchee, R.E., B.C. Alleman, R.E. Hoeppel and R.N. Miller, eds., CRC Press, Inc., Boca Raton, Florida.

58. Lu, C.J. and M.C. Hwang. 1992. "Effects of Hydrogen Peroxide on the *in situ* Biodegradation of Chlorinated Phenols in Groundwater. *Water Environ. Federation 65th Annual Conference*, Sept. 20-24. New Orleans, Louisiana.

59. Ma X, Novak PJ, Ferguson J, Sadowsky M, LaPara TM, Semmens MJ and Hozalski RM (2007). The Impact of H2 Addition on Dechorinating Microbial Communities. *Bioremediation Journal*, 11: 45-55.

60. Mangan, K.S. 1990. University of Texas Microbiologist Seeks to Persuade Skeptical Colleagues that Bacteria could be Useful in Cleaning Up Major Oil Spills. *Chron. Higher Education*. 37: A5-A9.

61. Mangan, K.S. 1990. University of Texas Microbiologist Seeks to Persuade Skeptical Colleagues that Bacteria could be Useful in Cleaning Up Major Oil Spills. *Chron. Higher Education*. 37: A5-A9.

62. Manning, J., Boopathy, R., Kulpa, C.F., 1995. A Laboratory Study in Support of the Pilot Demonstration of a Biological Soil Slurry Reactor. Report No. SFIM-AEC-TS-CR-94038. US Army Environmental Center, Aberdeen Proving Ground, MD.

63. Margesin, R. 2000. Potential of Cold-adapted Microorganisms for Bioremediation of Oil Polluted Alpine Soils. *Int. Biodet. Biodeg.* 46: 3-10.

64. Masai E, Yamada A, Healy JM, Hatta T, Kimbara K, Fukuda M, Yano K (1995) Characterization of Biphenyl Catabolic Genes of Gram Positive Polychlorinated Biphenyl Degrader *Rhodococcus* sp. RH1. Appl Environ Microbiol 61: 2079-2085.

65. Mearns A.J. (1997), Cleaning Oiled Shores: Putting Bioremediation to the Test. Spill Science and Technology Bulletin, 4 (4), pp. 209-217.

66. Mishra, S., J. Jyot, R.C. Kuhad, and B. Lal. 2001. *In situ* Bioremediation Potential of an Oily Sludge-degrading Bacterial Consortiium. *Current Microbiol.* 43: 328-335.

67. Nichols W.J. (2001), The United States Environmental Protection Agency: National Oil and Hazardous Substances Pollution Contingency Plan, Subpart J Product Schedule (40 CFR 300.900). Proceedings of the 2001 International Oil Spill Conference, March 26-29, 2001, Tampa, Florida, pp. 1479-1483.

68. Pardieck, D.L., E.J. Bouwer and A.T. Stone. 1992. Hydrogen Peroxide Use to Increase Oxidant Capacity for *in situ* Bioremediation of Contaminated Soils and Aquifers: A Review. *J. Contaminant Hydrol.* 9: 221-242.

69. Perry, J.J. 1984. Microbial Metabolism of Cyclic Alkanes. pp. 61-98 in *Petroleum Microbiology*, R.M. Atlas, ed., Macmillan Publishing Co., New York.

70. Prince R.C. (1993), Petroleum Spill Bioremediation in Marine Environments, Critical Reviews in Microbiology, 19, 4, pp. 217-242.

71. Prince, R.C., J.R. Clark, and J.E. Lindstrom. 1990. Bioremediation Monitoring Report in the U.S. Coast Guard. *Alaska Department of Environmental Conservation*, Anchorage, Alaska.

72. Pritchard, H.P. 1990. Bioremediation of Oil Contaminated Beach Material in Prince William Sound, Alaska. 199th National Meeting of the American Chemical Society, Boston, Massachusetts, 22-27 April, Abstract Environment 154.

73. *Pseudomonas* C12B, an SDS Degrading Strain, Harbours a Plasmid Coding for Degradation of Medium Chain Length n-alkanes. *Int. Biodet. Biodeg.* 42: 221-228. Leavitt, M.E. and K.L. Brown. 1994. Bioremediation Versus Bioaugmentation-three Case Studies. pp. 72-79 in *Hydrocarbon Bioremediation*.

74. Romanov V, Hausinger RP (1994) *Pseudomonas aeruginosa* 142 uses a Three Component *ortho*-halobenzoate 1, 2-dioxygenase for Metabolism of 2, 4-dichloro and 2-chlorobenzoate. J Bacteriol 176: 3368-3374.

75. Ruberto, L., S.C. Vazquez and W.P. Mac Cormack. 2003. Effectiveness of the Natural Bacterial Flora, Biostimulation and Bioaugmentation on the Bioremediation of a Hydrocarbon Contaminated Antractic Soil. *Int. Biodet. Biodeg.* 52: 115-125.

76. Saeed, T., S. Al-Muzaini, and A. Al-Bloushi. 1996. Post-Gulf War Assessment of the Levels of PAHs in the Sediments from Shuiba Industrial Area, Kuwait. *Water Sci. Technol.* 34: 195-201.

77. Šaššek, V., T. Cajthaml and M. Bhatt. 2003. Use of Fungal Technology in Soil Remediation: A Case Study. *Water, Air, Soil Pollut. Focus* 3: 5-14.

78. Schlegel, H.G. 1977. Aeration without Air: Oxygen Supply by Hydrogen Peroxide. *Biotechnol. Bioeng.* 19: 413.

79. Scragg, A. 1999. *Environmental Biotechnology*. Pearson Education limited. Essex, England.

80. Semprini, L. 1997. Strategies for the Aerobic Co-metabolism of Clorinated Solvents. *Curr. Opin. Biotechnol.* 8: 296-308.

81. Singh D, Fulekar MH. 2009. Benzene Bioremediation Using Cow Dung Microflora in Two Phase Partitioning Bioreactor. Journal of Hazardous Material, 175: 336-343

82. Singh D, Fulekar MH. 2010. Biodegradation of Petroleum Hydrocarbons by *Pseudomonas putida* Strain MHF 7109 Isolated from Cow Dung Microbial Consortium. Clean Soil, Air, Water, 38(8): 781-786.

83. Van Eyk, J. 1994. Venting and Bioventing for the *in situ* Removal of Petroleum from Soil. pp. 234-251 in *Hydrocarbon Bioremediation*, Hinchee, R.E., B.C. Alleman, R.E. Hoeppel, and R.N. Miller, eds., CRC Press, Inc., Boca Raton, Florida.

84. Vasudevan, N. and P. Rajaram. 2001. Bioremediation of Oil Sludge-contaminated Soil. *Environ. Int.* 26: 409-411.

85. Verstraete, W., R. Vanloocke, R. DeBorger, and A. Verlinde. 1976. Modelling of the Breakdown and the Mobilization of Hydrocarbons in Unsaturated Soil Layers. pp. 99-112 in *Proceedings of the 3rd International Biodegradation Symposium*, J.M. Sharpley and A.M. Kaplan, eds., Applied Science Publishers Ltd., London.

86. Vidali M (2001). Bioremediation An Overview. *Pure and Applied Chemistry* 73(7) 1163-1172. Weyens N, Van der Lelie D, Taghavi S and Vangronsveld J (2009). Phytoremediation: Plant–endophyte Partnerships take the Challenge. *Current Opinion in Biotechnology* 20: 248-254.

87. Watt, I. 1994a. Shorelines Clean-up Procedures. A Discussion Pertaining to the Gulf Sanctuary.

88. Xu, R, J.P. Obbard, and E.T.C. Tay. 2003. Optimization of Slow-release Fertilizer Dosage for Bioremediation of Oil-contaminated Beach Sediment in a Tropical Environment. *World J. Microb. Biotech.* 19: 719-725.

89. Yee DC, Maynard JA, Wood TK (1998) Rhizoremediation of Trichloroethylene by a Recombinant, Root-colonizing *Pseudomonas fluorescens* Strain Expressing Toluene *ortho*-monooxygenase Constitutively. Appl Environ Microbiol 64: 112-118.

90. Zucchi, M., L. Angiolini, S. Borin, L. Brusetti, N. Dietrich, C. Gigliotti, P. Barbieri, C. Sorlini, and D. Daffonchio. 2003. Response of Bacterial Community during Bioremediation of an Oil-polluted Soil. *J. Appl. Microbiol.* 94: 248-257.

91. Zwick, T.C., Foote E.A. and Pollack A.J. (1997), Effects of Nutrient Addition during Bioventing of Fuel Contaminated Soils in an Arid Environment. In: In-Situ and On-Site Bioremediation, Alleman, B.C. and Leeson A. (Eds.). Battelle Press, Columbus, pp. 403-409.

Pages: 81-97

AGRICULTURE, ENVIRONMENT AND NANO-SCIENCE
Edited by: Dr. Pawan Kumar 'Bharti'
ISBN: 978-93-5056-760-9
Edition: 2015
Published by: Discovery Publishing House Pvt. Ltd., New Delhi (India)

4

Constructed Wetlands

E. Parameswari; V. Davamani and A. Rathinasamy

INTRODUCTION

Wetlands, either constructed or natural, offer a cheaper and low-cost alternative technology for wastewater treatment. A constructed wetland system that is specifically engineered for water quality improvement as a primary purpose is termed as a 'Constructed Wetland Treatment System' (CWTS). In the past, many such systems were constructed to treat low volumes of wastewater loaded with easily degradable organic matter for isolated populations in urban areas. However, widespread demand for improved receiving water quality, and water reclamation and reuse, is currently the driving force for the implementation of CWTS all over the world..

Constructed wetland system are engineered systems that have been designed and constructed to utilize the natural process involving wetland vegetations, soils and their associated microbial assemblages to assist in treating waste water. They are designed to take advantages of many of the

Horticultural College and Research Institute, Periyakulam, Tamilnadu, (India).

process that occur in natural wetlands, but do so within a more controlled environment. Synonymous terms to constructed wetland include manmade, engineered or artificial wetlands.

WHY USE A CONSTRUCTED WETLAND

Constructed wetlands can treat wastewater from a variety of sources. One of the more common uses is to provide additional or advanced treatment of wastewater from homes, businesses and even communities. Wetlands treat wastewater that has already had most of the solid materials removed from it through some type of primary or secondary treatment.

Homes, businesses, farms, schools and other individual wastewater sources in rural areas sometimes can add a constructed wetland to a septic system or other onsite system to replace or assist a soil absorption field. Some onsite systems can be specifically designed from the start to use a constructed wetland in addition to a soil absorption field on properties with site constraints, such as tight or saturated soils.

Wetlands are good at handling intermittent periods of both light and heavy wastewater flows. Therefore, they often work well with wastewater treatment systems that serve hotels, campsites, resorts and recreational areas.

In environmentally sensitive areas, constructed wetlands can be used with onsite systems to improve the quality of the effluent before it is returned to the environment. They are also used on farms as an inexpensive way to provide extra treatment to animal wastes and by certain industries such as pulp and paper mills. Constructed wetlands are common in mining regions and are used to treat mine drainage.

Wetlands are not practical for treating industrial wastewater that includes pesticides, herbicides or large amounts of ammonia. Additionally wetland plants may accumulate high concentrations metals from some wastewater sources. This may affect the habitat value of the wetland.

Natural Wetlands Vs. Constructed Wetlands

Constructed wetlands, in contrast to natural wetlands, are man-made systems or engineered wetlands that are designed, built and operated to emulate functions of natural wetlands for human desires and needs. It is created from a non-wetland ecosystem or a former terrestrial environment, mainly for the purpose of contaminant or pollutant removal from wastewater (Hammer, 1994).

These constructed wastewater treatments may include swamps and marshes. Most of the constructed wetland systems are marshes. Marshes are shallow water regions dominated by emergent herbaceous vegetation including cattails, bulrushes, rushes and reeds.

Types and wise use of constructed wetland treatment systems.

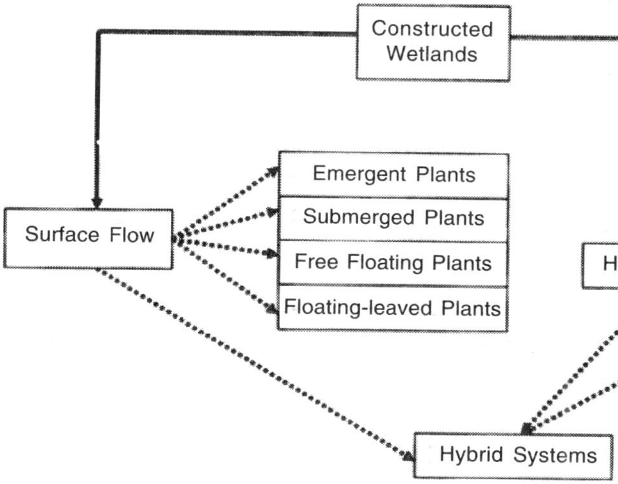

Fig. 4.1: Classification of Constructed Wetlands for Wastewater Treatment

Constructed wetlands could be classified according to the various parameters but two most important criteria are water flow regime (Surface and subsurface) and the type of macropytic growth (fig. 4.1). Different types of constructed wetlands may be combined with each other (so called hybrid of combined system) in order to exploit the specific advantages of the different systems. The quality of the final effluent from the systems improve with the complexity.

Horizontal flow system (HFS) is, wastewater is fed at the inlet and flows horizontally through the bed to the outlet. Vertical flow systems (VFS) are fed intermittently and drain vertically through the bed via a network of drainage pipes.

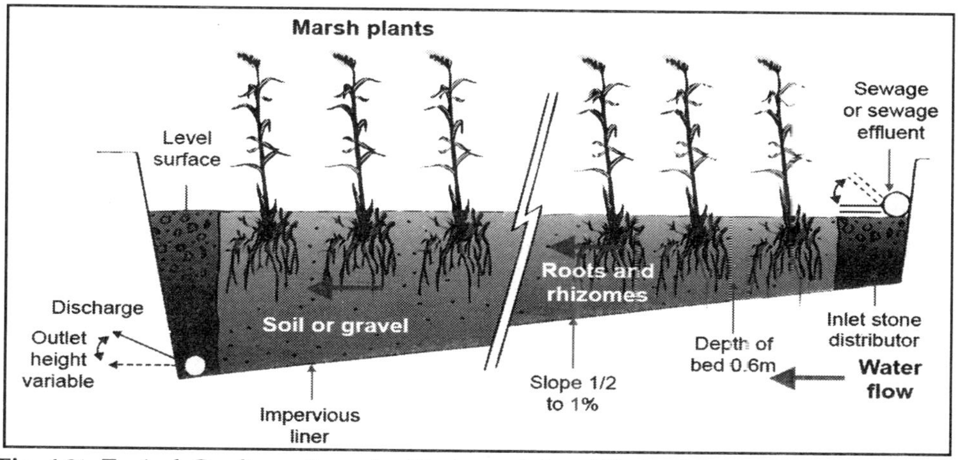

Fig. 4.2: Typical Configuration of a Horizontal-flow Wetland System (Modified from Cooper et al., 1996)

Surface Flow (SF)

The use of SF systems is extensive in North America. These systems are used mainly for municipal wastewater treatment with large wastewater flows for nutrient polishing. The SF system tends to be rather large in size with only a few smaller systems in use.

The majority of constructed wetland treatment systems are Surface-Flow or Free-Water surface (SF) systems. These types utilise influent waters that flow across a basin or a channel that supports a variety of vegetation, and water is visible at a relatively shallow depth above the surface of the substrate materials. Substrates are generally native soils and clay or impervious geotechnical materials that prevent seepage (Reed, *et al.*, 1995). Inlet devices are installed to maximise sheetflow of wastewater through the wetland, to the outflow channel. Typically, bed depth is about 0.4 m.

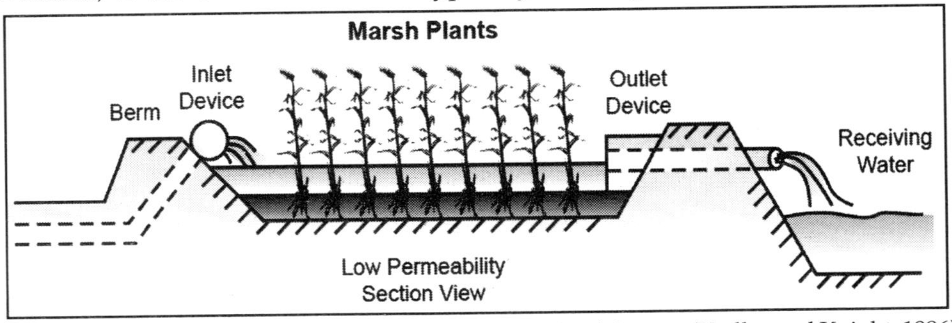

Fig. 4.3: Typical Configuration of a Surface Flow Wetland System (Kadlec and Knight, 1996)

Sub-surface Flow (SSF) system - The SSF system includes soil based technology which is predominantly used in Northern Europe and the vegetated gravel beds are found in Europe, Australia, South Africa and almost all over the world.

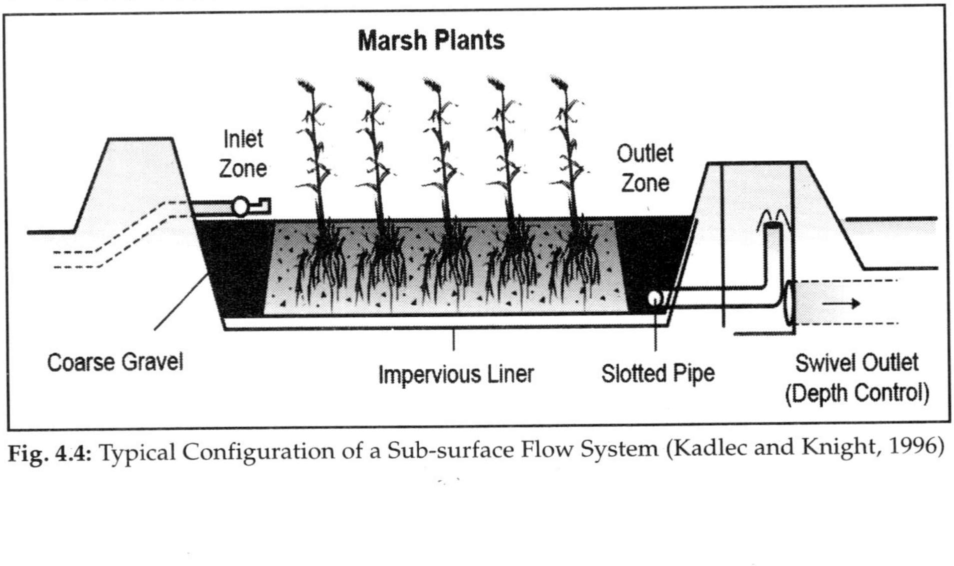

Fig. 4.4: Typical Configuration of a Sub-surface Flow System (Kadlec and Knight, 1996)

In a vegetated Sub-surface Flow (SSF) system, water flows from one end to the other end through permeable substrates which is made of mixture of soil and gravel or crusher rock. The substrate will support the growth of rooted emergent vegetation. It is also called "Root-Zone Method" or "Rock-Reed-Filter" or "Emergent Vegetation Bed System". The media depth is about 0.6 m deep and the bottom is a clay layer to prevent seepage. Media size for most gravel substrate ranged from 5 to 230 mm with 13 to 76 mm being typical. The bottom of the bed is sloped to minimise water that flows overland. Wastewater flows by gravity horizontally through the root zone of the vegetation about 100-150 mm below the gravel surface. Many macro and micro-organisms inhabit the substrates. Free water is not visible. The inlet zone has a buried perforated pipe to distribute maximum flow horizontally through the treatment zone. Treated water is collected at outlets at the base of the media, typically 0.3 to 0.6 m below bed surface.

Establishment of Constructed Wetland Treatment Systems

The creation of a constructed wetland treatment system can be divided into a wetland construction and vegetation establishment stage. Wetland construction includes pre-construction activities such as land clearing and site preparation, followed by construction of a wetland landform and installation of water control structures. In the stage of site clearing and grubbing, the site is cleared and existing vegetation is removed to allow construction of wetland cells. All tree root stumps and rubble below ground should be removed. Some endemic species with conservation values should be transferred off site for ex-conservation or protected intact on the site. For landforming, tractors are used to remove and stockpile topsoils from the created wetland to be reused. General contours of the wetland are graded, followed by the construction of wetland cell berms by compacting soil and installing of liners. Deep zones and islands will be created. Final site grading consists of leveling the wetland cell bottom to optimise the spreading and sheet flow of wastewaters in the completed wetland. The wetland cells are flooded to a 'wet' condition for planting. Wetland plants are transferred to the site and planted manually. After plants are established, water levels are gradually increased to normal water levels, and wetlands are completely created.

Roles of Wetlands Plants in Wastewater Treatment

In general, the most significant functions of wetland plants (emergents) in relation to water purification are the physical effects brought by the presence of the plants. The plants provide a huge surface area for attachment and growth of microbes. The physical components of the plants stabilise the surface of the beds, slow down the water flow thus assist in sediment settling and trapping process and finally increasing water transparency.

Wetland plants play a vital role in the removal and retention of nutrients and help in preventing the eutrophication of wetlands. A range of wetland plants has shown their ability to assist in the breakdown of wastewater. The Common Reed *Phragmites karka* and Cattail *Typha angustifolia* are good examples of marsh species that can effectively uptake nutrients. These plants have a large biomass both above (leaves) and below (underground stem and roots) the surface of the substrate. The sub-surface plant tissues grow horizontally and vertically, and create an extensive matrix, which binds the soil particles and creates a large surface area for the uptake of nutrients and ions.

Hollow vessels in the plant tissues enable oxygen to be transported from the leaves to the root zone and to the surrounding soil (Armstrong *et al.*, 1990; Brix and Schierup, 1990). This enables the active microbial aerobic decomposition process and the uptake of pollutants from the water system to take place.

The roles of wetland plants in constructed wetland systems can be divided into 6 categories:

(i) *Physical:* Macrophytes stablise the surface of plant beds, provide good conditions for physical filtration, and provide a huge surface area for attached microbial growth. Growth of macrophytes reduces current velocity, allowing for sedimentation and increase in contact time between effluent and plant surface area, thus, to an increase in the removal of Nitrogen.

(ii) *Soil hydraulic conductivity:* Soil hydraulic conductivity is improved in an emergent plant bed system. Turnover of root mass creates macropores in a constructed wetland soil system allowing for greater percolation of water, thus increasing effluent/plant interactions.

(iii) *Organic compound release:* Plants have been shown to release a wide variety of organic compounds through their root systems, at rates up to 25% of the total photosynthetically fixed carbon. This carbon release may act as a source of food for denitrifying microbes (Brix, 1997). Decomposing plant biomass also provides a durable, readily available carbon source for the microbial populations.

(iv) *Microbial growth:* Macrophytes have above and below ground biomass to provide a large surface area for growth of microbial biofilms. These biofilms are responsible for a majority of the microbial processes in a constructed wetland system, including Nitrogen reduction (Brix, 1997).

Plants create and maintain the litter/humus layer that may be likened to a thin biofilm. As plants grow and die, leaves and stems falling to the surface of the substrate create multiple layers of organic debris (the litter/humus component). This accumulation of partially decomposed biomass creates highly porous substrate layers that provide a substantial amount of attachment surface for microbial organisms. The water quality improvement function in constructed and natural wetlands is related to and dependent upon the high conductivity of this litter/humus layer and the large surface area for microbial attachment.

(v) *Creation of aerobic soils:* Macrophytes mediate transfer of oxygen through the hollow plant tissue and leakage from root systems to the rhizosphere where aerobic degradation of organic matter and nitrification will take place. Wetland plants have adaptations with suberised and lignified layers in the hypodermis and outer cortex to minimise the rate of oxygen leakage.

The high Nitrogen removal of *Phragmites* is most likely attributable to the characteristics of its root growth. *Phragmites* allocates 50% of plant biomass to root and rhizome systems. Increased root biomass allows for greater oxygen transport into the substrate, creating a more aerobic environment favoring nitrification reactions. Nitrification requires a minimum of 2 mg O2/l to proceed at a maximum rate. It is evident that the rate of nitrification is most likely the rate limiting factor for overall Nitrogen removal from a constructed wetland system (Sikora *et al.*, 1995).

(vi) *Aesthetic values:* The macrophytes have additional site-specific values by providing habitat for wildlife and making wastewater treatment systems aesthetically pleasing.

SELECTION OF WETLAND PLANTS

Floating and submerged plants are used in an aquatic plant treatment system. A range of aquatic plants have shown their ability to assist in the breakdown of wastewater. The Water Hyacinth (*Eichhornia crassipes*), and Duckweed (*Lemna*) are common floating aquatic plants which have shown their ability to reduce concentrations of BOD, TSS and Total Phosphorus and Total Nitrogen. However prolonged presence of *Eichhornia crassipes* and *Lemna* can lead to deterioration of the water quality unless these plants are manually removed on a regular basis. These floating plants will produce a massive mat that will obstruct light penetration to the lower layer of the water column that will affect the survival of living water organisms. This system is colonised rapidly with one or only a few initial individuals. The system needs to be closely monitored to prevent attack from these nuisance species. Loss of plant cover will impair the treatment effectiveness. Maintenance cost of a floating plant system is high. Plant biomass should be regularly harvested to ensure significant nutrient removal. Plant growth also needs to be maintained at an optimum rate to maintain treatment efficiency.

The Common Reed (*Phragmites* spp.) and Cattail (*Typha* spp.) are good examples of emergent species used in constructed wetland treatment systems. Plant selection is quite similar for SF and SSF constructed wetlands. Emergent wetland plants grow best in both systems. These emergent plants play a vital role in the removal and retention of nutrients in a constructed wetland. Although emergent macrophytes are less efficient at lowering Nitrogen and Phosphorus contents by direct uptake due to their lower growth rates (compared to floating and submerged plants), their ability to uptake Nitrogen and Phosphorus from sediment sources through rhizomes is higher than from the water.

Design and Principles of Constructed Wetland Systems

The principal design criterion for a constructed wetland system includes substrate types, pollutant loading rate and retention time. Some design criteria are discussed in detail as below. Choice of wetland plant species - The selected wetland plants are preferred because they have a rapid and relatively constant growth rate. In a tropical system, wetland plants have a higher growth rate. These wetland plants are easily propagated by means of runners and by bits of mats breaking off and drifting to new areas. This will help in increasing the capacity of pollutant absorption by the plants. The plants should also be able to tolerate waterlogged-anoxic and hyper-eutrophic conditions.

The plant species should be local species and widely distributed in the country. Use of exotic plants in constructed wetland systems should be avoided as they are highly invasive and difficult to control. The plant should be a perennial with a life cycle of more than one year or two growing seasons to ensure the sustainability of the constructed wetland system. Wetland plants with aesthetic appeal will provide a landscape-pleasing environment.

Substrates - Substrates may remove wastewater constituents by ion exchange/non-specific adsorption, specific adsorption/precipitation and complexation.

The choice of substrate is determined in terms of their hydraulic permeability and their capacity to absorb nutrients and pollutants. The substrate must provide a suitable medium for successful plant growth and allow even infiltration and movement of wastewater. Poor hydraulic conductivity will result in surface flow and channeling of wastewater, severely reducing the effectiveness of the system.

A successful operation requires a hydraulic conductance of approximately 10^{-3} to 10^{-4} m $^{-1}$ s^{-1}. The chemical composition of the substrate will also affect the efficiency of the system. Soils with low nutrient content will encourage direct uptake of nutrients from the wastewater by plants. Substrate with high Al or Fe content will be most effective at lowering Phosphate concentrations in the influent. Gravels are washed to reduce clogging (increase void spaces) for better filtration. The reed system on gravel reached better nitrification rates, while denitrification was higher in the soil-based reed system (Markantonatos *et al.*, 1996).

A mixture of organic clay soils, sand, gravels and crushed stones could be used to provide support for plant growth. These substrates are ideal reactive surfaces for ion complexation and microbial attachment, also provide a sufficiently high hydraulic conductivity to avoid short-circuiting in the system.

Area of reed bed - Most wastewater treatment wetlands have been designed for minimum size and cost to provide the required level of pollutant removal. However, operation and maintenance costs may be high. The creation of a maximum effective treatment area will reduce the short-circuiting problem. Generally, horizontal flow wastewater treatment systems should have a 3-4: 1 length to width ratio and be rectangular in shape if minimal treatment area is available. A long length-width ratio is required to ensure plug flow hydraulics (Miller and Black, 1985). The required surface area for a sub-surface flow system is calculated according to an empirical formula for the reduction of BOD_5 in sewage effluent.

$$A_h = KQ_d (\ln C_0 - \ln C_t)$$

Where A_h = surface area of bed, m^2

K = rate constant, $m\ d^{-1}$

Q_d= average daily flow rate of wastewater ($m^3\ d^{-1}$)

C_0 = average daily BOD_5 of the influent ($mg\ L^{-1}$)

C_t = required average daily BOD_5 of the effluent ($mg\ L^{-1}$)

The value of K = 5.2 was derived for a 0.6 m deep bed and operating at a minimum temperature of 80C. For less biodegradable wastewater, K values of up to 15 may be appropriate. Using this formula, a minimum area of 2.2 m^2 pe^{-1} is obtained for the treatment of domestic sewage. In practice, most design systems operate on the basis of 3-5 m^2 pe^{-1}.

Nature, loading and distribution of effluent - The long-term efficiency of an emergent bed system is improved if the effluent is pre-treated prior to discharge to the active bed. Suspended particles are settled during storage in a settlement tank or a pond for 24 hours. The BOD of the primary effluent may be reduced by 40%. The removal of Nitrogen and Phosphorus for secondary wastewater is higher.

The flow of wastewater through the emergent bed system is slow, giving a long retention time, therefore the flow must be regulated so that retention times are sufficiently long for pollutant removal to be efficient. A higher reduction efficiency for mass balances of N and P could be achieved by *Phragmites* if water retention time is more than 5 days. Shorter retention times do not provide adequate time for pollutant degradation to occur. Longer retention times can lead to stagnant and anaerobic conditions. Evapotranspiration can significantly increase the retention time.

Constructed Wetland Treatment Mechanisms

Wetlands have been found to be effective in treating BOD, TSS, N and P as well as for reducing metals, organic pollutants and pathogens. The principal pollutant removal mechanisms in constructed wetlands include biological processes such as microbial metabolic activity and plant uptake as well as physico-chemical processes such as sedimentation, adsorption and precipitation at the water-sediment, root-sediment and plant-water interfaces (Reddy and DeBusk, 1987).

Microbial degradation plays a dominant role in the removal of soluble/ colloidal biodegradable organic matter in wastewater. Biodegradation occurs when dissolved organic matter is carried into the biofilms that attached on submerged plant stems, root systems and surrounding soil or media by diffusion process. Suspended solids are removed by filtration and gravitational settlement.

A pollutant may be removed as a result of more than one process at work.

Nitrogen removal mechanisms: There are sufficient studies to indicate some roles being played by wetland plants in Nitrogen removal but the significance of plant uptake vis-à-vis nitrification/denitrification is still being questioned. Nitrogen (N) can exist in various forms, namely Ammoniacal Nitrogen (NH_3 and NH_4^+), organic Nitrogen and oxidised Nitrogen (NO^{2-} and NO^{3-}). The removal of Nitrogen is achieved through nitrification/ denitrification, volatilisation of Ammonia (NH_3) storage in detritus and sediment, and uptake by wetland plants and storage in plant biomass (Brix, 1993). A majority of Nitrogen removal occurs through either plant uptake or denitrification. Nitrogen uptake is significant if plants are harvested and biomass is removed from the system.

At the root-soil interface, atmospheric oxygen diffuses into the rhizosphere through the leaves, stems, rhizomes and roots of the wetland plants thus creating an aerobic layer similar to those that exists in the media-water or media-air interface. Nitrogen transformation takes place in the oxidised and reduced layers of media, the root-media interface and the below ground portion of the emergent plants. Ammonification takes place where Organic N is mineralised to NH_4^+-N in both oxidised and reduced layers. The oxidised layer and the submerged portions of plants are important sites for nitrification in which Ammoniacal Nitrogen (AN) is converted to nitrite N (NO_2-N) by the *Nitrosomonas* bacteria and eventually to nitrate N (NO_3-N) by the *Nitrobacter* bacteria which is either taken up by the plants or diffuses into the reduced zone where it is converted to N_2 and N_2O by the denitrification process.

Denitrification is the permanent removal of Nitrogen from the system, however the process is limited by a number of factors, such as temperature, pH, redox potential, carbon availability and nitrate availability (Johnston, 1991). The annual denitrification rate of a surface-flow wetland could be determined using a Nitrogen mass-balance approach, accounting for measured influx and efflux of Nitrogen, measured uptake of Nitrogen by plants, and sediment, and estimated NH_3 volatilisation (Frankenbach and Meyer, 1999).

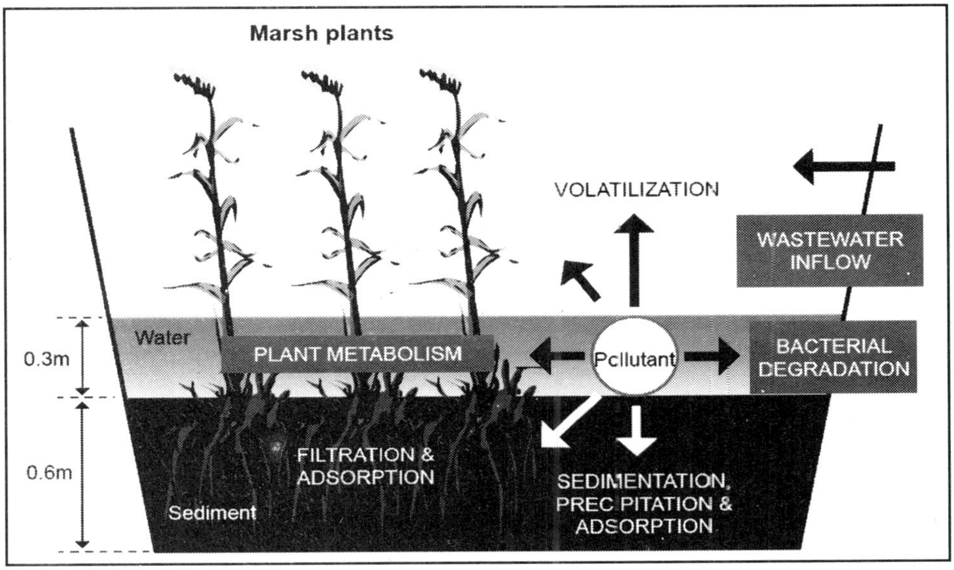

Fig. 4.5: Pollutant Removal Processes in a Constructed Wetland System

The extent of Nitrogen removal depends on the design of the system and the form and amount of Nitrogen present in the wastewater. If influent Nitrogen content is low, wetland plants will compete directly with nitrifying and denitrifying bacteria for NH_4^+ and NO_3-, while in high Nitrogen content, particularly Ammonia, this will stimulate nitrifying and denitrifying activity (Good and Patrick, 1987).

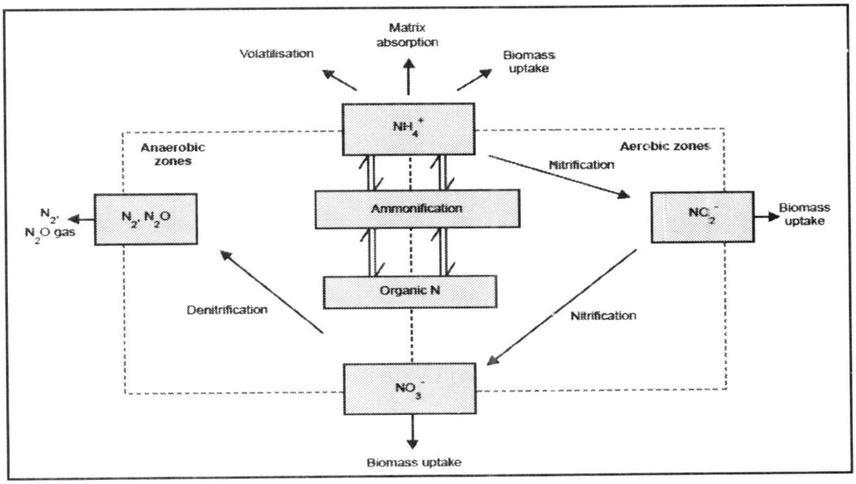

Fig. 4.6: Nitrogen Transformation in a Constructed Wetland Treatment System (Cooper *et al.*, 1996)

Phosphorus removal mechanisms - Phosphorus is present in wastewaters as Orthophosphate, Dehydrated Orthophosphate (Polyphosphate) and Organic Phosphorus. The conversion of most Phosphorus to the Orthophosphate forms (H_2PO_4-, Po_4^{2-}, PO_4^{3-}) is caused by biological oxidation.

Most of the Phosphorus component may fix within the soil media. Phosphate removal is achieved by physical-chemical processes, by adsorption, complexation and precipitation reactions involving Calcium (Ca), Iron (Fe) and Aluminium (Al). The capacity of wetland systems to absorb Phosphorus is positively correlated with the sediment concentration of extractable Amorphous Aluminium and Iron (Fe).

Although plant uptake may be substantial, the sorption of Phosphorus (Orthophosphate P) by anaerobic reducing sediments appears to be the most important process. The removal of Phosphorus is more dependent on biomass uptake in constructed wetland systems with subsequent harvesting.

Plant uptake - Nitrogen will be taken up by macrophytes in a mineralised state and incorporated it into plant biomass. Accumulated Nitrogen is released into the system during a die-back period. Plant uptake is not a measure of net removal. This is because dead plant biomass will decompose to detritus and litter in the life cycle, and some of this Nitrogen will leach and be released into the sediment. Johnston (1991) shows only 26-55% of annual N and P uptake is retained in above-ground tissue, the balance is lost to leaching and litter fall.

Metals - Metals such as Zinc and Copper occur in soluble or particulate associated forms and the distribution in these forms are determined by physico-chemical processes such as adsorption, precipitation, complexation, sedimentation, erosion and diffusion. Metals accumulate in a bed matrix through adsorption and complexation with organic material. Metals are also reduced through direct uptake by wetland plants. However over-accumulation may kill the plants. Pathogens - Pathogens are removed mainly by sedimentation, filtration and absorption by biomass and by natural die-off and predation.

Other pollutant removal mechanisms - Evapotranspiration is one of the mechanisms for pollutant removal. Atmospheric water losses from a wetland that occurs from the water and soil is termed as evaporation and from emergent portions of plants is termed as transpiration. The combination of both processes is termed as evapotranspiration.

Daily transpiration is positively related to mineral adsorption and daily transpiration could be used as an index of the water purification capability of plants. Precipitation and evapotranspiration influence the water flow through a wetland system. Evapotranspiration slows water flow and increases contact times, whereas rainfall, which has the opposite effect, will cause dilution and increased flow. Precipitation and evaporation are likely to have minimal effects on constructed wetlands in most areas. If the wetland type is primarily shallow open water, precipitation/evaporation ratios fairly approximate water balances. However, in large, dense stands of tall plants, transpiration losses from photosynthetically active plants become significant.

Wetland Monitoring and Maintenance

Monitoring and maintenance of the wetland areas is a key issue in maintaining wetland functioning. Wetland monitoring is required to obtain sufficient data to determine the wetland performance in fulfilling the objectives. Wetland maintenance is required to manage macrophytes and desirable species, to remove invading weeds, to remove sediment from the wetlands, and to remove litter from the wetlands (Beharrel *et al.*, 2002).

Effective wetland performance depends on adequate pretreatment, conservative constituent and hydraulic loading rates, collection of monitoring information to assess system performance, and knowledge of successful operation strategies. The CWTS system could be rather easy to design and construct, however it needs to be closely monitored and maintained.

Sustaining a dense stand of desirable vegetation within the wetland is crucial to ensure treatment efficiency. Aggressive species will out-compete less competitive ones and cause gradual changes in wetland vegetation. Certain undesirable plant species or weeds may be introduced to the wetland from the catchment. Natural succession of wetland plants will take place. However, some aquatic weeds may require maintenance by manually being removed. Weed invasion can dramatically reduce the ability of wetlands to meet its design objectives. For example, Pondweed (*Azolla*), Duckweed (*Lemna*), Water Fern (*Salvinia molesta*) and Water Hyacinth (*Eichhornia crassipes*) can form dense mats, exclude light and reduce dissolved oxygen in the water column, and increase the movement of nutrients through the system. Water level management is crucial to control weed growth.

Floods will cause plants to be scoured from the wetland and/or drowned. If a large area of plants is lost, re-establishment will need to be carried out. Small areas will generally recover naturally while larger areas above 5 m^2 may require replanting.

Plant viability is vital to water quality improvement in wetlands. Visible signs of plant distress or pest attack should be investigated promptly. Some common pest insects include Lepidopterrous Stem Borers on *Scirpus grossus*, aphids on *Phragmites karka* and Leaf Roller on *Phragmites karka*. Severe infestation could lead to severe stunting and death of plants. Biopesticides or narrow spectrum-pest specific insecticides could be used if pest population exceeds a certain threshold value. Other pests include the Golden Apple Snail *Pomacea sp*, which feeds actively on wetland plants.

Water levels are important in wetlands with effects on hydrology and hydraulics and impact on wetland biota. Water level should be monitored using water level control structures to ensure successful plant growth. A recirculation system should be in place to allow water from outlet points to be fed back to the wetlands to supplement catchment flows during dry periods. Suspended solids from effluents and litter fall from plants will accumulate in time and gradually reduce the pore space which has to be flushed to prevent short-circuiting. Monitoring of mosquito populations should be undertaken to avoid diseases, which can result in a local health problem.

Water Quality Monitoring

Water quality data are a good indication of wetland performance. Water quality should be monitored through assessment of inflow and outflow water quality parameters. Some important water quality parameters to be monitored include Dissolved Oxygen, redox potential, water temperature, pH value and turbidity, which are the in-situ parameters while laboratory analysis parameters include Total Suspended Solids (TSS), chemical conductivity, Ammoniacal Nitrogen (AN), Nitrate-Nitrogen, Phosphorus, Potassium, Magnesium, Soluble Fe, Mercury, Lead, Zinc, Iron, Cyanide, Arsenic, Phenols, Chemical Oxygen Demand (COD), Biological Oxygen Demand (BOD), Faecal Coliforms, and Oil and Grease.

Examples of Wetland Plants

There is a variety of marsh vegetation that is suitable for planting in a CWTS (Table 4.1). These marsh species could be divided into deep and shallow marshes.

Table 4.1: List of Emergent Wetland Plants Used in Constructed Wetland Treatment Systems (Lim *et al.*, 1998)

Planting Zones	Common Name	Scientific Name
Marsh and deep marsh (0.3-1.0 m)		
	Common Reed	*Phragmites karka*
	Spike Rush	*Eleocharis dulcis*
	Greater Club Rush	*Scirpus grossus*
	Bog Bulrush	*Scirpus mucronatus*
	Tube Sedge	*Lepironia articulata*
	Fan Grass	*Phylidrium lanuginosum*
	Cattail	*Typha angustifolia*
Shallow marsh (0-0.3 m)		
	Golden Beak Sedge	*Rhynchospora corymbosa*
	Spike Rush	*Eleocharis variegata*
	Sumatran Scleria	*Scleria sumatrana*
	Globular Fimbristylis	*Fimbristylis globulosa*
	Knot Grass	*Polygonum barbatum*
	Asiatic Pipewort	*Erioucaulon longifolium*

Table 4.2: Effectiveness of Reed Bed System in Various Effluent Treatments

Type of Flow	Effluent	Macrophytes	Effectivenes
Subsurface horizontal flow	Municipal wastewater	Phragmites australis *Typha latifolia Carex acutiformis*	Per cent reduction of BOD varied between 51 and 95 per cent. A wide variation was observed with respect to nutrients (Total-N: 10-88 per cent; Total-P: 11-94 per cent) [Brix,1987b]
Vertical and horizontal flow	Sewage effluent	*Phragmites australis* *Scirpus lacustris* *Iris pseudocorus*	The abatement of the organic loading (BOD and COD) reached 85 to 90 per cent and the rate of elimination of Total-N was near 50 per cent [Boutin, 1987].
Subsurface horizontal flow	Sewage effluent	*Phragmites australis*	The removal efficiency with respect to BOD was 70 to 90 per cent, Total-N was 25 to 50 per cent and Total-P was 20 to 40 per cent [Brix and Sehierup, 1989].
Surface flow	Sewage effluent	*Phragmites australis* *Typha latifolia*	The purification efficiencies were in the range of 60 to 80 per cent reduction in BOD, 25 to 50 per cent' reduction in Total-N and 6 to 57 per cent in Total-P [Schierup and Brix, 1990].
Subsurface flow	Combined sewage effluent	Pragmites communis *Typha latifolia*	Passing the effluent through a bed achieved reductions of 61to 99 per cent with respect to BOD and COD and elimination of nutrients varied between 5 and 100 per cent. Removal of pathogens was significant [Netter,1993].
Subsurface horizontal flow	Municipal waste dump leachate	*Phragmites australis*	The removal percentages for BOD, COD and TSS were 32, 36 and 73 per cent, respectively [Urbanc-Bercic, 1994].
Horizontal flow	Tannery effluent	Two species of *Glyceria maxima* and *Phragmites*	Passing the effluent through a bed achieved a reduction by 70 to 87 per cent with respect to COD [Daniels, 1998].

Advantages and Disadvantages

Advantages

- Constructed wetlands are typically inexpensive to build and maintain.
- They require little or no energy to operate.
- They can provide effective tertiary treatment
- They can provide additional wildlife habitat.
- They can be aesthetically pleasing additions to homes and neighborhoods.
- They are viewed as an environmentally friendly technology and are generally well received by the public.

Disadvantages

- Constructed wetlands require more land area than many other treatment options.
- Surface flow wetlands can attract mosquitoes and other pests.
- Wetlands are not appropriate for treating some wastewater with high concentrations of certain pollutants.
- The performance of wetlands may vary based on usage and climatic conditions.
- There may be a prolonged initial start-up period before vegetation is adequately established.

Case Study: Efficiency of Reed Bed System to Remove Pollutants

The ability of the reed bed method to remove organic load as well as as nutrients was conspicuous as given in Table 4.2. The presented cleaning efficiencies were BOD: 96 per cent; Total N: 92 per cent and Total P: 99 Per cent (Brix, 1987a). The removal efficiency was mainly depends on the pollution load, the season and the filter material (Netter, 1993). The purification rate is about 95 per cent with specific mass loading of 5 gm^{-1}.d with respect to BOD and it reaches 80 per cent with 10 gm^{-1}.d. Brix (1987b) observed a slight reduction in BOD (approximately 15 per cent) during winter season.

REFERENCES

Beharrel, M., Lim, W.H. and Gan, J. (2002). Good Practices in Wetland Management and Conservation. In: Proceedings of a Workshop on the Asian Wetlands: Bringing Partnerships into Good Wetland Practices. (eds Ahyaudin, A., Salmah, C.R., Mansor, M., Nakamura, R., Ramakrishna, S & Mundkur, T.). pp. 582-594.

Boutin, C. (1987). Domestic Waste Water Treatment in Tanks Planted with Rooted Macrophytes: Case Study; Description of the System; Design Criteria; and Efficiency. Wat. Sci.Tech.,19: 29-40.

Brix, H. (1987a). The Applicability of the Wastewater Treatment Plant in Othfresen as Scientific Documentation of the Root Zone - method. Wat.Sci.Tech.,19: 19-24.

Brix, H. (1987b). Treatment of Wastewater in the Rhizosphere of Wet Land Plants- the Root Zone Method. Wat. Sci.Tech., 19: 107-118.

Brix, H and H-H. Sehierup. (1989). Sewage Treatment in Constructed Reed Beds- Danish Experiences. Wat. Sci.Tech., 21: 1665-1668.

Brix, H. (1993). Wastewater Treatment in Constructed Wetlands: System Design and Treatment Performance. In: Constructed Wetlands for Water Quality Improvement (ed Moshiri, G.A.). CRC Press Inc., Boca Raton. pp. 9-22.

Brix, H. (1997). Do Macrophytes Play a Role in Constructed Treatment Wetlands? *Water Science and Technology* 35(5): 11-17.

Daniels, R. (1998). Investigation: The Potential of Reed Beds for Treating Waste Waters from Leather Manufacture. World Leather, 11: 48-50.

Frankenbach, R.I. and Meyer, J.S. (1999). Nitrogen Removal in a Surface-flow Wastewater Treatment Wetland. *Wetlands* 19(2): 403-412.

Good, B.J. and Patrick, J.R. (1987). Root-water-sediment Interface Processes. In: *Aquatic Plants for Water Treatment and Resource Recovery* (eds Reddy, K.R. & Smith, W.H.). Magnolia Publishing Inc., Orlando, Florida.

Hammer, D.A. (1994). Guidelines for Design, Construction and Operation of Constructed Wetland for Livestock Wastewater Treatment. In: *Proceedings of a Workshop on Constructed Wetlands for Animal Waste Management* (eds DuBowy, P.J. & Reaves, R.P.). Lafayette, IN. pp. 155-181.

Johnston, C.A. (1991). Sediment and Nutrient Retention by Freshwater Wetlands: Effects on Surface Water Quality. *Critical Reviews in Environment Control* 21: 461-565.

Lim, W.H., Kho, B.L., Tay, T.H. and Low, W.L. (1998). *Plants of Putrajaya Wetlands.* Putrajaya Corporation and Putrajaya Holdings. 154 pp.

Markantonatos, P.G., Bacalis, N.C. and Lazaras, G. (1996). Nutrient Removal Using Reed Bed Systems in Greece. Part A - Environmental Science and Engineering and Toxic and Hazardous Substance Control. *Journal of Environmental Science and Health* 31(6): 1423-1434.

Miller, I.W.G. and Black, S. (1985). Design and Use of Artificial Wetlands. In: Ecological Considerations in Wetland Treatment of Municipal Wastewaters. Van Nostrand Reinhold Co. NY. pp. 26-37.

Netter, R. (1993). Planted Soil Filter-a Waste Water Treatment System for Rural Areas. Wat.Sci.Tech., 28: 133-140.

Reddy, K.R. and De-Busk, T.A. (1987). State-of-the-art Utilisation of Aquatic Plants in Water Pollution Control. *Water Science and Technology* 19(10): 61-79.

Reed, S.C., Crites, R.W. and Middlebrooks, E.J. (1995). Natural Systems for Waste Management and Treatment. Second Edition. McGraw-Hill Inc. New York, NY. 433 pp.

Schierup, H-H and H. Brix. (1990). Danish Experience with Emergent Hydrophyte Treatment Systems (EHTS) and Prospects in the Light of Future Requirements on Outlet Water Quality. Wat.Sci.Tech., 22: 65-72.

Sikora, F.J., Tong, Z., Behrends, L.L., Steinberg, S.L. and Coonrod, H.S. (1995). Ammonium Removal in Constructed Wetlands with Recirculating Subsurface Flow: Removal Rate and Mechanisms (eds Kadlec, R.H. & Brix, H.). *Water Science and Technology* 32(3): 193-202.

Urbanc-Bercic, O. (1994). Investigation into the Use of Constructed Reed Beds for Municipal Dump Leachate Treatment. Wat.Sci. Tech.,19: 107-118.

Pages: 98-115

AGRICULTURE, ENVIRONMENT AND NANO-SCIENCE
Edited by: Dr. Pawan Kumar 'Bharti'
ISBN: 978-93-5056-760-9
Edition: 2015
Published by: Discovery Publishing House Pvt. Ltd., New Delhi (India)

5

Influence of Climate Change on Agricultural Crops

V. Davamani; E. Parameswari; P. Kalaiselvi[1] and S. Paulsebastian[1]

INTRODUCTION

The impacts of climate change on agriculture and human well-being include: (1) the biological effects on crop yields; (2) the resulting impacts on outcomes including prices, production, and consumption; and (3) the impacts on per capita calorie consumption and child malnutrition. The biophysical effects of climate change on agriculture induce changes in production and prices, which play out through the economic system as farmers and other market participants adjust autonomously, altering crop mix, input use, production, food demand, food consumption, and trade.

1. The Biological Effects of Climate Change on Yields

Rising temperatures and changes in rainfall patterns have direct effects on crop yields, as well as indirect effects through changes in irrigation water availability.

Horticultural College and Research Institute, Periyakulam, Tamilnadu, (India).

1 Department of Environmental Sciences, Tamil Nadu Agricultural University, Tamilnadu, (India).

Direct Effects on Yields: Rainfed and Irrigated Crops

The direct biological effects of the two climate-change scenarios on crop yields modeled directly with DSSAT for rainfed and irrigated crops in developing and developed countries, with and without CO_2 fertilization (CF and No CF).These results are created by "growing" each crop around the world at 0.5-degree intervals with 2000 climate, growing them again with a 2050 scenario value, and then calculating the ratio. In other words, no economic adjustments are included. The rainfed yield changes are driven by both precipitation and temperature changes; the irrigated yield effects are from temperature changes alone. In developing countries, yield declines predominate for most crops without CO_2 fertilization. Irrigated wheat and irrigated rice are especially hard hit. On average, yields in developed countries are affected less than those in developing countries. For a few crops, climate change actually increases developed-country yields. In calculating these projections, the East Asia and Pacific region combines China, which is temperate for the most part, and Southeast Asia, which is tropical. The differential effects of climate change in these two climate zones are concealed. In China, some crops fare reasonably well because higher future temperatures are favorable in locations where current temperatures are at the low end of the crop's optimal temperature.

Yields of important crops in Southeast Asia fall substantially in both scenarios unless CO_2 fertilization is effective in farmers' fields. South Asia is particularly hard hit by climate change. For almost all crops, it is the region with the greatest yield decline. With CO_2 fertilization, the yield declines are lower; in many locations, some yield increases occur relative to 2000. However, rainfed maize and irrigated and rainfed wheat still see substantial areas of reduced yields. Sub-Saharan Africa sees mixed results, with small declines or increases in maize yields and large negative effects on rainfed wheat. The Latin America and Caribbean region also has mixed yield effects, with some crops up slightly and some down.

Indirect Effects: Irrigated Crops

Climate change will have a direct impact on water availability for irrigated crops. Internal renewable water (IRW) is the water available from precipitation. Both climate scenarios result in more precipitation over land than would occur with no climate change. Under the NCAR scenario, all regions experience increased IRW. Under the CSIRO scenario, the average IRW increase is less than occurs with NCAR, and the Middle East and North Africa and Sub-Saharan Africa regions both experience reductions of about 4 percent. In addition to precipitation changes, climate change-induced higher temperatures increase the water requirements of crops. The ratio of water consumption to requirements is called irrigation water supply reliability (IWSR). The smaller the ratio, the greater the water stress on irrigated crop yields.

Across the group of developing countries, IWSR improves under the NCAR scenario and worsens under the CSIRO scenario. However, regional differentiation of climate-change effects is important. IWSR improves slightly for the Latin America and Caribbean region and for the Middle East and North Africa, but worsens slightly for Sub-Saharan Africa under both scenarios. For East Asia and the Pacific and for South Asia, reliability increases under the NCAR scenario but declines under the CSIRO scenario. Yield reductions of irrigated crops due to water stress are directly estimated in the hydrology portion of IMPACT, taking into account the growing demand for water outside agriculture as well as agricultural demands. As expected, irrigated yield losses due to water stress are relatively higher under the CSIRO scenario than the NCAR scenario. For example, in East Asia and the Pacific, with no climate change, the combined effects of nonagricultural demand growth and increased irrigated area result in an average 4.8 percent decline in irrigated rice yields. Under the NCAR scenario, that decline is only 1.2 percent. However, under the drier CSIRO scenario, the irrigated yield loss from water stress is 6.7 percent.

In East Asia and the Pacific, irrigated rice, wheat, and maize yield losses are all large under the CSIRO model. South Asia irrigated yields for all crops would experience large declines under both scenarios. In Sub-Saharan Africa, maize yields are less under both models, but the CSIRO effects are especially large. Latin America and the Caribbean yields are relatively unaffected, in part due to the small amount of irrigated production in that region.

2. Prices, Production, and Food Consumption

Prices

World prices are a useful single indicator of the effects of climate change on agriculture. The effects of the two climate-change scenarios on world food prices, with and without CO2 fertilization. It also reports the effects with no climate change. Demonstrate world price effects for livestock production and major grains, respectively, assuming no CO2 fertilization. With no climate change, world prices for the most important agricultural crops-rice, wheat, maize, and soybeans will increase between 2000 and 2050, driven by population and income growth and biofuels demand. Even with no climate change, the price of rice would rise by 62 percent, maize by 63 percent, soybeans by 72 percent, and wheat by 39 percent. Climate change results in additional price increases– a total of 32 to 37 percent for rice, 52 to 55 per cent for maize, 94 to 111 percent for wheat, and 11 to 14 percent for soybeans. If CO_2 fertilization is effective in farmers' fields, these 2050 prices are 10 percent smaller.

Livestock are not directly affected by climate change in the IMPACT model, but the effects of higher feed prices caused by climate change pass through to livestock, resulting in higher meat prices. For example, beef prices are 33 percent higher by 2050 with no climate change and 60 percent higher with climate change and no CO_2 fertilization of crops. With CO_2 fertilization, crop-price increases are less, so the beef price increase is about 1.5 percent less than with no CO_2 fertilization.

Production

The effects of climate change on crop production in 2050 compared to production without climate change, based on the NCAR and CSIRO scenarios, accounting for both the direct changes in yield and area caused by climate change and autonomous adaptation as farmers respond to changing prices with changes in crop mix and input use. The negative effects of climate change on crop production are especially pronounced in Sub-Saharan Africa and South Asia. In South Asia, the climate scenario results in a 14 percent decline in rice production relative to the no–climate-change scenario, a 44 to 49 percent decline in wheat production, and a 9 to 19 percent fall in maize production. In Sub-Saharan Africa, the rice, wheat, and maize yield declines with climate change are 15 percent, 34 percent, and 10 percent, respectively. For East Asia and the Pacific, the results are mixed and depend on both the crop and the model used. Rice production declines by around 10 percent, wheat production increases slightly, and maize production declines with the drier CSIRO scenario but increases with the NCAR scenario. Comparing average production changes, developing countries fare worse for all crops under both the CSIRO and NCAR scenarios than do developed countries.

Food Consumption

Agricultural output used for human consumption is determined by the interaction of supply, demand, and the resulting prices with individual preferences and income. Average per capita consumption of cereals and meat products in 2000 and in 2050 under the CSIRO and NCAR models, with and without CO2 fertilization. It also reports consumption with no climate change. Without climate change, rising per capita income results in reduced declines in per capita consumption of cereals in developing countries between 2000 and 2050 and increased meat consumption increases, with the meat increases more than offsetting the decline in cereals. Climate change reduces the growth in meat consumption slightly and causes a more substantial fall in the consumption of cereals. These results are the first indication of the negative welfare effects due to climate change. Both models have similar effects.

3. Per capita Calorie Consumption and Child Malnutrition

The primary measures used for the effects of climate change on human welfare are the change in calorie availability and the change in the number of malnourished children between 2000 and 2050 without climate change, and in 2050 using the two climate-change scenarios. The declining consumption of cereals translates into similarly large declines in calorie availability as the result of climate change. Without climate change, calorie availability increases throughout the world between 2000 and 2050. The largest increase, of 13.8 percent, is in East Asia and the Pacific, but there are gains for the average consumer in all countries–by 3.7 percent in Latin America, 5.9 percent in Sub-Saharan Africa, and 9.7 percent in South Asia. With climate change, however, calorie availability in 2050 is not only lower than the no-climate-change scenario in 2050–it actually declines relative to 2000 levels throughout the world. For the average consumer in a developing country, the decline is 10 percent relative to 2000. With CO2 fertilization, the declines are 3 per cent to 7 percent less severe, but are still large relative to the no-climate-change scenario. There is almost no difference in calorie outcome between the two climate scenarios.

Costs of Adaptation

Climate-change adaptation is increasingly on the agenda of researchers, policymakers, and programme developers who are aware that climate change is real and threatens to undermine social and ecological sustainability. In agriculture, adaptation efforts focus on implementing measures that help build rural livelihoods that are more resilient to climate variability and disaster. This section provides an assessment of the costs of productivity-enhancing investments in agricultural research, rural roads, and irrigation infrastructure and efficiency that can help farmers adapt to climate change. First, regardless of climate-change scenario, agriculture will be negatively affected by climate change.

Climate change increases child malnutrition and reduces calorie consumption dramatically. Thus, aggressive agricultural productivity investments are needed to raise calorie consumption enough to offset the negative impacts of climate-change on the health and well-being of children.

In order to assess the costs of adaptation alone, it is important to identify agricultural productivity investments that reduce child malnutrition with climate change to no-climate-change levels, holding all other macro changes constant, such as income and population growth. Two scenarios are assessed. The first focuses on developing countries and describes the investments needed to reduce childhood malnutrition close to level it would be without climate change. The cost estimates are based only on productivity-enhancing investments in developing countries. The second experiment involves including additional productivity enhancements in developed countries to assess the potential for spillovers in the developing world. The key messages embodied in these results point to the importance of improving the productivity of agriculture as a means of meeting the future challenges that climate change represents. The path to the needed agricultural productivity gains varies by region and to some extent, by climate scenario.

Rice Based Cropping System

Agricultural practices such as, rice based cropping system is considered as the major GHG emitter. Rice cultivation will continue to increase at or beyond its current rate to meet the rice supply of growing populations Furthermore, it emphasize on the various processes during rice cultivation contributing for gases emission and its possible mitigation options.

Rice based Cropping System and Global Warming

Rice (*Oryza sativa*) is the second largest crop in planting acreage after wheat in the global context. It is a staple food crop for more than a billion people in South and East Asia. Most of the world's population growth is in the rice growing countries. Paddy rice corresponds to approximately 10% of the global cultivated agricultural area, constitutes approximately 20% to the global natural freshwater wetland area. Paddy fields are one of the dominant anthropogenic sources of methane to the atmosphere (estimated as 15% of global methane emission (IPCC, 1994). Methane is an extremely heat trapping gas – one molecule of methane is 20 times more efficient at trapping infrared radiation from the earth's surface than a molecule of carbon dioxide.

Rice Plant as an Emitter of Methane

Rice cultivation encompasses the unique practices of flooding the soil unlike other crops. The rice fields are flooded with available irrigation water upto 4-6 cm depth. Being a semi aquatic plant and it also contributes in methane production like other aquatic plant measured the methane emission rate much higher than the calculated methane emission rate that would result from transpiration from rice. The main passage way of methane emission from anaerobic paddy soils to the atmosphere is through the arenchyma of the rice plant. Rice roots could absorb methane gas in the gas phase without water uptake. They suggested that methane dissolved in the soil water surrounding the roots diffuses into the cell-wall water of the root cells, gasifies in the root cortex, and then is mostly released through the micropores in the leaf sheaths.

Micro Organisms Involved in Methane Production

Microorganisms serve as an essential role in the ecosystem by recycling the carbon and mineral elements for reconversion into biomass. The energy stored in organic matter is released in oxidative reactions, in which oxygen serves as the ultimate electron acceptor.

When the food chain is disrupted due to localized exhaustion of the oxygen supply or to toxicity towards the microorganisms, the carbon - oxygen cycle is placed at risk. Microbial communities are a vulnerable part of ecosystem and any condition - that threatens them is very dangerous for the whole cycle. Due to flooding of soil in rice cultivation anaerobic condition is created in the root surface of the plant and consequently to the inhabiting microorganisms in the rhizosphere and nearby. In such condition anaerobic methanogenic bacteria produce methane as a product of their energy metabolism. The process is termed as methanogenesis. In well aerated land, aerobic methnotropic bacteria oxidize methane as an energy source with methanol as product. Hence methane production from well aerated land is much lower than from flooded land.

Nitrogen-gases from Rice Field

Among the nitrogen-gases, nitrous oxide (N2O) is a powerful greenhouse gas, about 310 times more effective at trapping heat than carbon dioxide on a molecular basis. This dangerous gas emission from rice field is mainly attributed to the heavy use of nitrogenous fertilizers. Formation and emission of N2O takes place wherever nitrogen occurs and is therefore more or less a function of the nitrogen turnover in agriculture. However, N2O emissions from paddy fields are considered to be very low. The importance of ammonia volatilization as a N loss mechanism from paddy fields has also been established in recent studies, though its environmental significance is not yet known.

Rice Straw Burning

There is a common practice of burning the crop residues such as straw. Burning of these materials converts a great deal of nitrogen and sulfur, and some phosphorus to gaseous form and they are lost from the site. It emits large quantities of carbon monoxide, CO2, fine particulate matter, and volatile hydrocarbons into the air, and somewhat lesser amounts of oxides of nitrogen and oxides of sulfur (Brady and Weil, 2002). These gases in the atmosphere enhance the atmospheric gases. There is common fallacy among the farmers that burning of straw in field adds nutrients than by incorporating. These residues if returned back to the soil, have immense potential for providing plant nutrient as well as adding organic matter to soil. Various scientists reported the increase in rice yield with the incorporation of straw in the rice field. They recommend incorporating the residues few weeks ahead of transplanting rice.

Decomposition of Incorporated Residues

Microbial decomposition proceeds most rapidly in the presence of plentiful supplies of oxygen. Oxygen supplies may deplete when soil pores are filled with water preventing the diffusion of O_2 to and from the atmosphere. The product of decomposition in such condition includes wide variety of organic compounds including methane gas. Anaerobic decomposition releases relatively little energy for the organisms involved therefore the end product still contains much energy. For example bio-gas and slurry from bio-gas chamber where anaerobic decomposition operates. The CH4 is the major product of anaerobic decomposition form the biogas chamber which is used for burning. Similarly, the bio gas slurry also contains the nutrients required by plant. Hence in the rice field, due to flooding residue incorporated undergoes anaerobic decomposition. The methane production from residue incorporated paddy field is higher than unincorporated. In well aerated condition the final product is mostly CO_2 instead of methane. Methane has higher potential for global warming than CO_2.

The Carbon: Nitrogen (C:N) ratio of the residues being incorporated also influence the quantity of gas to be produced. The rice or wheat straw with high C:N ratio are difficult to decompose and involves large number of microorganisms for longer period. In anerobic condition, the higher activity of mehtanogenic bacteria could produce higher methane than from low C:N ratio residues.

CONCLUSION AND RECOMMENDATION

Rice based agriculture plays a very important role in the global inventory of methane gas. Worldwide, irrigated rice cultivation is considered to be among the highest sources of atmospheric methane and to some extent nitrous oxide under certain water management regimes. Since rice is the staple food, neither its crop yield could be sacrificed nor could its pattern be changed to avoid green house gases emission. On the other hand, rise in earth's temperature enforces the soil to behave as sink for green house gases rather than source. The understanding of microbial processes and turnover of carbon and nitrogen in soil opens th possibility for reduction of green house gases emission. Some of the strategies to reduce green house gases emission from agricultural system are to practice Integrated Plant Nutrient System (IPNS) that includes use of nutrient enriched organic fertilizers. Soils can be modified and improved by the application of fertilizers designed to compensate for specific mineral deficiencies, inadequate soil drainage can be improved by tile drains, ditches. Cropping system based on nutrient supplying power of soil and low soil nutrient requiring crop in the marginal land should be selected as carbon sink. In the agricultural country like Nepal, India agricultural practices could be the major source of green house gases emission. The nation should think of reducing these gases with available technology and take an opportunity of selling these emission reduction units as per the Article 6.1 of the Kyoto Protocol.

Crop Ecosystem Response to Climate Change - Cotton

Cotton is a perennial with an indeterminate growth habit. Wild ancestors of cotton are found in arid regions often with high temperatures and are naturally adapted to surviving long periods of dry weather. Modern cultivars have inherited these attributes, making the cotton crop well adapted to intermittent water supply that occurs with rain-fed and irrigated production. Compared with other field crops however, its growth and development is complex. Vegetative and reproductive growth occur simultaneously making interpretation of the crop's response to climate and management sometimes difficult.

Impact of Climate Change on Cotton Production

Agriculture is extremely vulnerable to climate change. Higher temperatures will eventually reduce yields and increase the prevalence of pests and diseases. Changes in precipitation are likely to lead to crop failures and production declines. While there will be some gains depending on crops grown and regions, the overall impacts on agriculture are expected to be negative, thus threatening global food security. This assessment applies largely to the regional impacts of cotton production.

Impacts of Climate Change on Cotton Production by Country

Overall, the negative impacts of climate change on cotton production relate to the reduced availability of water for irrigation, in particular in Xinjiang (China), Pakistan, Australia and the western United States. Heat stress risks creating depressed yields in Pakistan in particular, while in other countries limited increases in temperatures could favour cotton plant growth and lengthen the cotton growing season.

Limited increases in atmospheric CO_2 could also favour cotton yields. The impacts of climate change on rainfall will likely be positive in the Yellow River area (China), in India, the south-eastern United States and south-eastern Anatolia (Turkey). Impacts on rainfall in Brazil and West and Central Africa are unclear.

Cotton is grown commercially in more than 70 different countries, mostly in the longitudinal band between 37°N and 32°S. Cotton is especially adapted to semi-arid and arid environments, where it is either grown rain-fed or through irrigation. About 53% of the world's cotton growth areas and 73% of all fibre growth areas benefit from full or supplementary irrigation. Cotton has a certain resilience to high temperatures and drought due to its vertical tap root. The crop is, however, sensitive to water availability, particularly at the height of flowering and boll formation. Rising temperatures favour cotton plant development, unless day temperatures exceed 32° C. Limited increases in atmospheric CO_2 also favour the cotton plant's development. Insects are expected to adapt to climate change through their capacity to adapt their body temperature to the temperature of the environment. The insects currently plaguing cotton are expected to continue to live and possibly thrive in new environmental conditions. Cotton supplies may benefit from higher temperatures as new production areas are established where cotton was not grown before. The overall impacts of climate change on cotton production and trade are very hard to predict, although certain observations can be made:

China is by far the largest cotton producer and consumer. Production in the western Xinjiang region depends almost entirely on irrigation. Water availability is expected to decrease and pressure on water use to rise. Production along the Yangtze River will likely decrease following relatively low yields and competition from food crops. Production along the Yellow River is very important and may come to benefit from a longer growing season as temperatures rise. Rainfall in China is expected to increase, which is favourable for production, particularly in combination with limited rises in temperature and atmospheric CO_2.

India is the second largest producer of cotton worldwide. Production is spread out over multiple regions and agro-ecological zones. Temperatures are expected to increase all over India. Rainfall intensity during monsoons may become an increasing problem. Higher temperatures in already hot areas may hinder cotton development and fruit formation. Rain-fed cotton production may suffer from higher climate variability leading to periods of drought or flooding. Irrigated cotton, particularly in northern India, may suffer from lower water availability due to the upstream reduction of snow and ice from Himalayan and Tibetan Plateau glaciers and snowfields.

The United States of America is the third largest producer country and the largest cotton exporter in the world. Cotton yields are expected to increase with limited increases in temperature and atmospheric CO_2. However, the number of very hot days is expected to increase. Climate change impacts on rainfall are regionally diverse. The mostly rain-fed cotton areas in the south-east and mid-south may see an increase in rainfall, but also an increase in extreme weather events. Production in the south-west and the west relies mostly on irrigation. Here, water availability is likely to become an ever bigger problem due to aggravating groundwater depletion and to reduced and more irregular meltwater in summer from the Rocky Mountains.

Pakistan is likely to be the country that will suffer most from climate change as far as agriculture and cotton production are concerned. In the country, agriculture is mostly dependent on irrigation with water from the Indus River, which will carry less water as the Himalayan and Tibetan glaciers and snowfields diminish in size. The Indus River is very important to agriculture in Pakistan. Here, cotton production already takes place in sub-optimal conditions with respect to high temperatures. Further increases in temperature during the growing season will depress yield.

Uzbekistan may benefit from limited temperature rises, provided soil salinization can be prevented. Higher soil temperatures following climate change may favour production through an earlier start and a later ending of the cotton growing season. Water availability is a crucial constraint as all Uzbek cotton is irrigated. Cross-boundary water distribution is the issue of concern. Finally, largescale monocropping of irrigated cotton has led to severe soil exhaustion and salinization. Climate change might intensify the salinization process with crop yield reduction as a result.

Brazil's cotton sector has grown rapidly over the last decade following the cultivation of new lands in the *cerrado,* a vast tropical savannah particularly in Mato Grosso. Projections are that temperatures will rise with climate change. The impacts on rainfall are unclear, however, because climate models are not yet sufficiently sophisticated to paint a clear picture. Predictions for Central and tropical South America range from a reduction of 20% to 40% to an increase of 5% to 10% for 2080. Future development of cotton in Brazil will generally depend in particular on the rate of deforestation in the '*cerrado*', the future of competing soy production, and the long-term soil fertility of newly cultivated lands.

Cotton is the economic driver of the rural economies in many French-speaking countries in *West and Central Africa*. Unfavourable exchange rates policies currently discourage exports, and problems in sector organization and restructuring hamper cotton production growth. Temperatures are expected to rise due to climate change. The impact on rainfall patterns, however, is unclear for this part of Africa.

Cotton production in *Turkey* is on the decline due to relatively high costs. Cotton consumption relies heavily on imports from the United States. All cotton in Turkey is irrigated. Half of the cotton is grown close to the Mediterranean, in the Aegean region and around Antalya. Temperature rises in Turkey will be more severe in the Aegean region. Precipitation will decrease along the Aegean and Mediterranean coasts. However, most cotton is now grown in south-eastern Anatolia, where water availability for irrigation is expanding due to the construction of new dams. Here, temperatures and precipitation are expected to increase, yet meltwater from snow and ice will decline.

Australia cotton production is in the hands of a relatively small number of farmers (about 1,200). Production is large-scale and capital-intensive. Eighty percent of production is irrigated. Water availability is a serious problem in New South Wales and Queensland. River systems are currently over-exploited. Drought in recent years has further aggravated the water problem and severely limited production. Climate change is expected to increase temperatures such that the growing season may start earlier and end later, while the number of 'cold shock' events will decline, and new production areas may be developed in the North, provided water is available. Heat stress, however, is also likely to increase and may depress cotton development and fruit formation.

Options to Adapt to Climate Change

Climate change is changing the economics of production, forcing rural cotton farming communities to consider multiple livelihood strategies including planting different crops and seeking alternative non-farm income streams. This entails complex and resource intensive responses from government and international aid flows. With respect to production, cotton has limited capacity to respond to heat stress, through 'compensatory growth'. Its vertical tap root also provides resilience against spells of drought, but also makes it vulnerable to water-logging. Cotton relies heavily on irrigation and thus groundwater or freshwater availability. A number of adaptation strategies include:

- Maximizing plant diversity
- Flexibility of sowing dates
- Maintaining soil cover
- Minimizing soil tillage
- Breeding more resistant cotton varieties

Impact of Climate Change in India

The UNFCCC (2008) expects that climate change in Southern Asia will lead to warming above the global mean. Precipitation will increase, and the frequency of intense precipitation will increase in parts of Southern Asia. The reduction of snow and ice in Himalayan and Tibetan Plateau glaciers will decrease freshwater availability for irrigation, particularly in the large river basins in northern India (UNFCCC, 2008).

The annual global average surface air temperature has increased significantly in the past one hundred years (0.4° C). The annual India-wide average monsoon rainfall has been without any trend in the same period; however increases in monsoon seasonal rainfall have been recorded along the West coast, in North Andhra Pradesh and northwest India (10%-12% higher than normal over 100 years) and decreasing trends in East Madhya Pradesh and adjoining areas, in northeast India and in parts of Gujarat and Kerala (6%-8% lower than normal over 100 years).

A marked increase in seasonal surface air temperature is projected in the future, becoming conspicuous after the 2040s. Projections indicate increases in both maximum and minimum temperatures in the region south of 25°N. Maximum temperatures are projected to increase by 2° C-4° C by the 2050s. In the northern region the increase in maximum temperatures may exceed 4° C. Minimum temperatures would increase by 4° C all over the country.

Little change in monsoon rainfall is projected India-wide up to the 2050s. However, the number of rainfall days will decrease over a major part of the country. This decrease is greater in the western and central parts (>15 days) while near the Himalayan foothills (Uttaranchal) and in northeast India the number of rainfall days may increase by 5-10 days. Rainfall intensity will increase throughout India by 1-4 mm per day, except for small areas in northwest India where rainfall intensity may decrease by 1 mm per day.

Climate change will likely significantly change the hydrological cycle. The severity of droughts and the intensity of floods are likely to increase, and the quantity of available runoff to decrease. The Sabarmati and Luni river basins, which cover about a quarter of Gujarat and 60% of Rajasthan, are likely to experience acute water-scarce conditions, and the Mahi, Pennar, Sabarmati and Tapi river basins constant water scarcity. The Cauvery, Ganga, Narmada and Krishna river basins are likely to experience seasonal or regular water-stressed conditions. The Godavari, Brahmani and Mahanadi river basins are projected to experience water shortages only in a few locations (India, 2004).

Simulations show a decrease in crop yields as temperatures increase. Decreases are generally offset by increases in CO_2, yet the magnitude of this response varies with crop and region. Irrigated rice yields may slightly improve throughout India, whereas wheat yields in central India may drop 2% or increase 6%, depending on scenario. Sorghum, a C4 plant, does not show any significant response to CO_2 increases. If temperatures increase further, western India may experience lower productivity due to a reduced crop duration (India, 2004).

The Central Institute for Cotton Research (CICR) found that selected conventional cotton varieties/hybrids are well adapted to elevated CO_2 levels alone – due to better morpho-physiological and biochemical attributes. The productivity of cotton in terms of total number of bolls and weight increased significantly (73%). Fibre quality also improved significantly.

Elevated CO_2 levels in the atmosphere of up to 650 ppm and temperature of 40° C was found to be optimum for cotton plant growth. It thus appears that cotton will benefit from the changed atmospheric scenario during the later part of the 21st century, yet studies indicate that the pest problem will be aggravated. By and large, though, research in India indicates that the impact of climate change on cotton production and productivity will be favourable (Kranthi, 2009).

Climate change impacts on cotton growth and development that influence yield and fibre quality will most likely be a result of the net effects of:

- Increases in CO_2 concentration.
- Reduced water availability and increased atmospheric evaporative demand as a result of lower rainfall and relative humidity.
- Increases in temperature.

Increase in CO_2

Through the process of photosynthesis, plants synthesize organic compounds used for growth using water and CO_2 using energy absorbed by chlorophyll from sunlight. Two sources of research are currently available that discuss the impact of CO_2 on cotton's growth and development. The first block of research summarised by Reddy et al. (1996) discusses impacts of CO_2 increase on cotton in growth chambers. This work showed that doubling CO_2 concentrations in the atmosphere increased photosynthesis by about 40 per cent which led to increased growth and yield in well watered environments (see Figure 5.1). This work also showed that increasing CO_2 increased water use — but the efficiency of water use was improved. From their studies they postulated that increased growth and yield would occur with higher CO_2 concentrations even in dry or nutrient deficient situations. Using this work we could assume that with an increases in CO_2 to levels predicted for 2020 (406 to 415 ppm) and 2050 (473 to 555 ppm), photosynthesis would increase by approximately 23 and 29 per cent respectively.

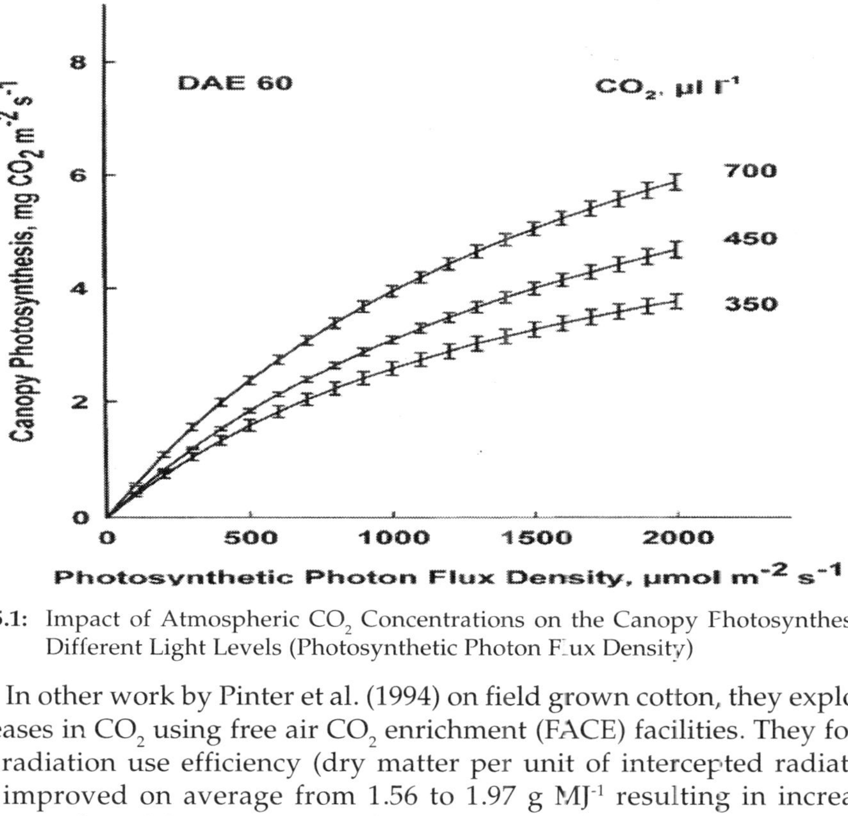

Fig. 5.1: Impact of Atmospheric CO_2 Concentrations on the Canopy Photosynthesis at Different Light Levels (Photosynthetic Photon Flux Density)

In other work by Pinter et al. (1994) on field grown cotton, they explored increases in CO_2 using free air CO_2 enrichment (FACE) facilities. They found that radiation use efficiency (dry matter per unit of intercepted radiation) was improved on average from 1.56 to 1.97 g MJ^{-1} resulting in increased biomass when CO_2 was increased to 550 ppm. They also investigated the impact of CO_2 elevation with different irrigation regimes. They found that regardless of irrigation treatment (wet or dry), radiation use efficiency was increased in CO2 elevated treatments. This suggested that a rise in atmospheric CO2 concentrations may partially compensate for plant stress caused by water shortages. As a consequence, lint yield on average was increased by 43 per cent – due to increased early leaf area and a longer flowering period.

Reduced Water Availability and Higher Evaporative Demand

Less water for irrigation will mean lower cotton yields unless farm and agronomic water use efficiencies can improve. Water stress in cotton restricts both vegetative and fruit growth. Cotton's response to stress varies on the stage of growth, the degree of stress, and the length of time imposed. Research in Australia has shown that to prevent yield reductions, cotton crops generally require enough water to allow 700 mm of evapotranspiration (transpiration plus soil evaporation. Lower relative humidity caused by climate change will increase evaporative demand by the atmosphere surrounding crops. Changes in evaporative demand will influence the amount of evapotranspiration – affecting both transpiration and soil evaporation.

Transpiration is used by crops to regulate temperature of their canopies. Higher evaporative demand in well watered crops has the potential to increase transpiration and soil evaporation – lowering water use efficiency. In situations where water is limited and there is high evaporative demand, crops will struggle to transpire enough to keep the canopies cool. Leaf temperatures are then increased to a point where photosynthesis and growth are impaired. Recent research in cotton has shown that regardless of the water availability in the soil there is an increase in plant stress associated with higher evaporative demands. Research is continuing to quantify the effects of relative humidity on cotton growth on soils with different water holding capacities.

Increase in Temperature

Temperature has two main influences on cotton growth and development. Firstly it determines the rates of morphological development and crop growth (eg. node development, rate of fruit production, photosynthesis and respiration). Secondly, it also helps determine the start and end of a growing season. Climate change raising temperatures may:

- Increase average daily temperatures warming both the start and end of cotton seasons allowing for longer and better cotton growth (a positive effect).
- Increase average temperatures during boll filling predisposing crops to high micronaire issues (a negative effect).
- Increase the number and severity of days with very high temperatures during the cotton season (negative effect).

Increase in Frequency of Very Hot Days

Many areas in which cotton is grown in Australia already experience extremely high temperatures during the growing season, particularly during flowering and boll development. Climate change may increase the frequency of these high temperatures. Cotton plants maintain optimum growing temperatures by opening stomata's in the leaves, allowing water to pass out

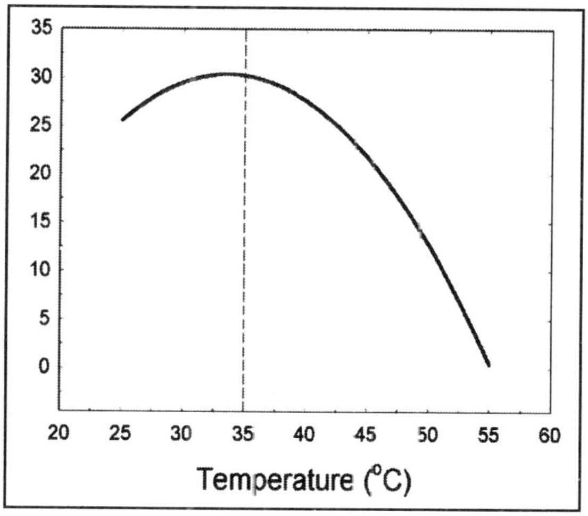

Effect of High Temperatures on Leaf Photosynthesis

and evaporate, thus cooling leaves (transpiration). Excessively high temperatures (greater than 35°C) during the day can reduce photosynthesis while warm nights (above 25°C) mean that leaf temperature remains high, and respiration remains high, consuming stored assimilates. Maintenance respiration approximately doubles for every 10°C rise in temperature. Both situations reduce the amount of Effect of high temperatures on leaf photosynthesis assimilates available for growth, and in turn reduce yield by:

- Causing increases in square and boll shedding
- Reducing seed number per boll.
- Loss of fruit may cause the crop to grow excessively vegetative (rank) following the period of heat stress.

In addition to reductions in assimilates available for growth, heat stress can also directly damage cotton plant tissue. At night the plant loses the ability to cool evaporatively (no transpiration), so tissue temperatures approach air temperature. During the day very high relative humidity (which restricts evaporative cooling) in combination with clear skies can also increase tissue temperature to approach or exceed air temperature. Two known consequences of direct tissue damage from severe heat stress are:

- **Parrot beaked bolls:** High temperatures reduce the viability of the pollen at flowering. This reduces boll size and can reduce yield. The result is small bolls with uneven seed numbers between the locks caused by poor pollination/seed set particularly in one lock. There are no known studies to show if the plant compensates for parrot beaked bolls by having other normal bolls grow bigger.
- **Boll freeze or cavitation or boll dangle:** This occurs when young bolls die before the abscission layer forms. Again this loss of fruit may cause the crop to grow excessively vegetative (rank) following these symptoms.

Large increases in temperature also reduce the interval between flowering and boll opening, shortening the time to maturity and reducing yield. This may increase final micronaire by limiting the number of late set bolls that can have lower micronaire Fibre length can also be affected by sustained periods of high temperatures as the time required for fibre elongation is reduced, not allowing for the genetic potential of fibre length to be reached. Fibre length is reduced as boll temperatures increase above 32°C. The consequences of hot conditions for yield and quality are exaggerated if water stress also occurs during these periods.

Warming the Start and End of Cotton Seasons

Increased average temperatures especially at the start and end of the cotton season can have positive effects on growth, development and ultimately yield. Low temperatures after sowing increase the time to emergence and reduce cotton seedling vigour – often leading to poor establishment, poor early growth and increased risk of seedling diseases. A key indicator used in the Australian cotton industry of the degree of very cold temperatures that contribute to the conditions mentioned above is the 'cold shock' concept. A cold shock is defined as when minimum daily temperatures are below 11°C and each event extends the duration to flowering by 5.2 day degrees.

In some cotton producing regions in Australia early in cotton growth the number of cold shocks can be on average as frequent as 40. In an analysis prepared for the Australian Cotton Conference (2006) by Chris Mitchell, CSIRO, he showed that climate change had the potential to raise minimum temperatures and significantly reduce the number of cold shocks. Cotton is a perennial crop. Warmer temperatures at the start and the end of cotton seasons will increase the length of time cotton has to grow and produce yield, provided adequate water and crop nutrition are available. For every extra week that the growth period (time between sowing and maturity) may be allowed to be extended through warmer temperatures it has the potential to increase lint yield by 68 and 136 kg per hectare.

Warmer Temperatures during Boll Filling

A key factor effecting micronaire is the temperature during boll filling. Micronaire is a measure of fibre fineness and maturity. Finer fibres means that there are more fibres in the cross section of a yarn when it is spun and the yarn is stronger. The degree of fibre maturity impacts dye absorbency and retention. Fibre fineness is determined primarily at fibre initiation on a seed. Fibre maturity is the proportion of fibre cross section occupied by cellulose and is influenced by impacts on photosynthesis and demand for resources by the developing bolls. As photosynthesis increases with temperature in the absence of water stress, more resources are available to mature the fibres thus increasing micronaire. Situations where seasons are warmer more often during boll filling predispose crops to situations where high micronaire will be more likely to occur.

SUMMARY

As there are many facets of cotton physiology potentially impacted by climate change, assessing the overall impact will be complex. There will be a need to investigate the impacts of changes in rainfall, rises in temperature, increases in CO_2, and evaporative demand together to establish if climate change will substantially impact cotton growth, development, and yield in a positive or negative way. There will also be a need to identify the degree to which these impacts may occur with growing cotton in different regions. Some further studies of cotton physiology in Australian conditions with climate change scenarios will be needed – especially the relative impact of lower water availability, high-temperature, increased evaporative demand, and higher CO_2 together. But the Ozcot cotton crop simulation model will be a powerful tool coupled together with predictions of climate change to investigate management practices that may be adapted to offset impacts of climate change. Research is progressing to update to assess these impacts in an integrated way.

REFERENCES

Australia (2008). Australia Statement. *In:* ICAC (2008). *Statement to the 67th ICAC Plenary Meeting,* pp. 60-63. International Cotton Advisory Committee (ICAC). Washington, D.C., United States of America. November 2008.

Australia (2009). Statement at the 68th ICAC Plenary Meeting. *In:* ICAC (2009). *The Role of Cotton in Economic Development and Ensuring Food Security during a Period of Global Economic Crisis,* pp. 94-97. International Cotton Advisory Committee (ICAC). Washington, D.C., United States of America. September 2009.

Bange, M. (2007). Effects of Climate Change on Cotton Growth and Development. *In: The Australian Cotton Grower* (June-July 2007). pp. 41-45.

Chaudhry, R. and A. Guitchounts (2003). *Cotton Facts.* International Cotton Advisory Committee (ICAC). Washington, D.C., United States of America, 158 p.

CICR (2009). *Constraints Analysis of Cotton in India.* Central Institute for Cotton Research (CICR). India.

Wu G., F.J. Chen, F. Ge and Y.C.Sun (2007). Effects of Elevated Carbon Dioxide on the Growth and Foliar Chemistry of Transgenic Bt Cotton. *In: Journal of Integrative Plant Biology 49(9).* 1361-1369.

Pages: 116-151

AGRICULTURE, ENVIRONMENT AND NANO-SCIENCE
Edited by: Dr. Pawan Kumar 'Bharti'
ISBN: 978-93-5056-760-9
Edition: 2015
Published by: Discovery Publishing House Pvt. Ltd., New Delhi (India)

6

Metallothioneins
A Novel Metal Binding Proteins

E. Parameswari; V. Davamani; T. Anitha and A. Rathinasamy

ABSTRACT

Metallothioneins (MTs) are a family of cysteine (Cys) rich, low molecular weight proteins which are found ubiquitously in animals, fungi, cyanobacteria and plants. They are grouped into class I, II and III. Class I and II MTs are polypeptides which are direct gene products, class III MTs are non-translational cysteine-rich molecules named phytochelatins. Metal ions are sequestered by MTs through complexation with the -SH group of the Cys rich motifs. All cysteines occur in the reduced form and are coordinated to the metal ions through mercaptide bonds, giving rise to spectroscopic features characteristic of metal-thiolate clusters. The cysteines in MTs are absolutely conserved across species, it was suspected that the cysteines are necessary for function and MT is essential for life.

The various physiological and toxicological factors stimulating the biosynthesis of MTs, makes it difficult to pinpoint a specific biological role. In fact, more

Horticultural College and Research Institute, Periyakulam, Theni (Dt.) - Pin: 625 604 (Tamilnadu) (India).

than five decades after their discovery, their functional significance is still a topic of discussion. According to hypothesis, MTs are commonly believed to be involved in essential metal homeostasis and the detoxification of toxic heavy metals. Under normal conditions, MTs function in the storage and mobilization of essential metals such as Zn and Cu. However, when the organism faces a toxic metal such as Cd, it acts as scavengers to protect cells against metal toxicity. MTs are still the only biological compounds known to contain this metal. However, Cd is one of several optiona metallic components, the others being most commonly Zn and Cu. The conservation of the structure of MTs in evolution, their ubiquitous occurrence, the redundancy of genes and the programmed synthesis of MTs in the development, regeneration and reproduction of living organisms are weighty arguments for suspecting MTs to also serve other and perhaps more specific metal-related cellular roles.

INTRODUCTION

The discovery of cadmium (Cd)-binding, cystein-rich protein from horse kidney by Margoshes & Vallee was the seminal finding that marked the birth of a field of research focused on the study of a new polypeptide super family, the metallothioneins (MTs). Metallothioneins (MTs) are a family of cysteine (Cys)-rich, low molecular weight (6-7 kDa), nonenzymatic proteins that are found ubiquitously in animals, in higher plants, in eukaryotic microorganisms, and many prokaryotes. MTs have an unusual amino acid composition as they do not contain aromatic amino acids, and most important, one third of its residues are cysteines. Moreover, MTs show spectroscopic features of metal thoilates (mercaptides) (Messerle *et al.*, 1990). MTs can bind Zn, Cd, Ni, Pb, and Cu with affinities that depend on the concentration and bioavailability of the heavy metals. Three major groups of scientist have contributed to our knowledge of MT:

1. Physiologists and toxicologists interested in its role in heavy metal metabolism and detoxification.
2. Protein chemists and spectroscopies intrigued by its usual structural features, and most recently.
3. Molecular biologist interested in gene regulation and the use of MT (promoter) sequences for genetic engineering experiments.

Nevertheless, although MTs were discovered over 40 years ago, their physiological functions are still unclear

HISTORY OF METALLOTHIONEIN

Scientific research history of metallothionein begins in the 1950s almost 50 years ago. Development of MT research include contributions from scientists in the fields of biochemistry, environmental hygiene/medicine, medicine, toxicology, pathology and nutrition and is best illustrated by the number of articles that have been published. There has been a considerable development of methods in protein research, including isolation and analytical methods for identification during this time. Interest in MT was in the beginning focused mainly on two topics. The main interests were the strict protein chemistry and the toxicological, i.e. the metabolic pathways for metal toxicology particularly with regard to cadmium kinetics. Later on other interests and aspects on MT have expanded the field. In recent years important contributions have been brought in from molecular biology. Consensus and conclusions reached at several scientific meetings on metallothionein based on published data have been published as depicted in Table 6.1.

Table 6.1: History of Metallothionein

1960, 1961	Metallothionein
1964	Induction by cadmium
1971	Modification of Cd-toxicity
1972	Amino acid composition
1976	Sequence
1979	1st international meeting Consesus nomenclature
1979	Radioimmunoassay
1983	International meeting Metallothionein and nephrotoxicity
1985	2nd International meetingon metallothionein
1992	3rd International meetingon metallothionein
1996	Workshop on metallothionein

In 1957 data on cadmium binding protein in equine tissue was published. However this study was initiated by a report in the form of an abstract dealing with cadmium in human organs. Small amounts of cadmium had been shown to be present in tissues and body fluids in several animal species. Hypotheses were postulated to explain this unexpected finding. Either cadmium could be present as bound to a macromolecule and therefore have a natural function in biological system or cadmium could also be just a contaminant. In 1960 the first report on metallothionein was published (Kagi and Schafer, 1988). This was the first time that the cadmium containing protein, isolated from equine renal tissue, was named 'metallothionein' based on an extremely high content of sulphur of 4.1% g^{-1} dry weight and 2.9% of Cd and 0.6% Zn. Isolation was performed from five frozen horse kidneys with for that time conventional methods. Later studies reported data on physical properties; molecular weight was estimated to be 10000 ± 260. Specific absorption at 250 nm was explained by cadmium mercaptide bonds. Metallothionein was assumed to lack aromatic amino acids as indicated by absence of absorption at 280 nm. This was later verified by aminoacid analyses. The high concentration of sulphur of 8.5% is explained by aminoacid analyses that revealed high content of cysteine. At this time reactive protein mercapto groups were determined by titration with silver ions, CMB and N-ethylmaleimide. Aminoacids were determined by two dimensional paper chromatography and ion exchange chromatography. Cysteine residues were determined as cysteic acid after oxidation of metallothionein with performic acid and as derivatives of N-ethylmaleide. Sedimentation constant was determined via Schlieren diagram by use of sedimentation by ultracentrifugation to 1.75 (S_{020w}). Diffusion constant, partial specific volume and friction ratio was reported. The estimated molecular weight of the protein was still varying from 9790-10500. This was partly explained by various artefacts during preparation. Metal analyses for cadmium and zinc reported 5.2 g atoms mol^{-1} and 5.9% of MT weight for cadmium and for zinc 3.3 g atoms mol^{-1} and 2.2% by weight. Some exchange between zinc and cadmium was obviously taking place. It was suggested that bonding with three SH-groups together with one atom of either cadmium or zinc was formed.

In the 1970s and early 1980s, there were only a limited number of research groups performing research related to MT. An increasing number of publications in which different nomenclature for MT was used made it clear that an evaluation of the knowledge available at that time would be of importance. A workshop with approximately 25 invited participants who had submitted background manuscripts was arranged and a tentative report (Nordberg *et al.*, 1979) was prepared and distributed in advance to each participant. A consensus report was agreed during the meeting held in 1978.

During this first international meeting on MT, held in Zurich consensus was reached about, e.g. nomenclature and methods for preparing the protein. This first meeting has been followed by one more meeting in Zurich 1985 which was more open but still with a workshop consensus. In between, a meeting was arranged in Aberdeen in1981.

STRUCTURE AND OCCURRENCE OF METALLOTHIONEIN

The structure of MTs was first described by Kagi *et al.*(1987) (Fig. 6.1). MTs have two domains consisting of one cluster with three and one with four metal atoms. The gene is located on chromosome 16. This protein consists of a number of isoforms coded by various alleles. The ratio of mRNA for MT-I and MT-II genes remains constant during induction by metals, e.g. Cd, Zn, and Cu.

Metallothioneins from mammals contain 20 cysteins residues and bind seven cadmium or zinc ions in two discrete clusters. The thiolate side chains of these proteins act as bridging and terminal ligands to form Cd3SCy9 and Cd4 SCy11 clusters.

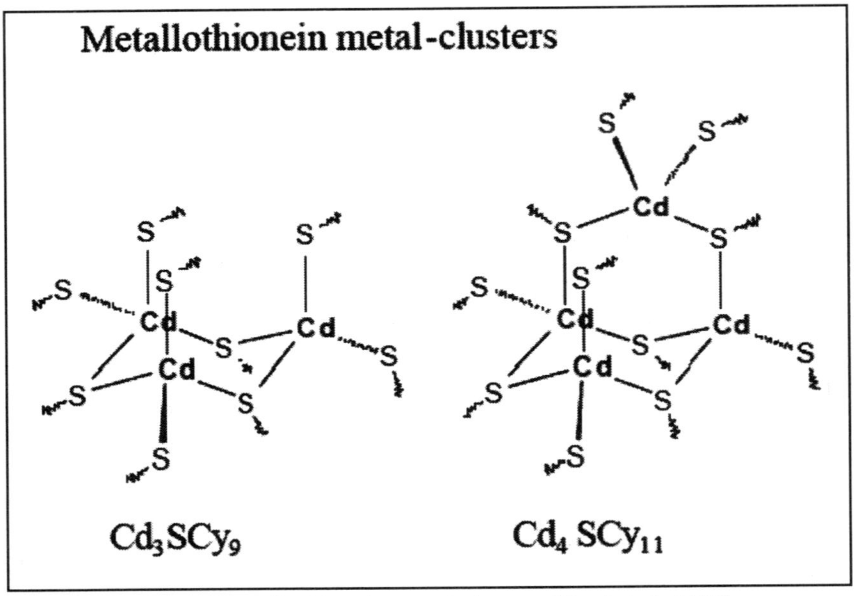

Fig. 6.1: Metallothionein metal-clusters (Kagi *et al.*, 1987)

The amino acid sequences of MTs from many mammalian sources reveal that all contain approximately 61 amino acids of remarkably similar composition. More important, all contain 20 cysteine residues that remain invariant along the amino acid sequence. All cysteines are known to participate in the coordination of 7 moles of Cd or zinc (Zn) per mole of MT. MTs are cytoplasmic proteins; however, their occurrence in the nucleus during fetal development has been shown by immuno histochemistry. MTs from eukaryotic and prokaryotic microorganisms and from plants resemble mammalian MTs on their conspicuous metal and cysteine content and on the occurrence of metal-thiolate cluster structures. Plant MTs first recognized in the roots of a copper-resistant strain of the grass *Agrotis gigantean* and in the roots of tomato plants exposed to elevated concentrations of $CdCl_2$ in the medium have now been found in a number of other plants including Cd-treated maize, cabbage, tobacco, rice and wheat and others, as well as in plant cell suspension cultures.

Classes of Metallothionein

Based on their structural similarities, MTs have been divided into three classes:

1. *Class I:* (Cys-Cys), occur in mammalians, some fishes, crabs, oysters and mussels.
2. *Class II:* (Cys-x-Cys), occur in yeasts, plants, fungi, nematodes, cyanobacteria and Drosophila.

3. *Class III:* (Cys-x-x-Cys) includes the phytochelatins that are occurring in all plants, algae and in some fungi.
   (x): any amino acids other than Cys

Metallothioneins belonging to class I and II are biosynthesized by direct translation of mRNA. On the other hand, class III metallothioneins are a group of metal-binding polypeptides containing peptide bond that are biosynthesized as enzymatic products. All vertebrates examined contain two or more distinct MT isoforms, which are grouped into two classes, designated MT-I and MT-II, depending on the elution position from DEAE cellulose. In many cases each class actually consists of several different proteins, which are designated MT-IA, MT-IB, MT-IC, etc.

Class I

Comprises mammalian metallothioneins with 20 cysteines and closely related metallothioneins such as the 18-cysteine metallothioneins of crustaceans. Mammalian MTs are a 61- or 62-amino-acid peptide containing 20 cysteines, 6-8 lysines, 7-10 serines, a single acetylated methionine at the amino terminus, and no aromatic amino acids or histidines. Metals are associated with MTs exclusively through thiolate bonds to all 20 cysteine residues. Mammalian tissues usually contain two major fractions, i.e. MT-1 and MT-2, differing at neutral pH by a single negative charge. Within these fractions, isoforms identified by letters such as MT-1a, MT-1b could be resolved by high-performance liquid chromatography. An excess of heavy metal ions such as Cd^{2+} or Cu^{2+} induces the expression of mammalian MTs. However, hormones, cytokines, growth factors, tumour inducers and chemical and physical stresses may also induce expression of MTs.

Class II

Metallothioneins isolated from non-animal sources such as the yeasts *Saccharomyces cerevisiae*, *Candida glabrata*, *Candida albicans*, algae, cyanobacteria (*Synechococcus* sp.) or plants (*Triticum aestivum*, *Zea mays*) belong to the class II of MTs. Thus far, the only lower organisms possessing a class I MT is the ascomycete *Neurospora crassa*. A well-known class II member is CUP1, the MT of *S. cerevisiae*. It is mainly responsible for copper tolerance and its structural gene is located in the CUP1 locus (chromosome VIII) that may amplify upon Cu^{2+} exposure. The CUP1 binds, however, both Cd and Zn (4 equivalents per molecule) besides 8 equivalents per molecule of monovalent ions. In the case of yeast protein there is no evidence of formation of two separate metal binding domains. In contrast to mammalian MTs, processing of the primary translation product results in the removal of 8 amino acids from the N-terminus. Polypeptides, such as yeast metallothioneins, show location of cysteines only distantly related to mammalian metallothioneins.

Class III

Enzymatically synthesized peptides such as the poly (?-glutamylcysteinyl) glycines are known as phytochelatins (PCs) and cadystins. The synthesis of phytochelatins is induced not only by Cd^{2+} but also by other heavy metal ions such as Cu^{2+}, Hg^{2+}, Pb^{2+} and Zn^{2+}. PCs have the general structure (?-Glu-Cys) n-Gly, where n= 2-11, and they are also called class III metallothioneins (MTs). Although the synthesis of class I and II MTs in animals and yeast (*Saccharomyces cerevisiae*), respectively, is controlled by genes and performed on ribosomes, the ?-carboxyamide bond involved in the class III MT is not synthesized on ribosomes. That is, the synthesis of PCs is not controlled genetically.

Physical and Chemical Characterization of MTs

General Characteristics of Metallothioneins are:

1. MT I and MT II's molecular weight is 6-7 kDa, 61 amino acids, 20 Cysteine (30%), N-acetylmethionine, C-alanine, no aromatics, no histidine.
2. Unique amino acid sequence,tertiary structure/metal clusters.
3. Metal content; Cd, Zn, Cu, Hg; 5-10% W/w.
4. Light absorption 250 nm (Cd), 225 nm (Zn), 275 nm (Cu), 300 nm (Hg).
5. Induced synthesis by Cd, Zn.
6. No disulfide bonds, heat stability.
7. Cytoplasmic localization.
8. Isoforms.
9. Localization on chromosome.

Degradation of MT protein is also an important aspect of MT regulation. There are tremendous differences in the half- lives of MT synthesized as a result of chemical induction of the MT gene. For example, the half- life of Zn-MT is approximately 18-20h, whereas that of Cd-MT is about 3 days. All class II MTs and I characterized thus far single chain proteins with chain weights of 6000 or less. However, on gel filtration mammalian and crustacean MTs are eluted at a position corresponding to that of a globular protein of molecular weight 10, 000. This discrepancy has been attributed to their nonglobular shape. Class III MTs may occur in oligomeric structures composed of two or more chains differing in chain weight from 500 to 2000 Daltons depending on the source. In these aggregates the chains proposed to be linked via metalthiolate bridges and/or via disulfide bonds. Their apparent molecular size is strongly dependent on salt concentration.

Functions of Metallothioneins

1. Transport and storage of metals
2. Protection from metal toxicity

3. Free radical scavenger
4. Immune response
5. Genotoxicity and carcinogenicity

METALLOTHIONEIN REDOX CYCLE AND FUNCTION

MT redox cycle may play a crucial role in MT biologic function. It may link to the homeostasis of essential metals, detoxification of toxic metals and protection against oxidative stress. The most critical advance in MT research is the demonstration of the redox regulation of Zn-S interaction and the coupling of zinc and redox metabolism. The cluster structure of Zn-MT provides a chemical basis by which the cysteine ligand can induce oxido reductive properties. This structure allows for thermodynamic stability of zinc in MT while permitting zinc to retain kinetic lability. The sulfur ligand confers the redox activity on the zinc-MT complex and can be oxidized and reduced with concomitant release and binding of zinc in an oxidoreductive environment. The release of zinc from MT makes zinc available for the functional demand of other molecules. The reduction of the oxidized MT restores the zinc binding capacity and, thus, the repletion of the endogenous zinc reservoir. This process constitutes a MT redox cycle, as shown in Figure 6.2, which provides an alternate perspective on biologic function of MT.

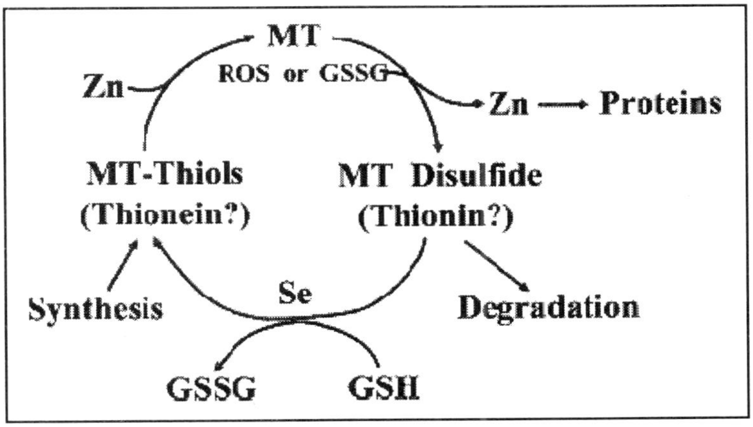

Fig. 6.2: Schematic Presentation of MT Redox Cycle

Zinc Release from MT

Early studies have shown that there is fast zinc exchange between MT isoforms, between MT and the zinc cluster in the Gal4 transcription factor and between MT and the apoforms of various zinc proteins. Importantly, zinc release from MT is modulated by both glutathione (GSH) and glutathione disulfide (GSSG). GSH inhibits zinc release in the absence of GSSG, indicating that MT is stabilized at relatively high cellular GSH concentrations. The presence of GSSG results in zinc release. The rate of zinc release depends linearly on the amount of GSSG: the more oxidative the redox state becomes, the more efficiently zinc is released from MT. Moreover, cellular disulfides other than GSSG also react with MT to release zinc with high efficiency.

Under physiologic conditions, zinc bound to MT is released through oxidation of the thiolate cluster when the environment becomes oxidized. Formation of MT-disulfide or thionin (if all metals are released from MT) follows zinc release. MT-disulfide or thionin would be subjected to degradation, however, when the oxidized environment became reduced through, for example, an increase in GSH/ GSSG ratio MT-disulfide or thionin is reduced to MT-thiol or thionein. This reduction process is greatly enhanced in the presence of selenium catalyst or other unidentified catalytic agents. In the presence of zinc, MT is quickly reconstituted. This process constitutes MT redox cycle, which plays a crucial role in the biologic function of MT.

Formation of MT-Disulfides

Attempts to demonstrate the formation of MT-disulfide bonds *in vivo* were impractical in the past, largely due to the fact that the tissue concentrations of MT were insufficient. This limitation is now overcome by the availability of MT over expressing transgenic mice. A strategy of differential alkylation of cysteine residues in MT to identify disulfide bond formation *in vivo* has been developed (Feng *et al.,* 2006). A pH of 6.0 and nitrogen-flushed buffer is used for tissue homogenization immediately after tissue harvest, in the presence of N-ethylmaleimide (NEM), to trap the sulfhydryl groups of cysteine residues that are not present as disulfide bonds *in vivo.*

Reduction of MT-Disulfides

Coordination of zinc to the thiol group of cysteine residues in MT and the low redox potential of the thiolate clusters make the coupling between zinc and redox metabolism possible. A number of mild cellular oxidants can oxidize the thiolate clusters, leading to zinc release. Among that physiologic oxidants is GSSG. It has been shown that changes in the GSH/GSSG ratio modulate zinc transfer from MT to other zinc-binding proteins. Therefore, the changes in the cellular redox state serve as a signal for zinc mobilization and distribution through the redox reaction of thiol clusters in MT.

Possible Link Between MT Redox Cycle and Biologic Function

Many studies have implicated three major biologic functions of MT, including homeostasis of essential metals, detoxification of toxic metals, and protection from oxidative stress. However, the lack of a sufficient mechanistic understanding of the action of MT makes the study of biologic function of MT progress with uncertainty. The MT redox cycle described above may provide an alternative perspective on this perplexing topic. The chemical properties of the MT redox cycle have potential links to the biologic function.

MT Redox Cycle and Zinc Homeostasis

Several zinc transporters have been identified and characterized and they participate in mammalian zinc metabolism by transporting zinc across plasma membranes. These proteins belong to two solute-linked carrier (SLC) gene families, ZnT (SLC30) and Zip (SLC39). All of these proteins have transmembrane domains and it appears that ZnT proteins transport zinc from cytosol to extracellular space or to intracellular vesicles and Zip proteins promote extracellular zinc uptake and zinc release from vesicles to cytoplasm. As described above, zinc movement in the cell is tightly regulated and intracellular free zinc is very limited.

MT Redox Cycle and Metal Detoxification

The earliest suggested and most consented function of MT is its role in detoxification of metals. The discovery of MT was associated with cadmium binding. Since then, the effect of MT on cadmium metabolism and toxicity has been studied extensively. Such studies continue along with advances in biochemical and molecular techniques and instrumentation invention. The binding of cadmium to MT and the structural characteristics of cadmium-MT have been a topic since the discovery of MT. These structural studies have unambiguously demonstrated the interaction between cadmium and MT.

MT Redox Cycle and the Antioxidant Function

The hypothesis that MT functions as an antioxidant against reactive oxygen and nitrogen species has received extensive experimental support from many in vitro studies. Studies using a cell-free system have demonstrated the ability of MT as a free radical scavenger. The first suggestion of the antioxidant function of MT was obtained from a study examining the effects of MT on the radiosensitivity of a cultured human epithelial (HE) cell line and mouse fibroblast (C1 1D) cells. Further studies showed that MT containing zinc and/or cadmium can scavenge hydroxyl and superoxide radicals produced by the xanthine/xanthine oxidase reaction system.

PLANT METALLOTHIONEINS

After the discovery of PCs as an important metal ligand required for tolerance of plants to Cd, a MT protein was identified in wheat. and a number of MT genes were isolated from plants. The plant Class II MT proteins can be further classified based on amino acid sequence. Robinson *et al.* (1993) first identified two plant MT types based on the position of cysteine residues in the predicted proteins. Since then, the number of characterized plant MT genes has increased dramatically, and because many do not conform to these two groups, additional categories have been added.

Other classifications have been proposed (Liu *et al.*, 2000). However, the system presented below builds on the one developed by Robinson *et al.* (1993) and is able to place almost all of the known plant MT genes into four categories based on amino acid sequence. Type 1 and Type 2 MTs follow the classification of Robinson *et al.* (1996), Type 3 includes many MTs expressed during fruit ripening, and Type 4 is exemplified by the wheat Ec protein, the first characterized plant MT protein.

Type 1 MTs contain a total of six Cys-Xaa-Cys motifs (where Xaa represents another amino acid) that are distributed equally among two domains. In the majority of Type 1 MTs, the two domains are separated by approximately 40 amino acids that include aromatic amino acids. This large spacer is a common feature of plant MTs and contrasts with most other MTs in which cysteine-rich domains are separated by a spacer of less than 10 amino acids that do not include aromatic residues. Within the Type 1 MTs, those from various Brassicaceae (*Arabidopsis* and *Brassica* species) have a number of distinguishing features, including a much shorter spacer between the cysteine-rich domains and an additional Cys residue.

Type 2 MTs also contain two cysteine-rich domains separated by a spacer of approximately 40 amino acid residues. However, the first pair of cysteines is present as a Cys-Cys motif in amino acid positions 3 and 4 of these proteins. A Cys-Gly-Gly-Cys motif is present at the end of the N-terminal cysteine-rich domain. Overall, the sequences of the N-terminal domain of Type 2 MTs are highly conserved (MSCCGGNCGCS). The C-terminal domain contains three Cys-Xaa- Cys motifs. By contrast, the spacer region separating these domains in Type 2 MTs is much more variable between species.

Type 3 MTs contain only four Cys residues in the N-terminal domain. The consensus sequence for the first three is Cys-Gly-Asn-Cys-Asp-Cys. The fourth cysteine is not part of a pair of cysteines but is contained within a highly conserved motif, Gln-Cys-Xaa-Lys-Lys-Gly. The six Cys residues in the C-terminal cysteine-rich domain are arranged in Cys-Xaa-Cys motifs. As with the majority of Type 1 and Type 2 plant MTs, the two domains are separated from each other by approximately 40 amino acid residues.

Type 4 MTs differ from other plant MTs by having three cysteine-rich domains, each containing 5 or 6 conserved cysteine residues, which are separated by 10 to 15 residues. Most of the cysteines are present as Cys-Xaa-Cys motifs. Although a large number of Type 4 MTs have not been identified, compared to those from monocots, Type 4 MTs from dicots contain additional 8 to 10 amino acids in the N-terminal domain before the first cysteine residue.

Plant Genes with Similarity to Metallothionein Genes

Genes that encode proteins with (some) sequence similarity to metallothioneins have been isolated from several plant species. All of these genes encode predicted proteins with two Cys-rich domains containing Cys-Xaa-Cys motifs (where Xaa is an amino acid other than Cys). Computer based searches select metallothionein as the most similar known proteins.

Comparison (DNASTAR software) of the predicted protein from *Mimulus guttatus* with sequences in the NBRF protein database identified 19 of the top 23 matches as metallothioneins. Similar analysis (Fast P software) of the predicted translational product of the pea gene, PsMTA, also selected metallothioneins as the top 10 best matches. Matrix comparisons of the amino acid sequences of the predicted PsMTA protein and class I metallothionein from *Neurospora crassa* identify two regions of sequence similarity (amino acids 4-18 and 61-74 in the predicted pea protein), that correspond to the Cys-rich terminal domains. These two domains are linked by a central 'spacer' region of approx. 40 amino acids that is devoid of Cys residues. The Cys rich terminal domains in the predicted sequences from different species are somewhat more conserved than the central 'spacer' regions (table 6.2).

MT Proteins

The wheat Ec Type 4 MT protein was purified from embryos as a zinc binding protein and provided the first evidence that plants contained not only PCs but also MTs as cysteine-based metal ligands. At present, the wheat Ec protein is the only plant protein that can be unequivocally designated a metallothionein. While 'metallothionein- like' plant genes have been isolated from other species (Figure 6.1), and data indicate that these genes have roles in metal metabolism, their translational products remain to be purified from plant material and sequenced. The ensuing flood of information about plant genes and cDNAs encoding MT proteins has not been accompanied by a corresponding increase in knowledge about the expression or distribution of MT proteins.

MT Gene Expression

In attempting to shed light on their function, investigators have relied primarily on RNA blot hybridization to study the expression of MT genes during development and in response to various environmental factors. More detailed localization of MT mRNAs or MT gene promoter activity has been obtained in a small number of cases through *in situ* hybridization and reporter gene expression studies. Many MT genes are expressed at very high levels in plant tissues, at least in terms of transcript abundance. Direct evidence comes from gene profiling experiments in rice using the serial analysis of gene expression (SAGE) protocol. Transcripts from four MT genes comprised almost 3% of the transcripts in two-week-old seedlings. A Type 2 MT gene contributed 1.26% of all transcripts, the single most abundantly expressed gene in this tissue. Transcripts of two Type 3MT genes accounted for an additional 1.25% of the mRNAs. Furthermore, ESTs for MT genes are among the most prevalent in randomly sequenced cDNA libraries from a number of plants.

Table 6.2: Expression of Genes with Similarity to Metallothionin Genes in Different Plants

Plant	Trandance Abundance										
	Localization			Elevated Metal							
	Root	Leaf	Seed	Zn	Cu	Cd	Fe	Fe+ Cu	Hormone ABA	ABA Element	Metal Binding
Pea	High	Low	Low	–	No	–	Down	Up	–	No	Cu>Cd>Zn
Mimulus		Low	–	Down	Down	–	–	–	–	–	–
Maize	High		Very Low	–	–	–	–	–	–	No	–
Barley	High	On	–	–	–	–	Down	–	–	–	–
Arabidopsis	–	On	–	–	–	Down	–	–	–	–	–
Caster bean	–	High	–	–	–	–	–	–	–	–	–
Soybean	Low	–	–	–	Down	–	–	–	–	–	–
Wheat	–	–	High	No	–	–	–	–	Up	Yes	Zn

(Robinson *et al.*, 1993)

Differential Expression of Class I MTS

The class I MTS reported so far can be divided into five type. Many pieces of evidence support the idea that type I MTs are the most abundant in roots Evans *et al.* (1992) characterized the type 1 PSMTA in pea, which was highly expressed in roots, weakly expressed in green and etiolated leaves, and most weakly expressed in developing cotyledons. The mRNA of the maize MT-L (type l) gene was the most abundant in roots, less abundant in green leaves and pith, and much less abundant in kernels.

In addition, tvpe 2 MT transcripts preferentially accumulate in aerial tissues, especially leaves, as in soybean MT, rice OSMT-2 and LeMTA, LeMTB from tomato. In *Vicia faba*, Evans *et al.* (1992) demonstrated through Northern blot analysis that type 2 MT was expressed abundantly in leaves, stems and flowers, and at a low level in roots, but was absent in mesophyll protoplasts. Moreover, using ^{32}P-labeled MT transcripts as probes, they performed *in situ* hybridization on leaf sections and observed predominant signals at the site of trichome. In kiwifruit, the type 2MT pKIWI204 was expressed most abundantly in young fruit (6 days after anthesis).

Type 3 MTS have been reported only in *Arabidopsis* and rape. The differential expression of the MT I (type 3) gene was investigated in Arabidopsis. A higher level of transcripts was observed in roots than in leaves in both young and mature plants. On the other hand, the LSC54 in *Brassica napus* showed pronounced expression in senescing leaves and nearly no expression in roots, even though it is a type 3 MT with the same Cys arrangement in the two Cys-rich domains as *Arabidopsis* MT I. The ricMT in rice is the onlv type 4 MT gene for which the expression pattern has been investigated. This gene seems to be expressed constitutively, and the strongest transcription signal for ricMT was detected in stems, at a level dozens of times higher than that in green leaves. A low level of ricMT transcript was observed in roots and endosperms.

A type 5 MT gene has been reported in kiwifruit, and the mRNA level was high in the late stage of fruit development. Another type 5 MT was extracted from *Arabidopsis* as MT 3, but little is known about its expression pattern.

Generally, class I MT genes are expressed constitutively in plants, with tissue-specific patterns. This differential expression depends on the features of the Cys-rich domain in type I and type 2, but varies in tvpe 3. An analysis of the genomic structure of MTS and of the mechanism of genetic regulation may help to explain the relationship between the structure and the expression pattern of MTs.

Expression Pattern Under the Influence of Various Factors

Metal ions

As homologs of animal MTs, it would be reasonable to assume that the MTs in plants are related to metal metabolism and the detoxification of excess metal ions. Indeed, the expression of both Ec proteins and several class I MT genes vary under metal treatment. The wali l (type 2) in wheat was originally isolated as an aluminum-induced gene. Its expression is also increased by treatment with other toxic metal ions such as Cd, Fe, Zn, Cu, Ga, In and La.

Senescence

Coupe *et al.* (1995) isolated the type 2 MT gene JET12 from the abscission zones of ethylene-treated *Sambucus nigra* L. leaves. Northern analysis revealed that the JET12 gene was expressed only in senescent leaves, and in the ethylene-treated abscission zone. Similarly, the type 3 MT LSC54 in rape (*Brassica napus*) was expressed during leaf senescence, and as senescence progressed, the mRNA level of LSC54 increased. Hsieh *et al.*(1995) showed that the expression of rgMT (type 1) increased as young leaves progressed to senescence. These results suggest that these MT genes may play a role in the senescence-associated metabolism of plants.

Other Stresses

Considerable effort has been made to clarify the relationships between plant MTs and environmental factors other than metal ions. The expression of type 2 MT seems to be easily affected by stresses- For example; the MT in tobacco was strongly induced by tobacco mosaic virus and wounding and the expression of MT in *Vicia faba* was reduced when plants were treated with salt, cold, salicylic acid or UV-light. Furthermore, transcripts of OsMT-2 in rice could be induced by sucrose starvation, heat shock and abscisic acid and the expression of wali l in wheat was increased by low-nutrient conditions and wounding.

Class III Metallothioneins

y-glutamyl isopeptides, cadystins, phytochelatins, poly (y-glutamylcysteinyl) glycines.

Class III metallothioneins differ markedly from class I and II metallothioneins. They are enzymically derived and are most commonly composed of poly (γ -glutamylcysteinyl)glycine, (γ -Glu-Cys).Gly, where n = 2-11 depending on the organism, although the most common forms have n = 2-4. However, class III metallothioneins isolated from the Fabaceae contain, 8-alanine in the C-terminal position and these species produce predominantly homoglutathione (γ-glutamylcysteinyl-β-alanine) rather than glutathione (y-glutamylcysteinylglycine). Des-glycine forms of class III metallothioneins have also been described.

Metal complexes containing these y-glutamyl isopeptides have apparent native M_rS ranging from 2000 to 10000 depending upon the source and method of isolation, and include multiple polypeptides in a cluster. Sulphide is sometimes present in Cd^{2+} complexes in varying amounts but has not been found in copper complexes. High-Mr sulphide-containing complexes show enhanced affinity for metals. The structure of such complexes is of interest, being composed of a CdS quantum semiconductor crystallite core surrounded by polypeptides.

Biosynthesis

Structural similarities between glutathione and class III metallothioneins suggest that the latter are synthesized from the former or its precursors. *In vivo* experiments demonstrate a significant reduction of free glutathione upon exposure of plant cell cultures to Cd^{2+}. Pulse-chase experiments, where the cellular glutathione pool is tagged with 36S, show loss of radiolabel from glutathione with a concomitant increase in radiolabelled class III metallothioneins. Treatment of cell cultures with buthionine sulphoxamine, a potent inhibitor of ã- glutamylcysteine synthetase, results in the loss of metal tolerance and an inability to synthesize class III metallothioneins. In addition, mutants of the fission yeast deficient in enzymes of glutathione synthesis are unable to produce class III metallothioneins and are hypersensitive to Cd^{2+}.

Localizaton

In Cd^{2+} exposed hydroponically grown *Nicotiana rustica* var. *Pavonii*, the main Cd^{2+} binding components were $(\gamma\text{-Glu- Cys})_3\text{Gly}$ and $(\gamma\text{-Glu-Cys})_4\text{Gly}$. The location of these polypeptides was determined following isolation of protoplasts and vacuoles from leaves of Cd^{2+} exposed seedlings. Both class III metallothioneins and Cd^{2+} were found in the vacuoles.

These thiol-rich compounds are also known as cadystins and phytochelatins. Cd^{2+} complexes contain multiple polypeptide molecules and some complexes also contain inorganic S^2 within the metal core. Vacuolar accumulation of such complexes has been observed in plants and in *S. pombe*. The product of the hmtl gene, localized to the vacuolar membrane, is required for the accumulation of these complexes in vacuoles of *S. pombe* (Ortiz *et al.*, 1992). The predicted sequence of HMT1 is similar to those of ABC-type membrane transporters but it remains to be established which component(s) of the Cd^{2+} complexes (or their precursors) it transports. Red circles, cysteine residues; black circles, glutamate residues; white circles, glycine residues.

The recent observations of Ortiz *et al.* (1992) indicate that there is a specific transporter, designated HMT1, required for the accumulation of high-M_r CdS-(class III metallothionein) complexes in the vacuole of *S. pombe* cells, A Cd^{2+} sensitive mutant of *S. pombe*, designated LK100, was isolated that accumulated less of these complexes than the wild type. LK100 cells transformed with hmt FI showed restored (increased) Cd^{2+} accumulation. The amino acid sequence deduced from hmtl cDNA suggests that its product is similar to ABC (ATP-binding cassette)-type membrane transport proteins (Ortiz *et al.*, 1992). Subcellular fractionation of extracts from *S. pombe* containing an hmtl-lacZ fusion indicated that the encoded fusion protein is localized in the vacuolar membrane. At present it is not clear which of the components of the complex (Cd^{2+}, S^{2-}, polypeptides or their precursors) is transported into the vacuole via HMT1 (Figure 6.3).

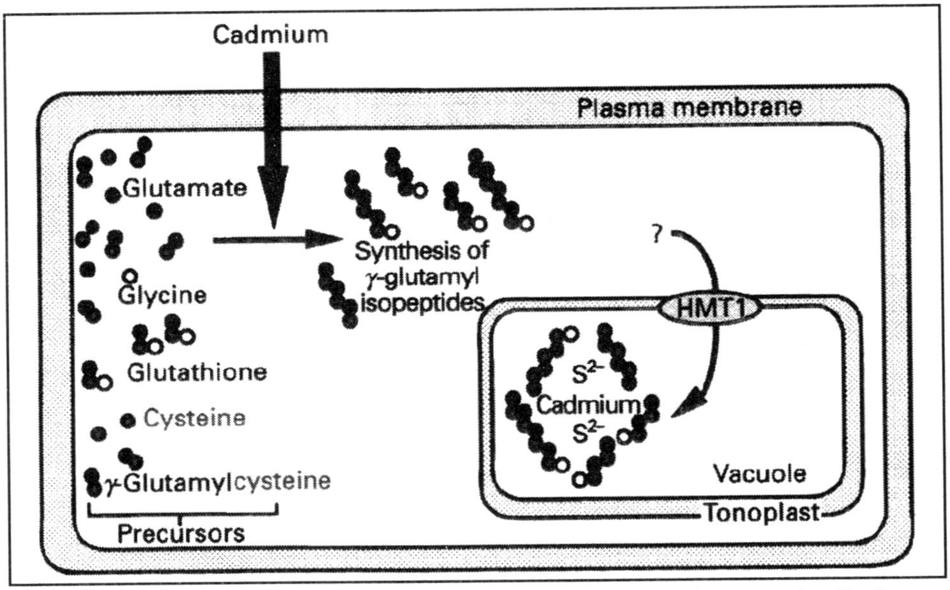

Fig. 6.3: Plants and Certain Species of Yeast accumulate y-glutamyl Isopeptides, Designated Class III Metailothioneins, when Exposed to Cd^{2+}

Phytochelatins: Structure and Biosynthetic Pathway

Phytochelatins (PCs) form a family of structures with increasing repetitions of the γ-GluCys dipeptide followed by a terminal Gly; (γ-GluCys)n-Gly, where n is generally in the range of 2 to 5. PCs have been identified in a wide variety of plant species and in some microorganisms.

As a composite of various functions identified through the isolation of Cd-sensitive mutants of different organisms that express PCs. Gene loci are shown in italics: CAD1 and CAD2/RML1 are in *Arabidopsis*; hmt1, hmt2, ade2, ade6, ade7, and ade8 are in *S. pombe*; ycf1 is in *S. cerevisiae*; and hem2 is in *C. glabrata*. Enzyme abbreviations: GCS, γ -glutamylcysteine synthetase; GS,glutathione synthetase; PCS, phytochelatin synthase.

In addition, a number of structural variants, for example, (γ- GluCys)n-Ala, (γ-GluCys)n-Ser and (γ-GluCys)n-Glu, have been identified in some plant species. PCs are structurally related to glutathione (GSH; γ-GluCysGly), and numerous physiological, biochemical, and genetic studies have confirmed that GSH (or, in some cases, related compounds) is the substrate for PC biosynthesis (Fig. 6.4).

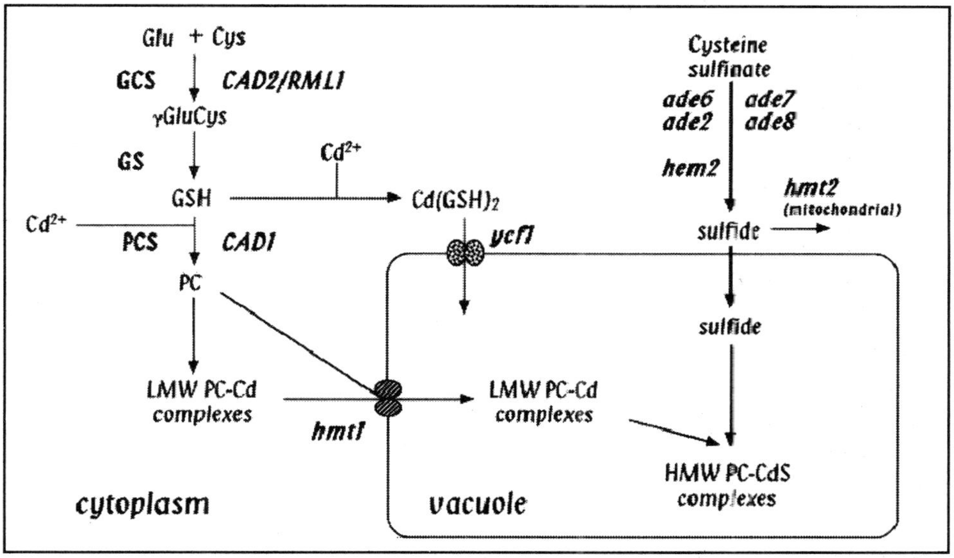

Fig. 6.4: Genes and Functions Contributing to Cd detoxification in Plants and Fungi

Sequestration to the Vacuole

In both plant and yeast, PC-Cd complexes are sequestered to the vacuole. In *S. pombe*, this process has been most clearly demonstrated through studies of the Cd-sensitive mutant hmt1. In extracts of *S. pombe*, two PC-Cd complexes (referred to as HMW and LMW) can be clearly resolved using gel-filtration chromatography. The hmt1 mutant is unable to form the HMW complexes. The Hmt1 gene encodes a member of the family of ATP-binding cassette (ABC) membrane transport proteins that is located in the vacuolar membrane. Both HMT1 and ATP are required for the transport of LMW PC-Cd complexes into vacuolar membrane vesicles (Fig. 6.4). In *S. cerevisiae*, which appears not to express a PC synthase, YCF1 is also a member of the ABC family of transporters and carries (GSH) 2Cd complexes to the vacuole. Interestingly, in *C. elegans*, various mutations affecting ABC transporter proteins also confer heavy metal sensitivity. It is possible that these transporters are involved in the sequestration of PC metal complexes in *C. elegans*.

Sulfide Ions and PC Function

In some plants and in the yeasts *S. pombe* and *Candida glabrata*, sulphide ions play an important role in the efficacy of Cd detoxification by PCs. HMW PC-Cd complexes contain both Cd and acid-labile sulfide. The incorporation of sulfide into the HMW complexes increases both the amount of Cd per molecule and the stability of the complex. Some complexes with a comparatively high ratio of S^{2-}: Cd consists of aggregates of 20A° diameter particles, which themselves consist of a CdS crystallite core coated with PCs. The analysis of Cd-sensitive mutants of *S. pombe* deficient in PC-Cd complexes has provided evidence for the importance of sulfide in the function of PCs.

Metals Other than Cd

Although both induction of PCs *in vivo* and activation of PC synthase *in vitro* is conferred by a range of metal ions, there is little evidence supporting a role for PCs in the detoxification of such a wide range of metal ions. For metals other than Cd, there are few studies demonstrating the formation of PC-metal complexes either *in vitro* or in vivo. PCs can form complexes with Pb, Ag and Hg *in vitro*. Maitani *et al.*used inductively coupled plasma-atomic emission spectroscopy in combination with HPLC separation of native PC-metal complexes in the roots of *Rubia tinctorum*. PCs were induced to varying levels by a wide range of metal ions tested. The most effective appeared to be Ag, arsenate, Cd, Cu, Hg, and Pb ions. However, the only PC complexes identified *in vivo* were with Cd, Ag, and Cu ions.

Multiple Metallothioneins from Hybrid Poplar

Kohler *et al*., (2004) characterized six metallothionein genes (PtdMTs) in the hybrid cottonwood, *Populus trichocarpa* × *deltoids*. cDNA microarrays and reverse transcriptase-polymerase chain reaction were used to examine PtdMT expression in poplar tissues. They displayed differential gene expression patterns, which may be associated with the diverse roles and functions PtdMTs have in coping with particular developmental (e.g. root development and leaf senescence) and environmental cues. The heterologous expression in cadmium (Cd)-hypersensitive yeast mutant showed the ability of PtdMT cDNAs to confer Cd tolerance. The concentration of PtdMT mRNAs were increased by zinc, but not by copper and Cd.

Multiple Isoforms of MTs in Poplar

Metallothionein is encoded by a small gene family in hybrid poplar and six different MT sequences from root and leaf cDNA libraries of *P. trichocarpa* × *deltoids* were identified. They were further divided into three subgroups, corresponding to the previously described type 1, type 2 and type 3 MTs from other plants. Type 4 MT sequences were not found in our cDNA libraries and the NCBI poplar ESTs, but their expression seems to be clearly restricted to developing seeds.

Role of Poplar MTs in Heavy Metal tolerance

Using the yeast yap-1Δ mutant, which is particularly sensitive to Cd, Kohler *et al.* (2004) showed that PtdMTs were capable of restoring Cd tolerance (Fig. 6.5). We further investigated whether PtdMT gene expression was regulated by heavy metals. In poplar roots, only treatment with Zn had a stimulating effect on type 1 and type 2 MT gene expressions. PtdMT3a gene expression was not effected by the Zn treatment, whereas PtdMT3b expression was weakly affected. By contrast, Cu (50 µM) and Cd (25 µM) only slightly enhanced the transcript levels of PtdMTs compared with the transcript levels in untreated roots and they repressed MT expression.

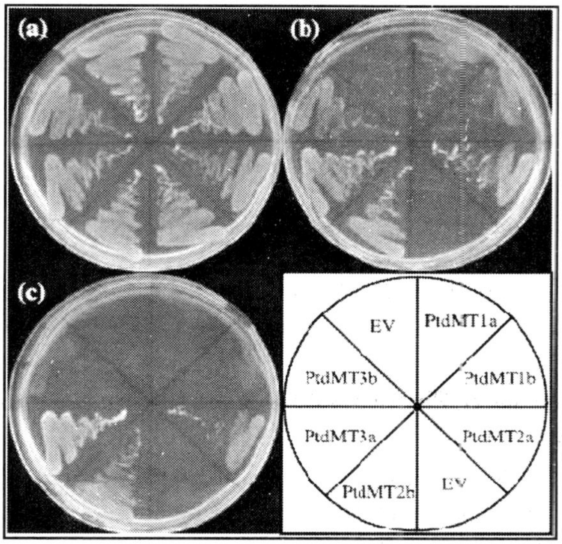

Fig. 6.5: Growth of yap-1Δ Yeast Cells Expressing PtdMTs Under Various Cadmium (Cd) Concentrations

The Cd-sensitive yap-1Δ strain was transformed either with the pYES2 empty vector (EV) or with the different pYES2–PtdMT constructs. Cells were grown on normal SD medium (a) or supplemented with 75 µM (b) or 125 µM (c) Cd. Plates were incubated for 5 d at 30°C. Equivalent data were obtained in two other replicate experiments with independent transformants higher concentrations.

Results suggest a role for poplar PtdMTs mainly in Zn metabolism/detoxification rather than in Cd or Cu metabolism/detoxification, but further experiments will be necessary to establish the exact function of PtdMTs. The occurrence of multiple MTs in poplar (and other plants) may reflect the diversity of their functions in heavy metal sequestration, but also other mechanisms essential for plant growth and development.

MT Expression is Regulated by Root Development

The expression patterns of the various types of *Ptd*MTs are dramatically altered by the adventitious root development. As stressed above, all *Ptd*MTs transcripts were very abundant in the bark tissues of dormant cuttings. When root development initiated, the expression of all *Ptd*MTs dropped down. In poplar roots incubated in the presence of auxins, a decreased expression of type 1 and type 2 MT genes was also observed (*A. Jambois*, UMR IaM, INRA, Nancy, France, unpublished data), suggesting that *Ptd*MT expression in developing roots was regulated by auxins.

MTs in Senescing Leaves

Previous studies demonstrated that MT expression was induced during leaf senescence (Andersson *et al.*, 2004). It has been argued that during senescence metal ions are transported from leaves to other parts of the plant to be recycled and that MTs are involved in the cellular protection against elevated metal concentration during this process. In hybrid poplar, all *Ptd*MTs were expressed at higher levels in senescing leaves than in young leaves (Fig. 6.4). However, a different expression pattern was obtained during autumn senescence in aspen leaves. The mRNA of aspen PMt4, which shares a high homology with PtdMT2b, decreased in expression when senescence proceeded. Perhaps the discrepancy between expression patterns results from the fact that Andersson *et al.* (2004) used leaves from an adult aspen tree (> 30 yr old), while we harvested leaves from a 5-month-old glasshouse-grown poplar.

Coordinated Responses of Phytochelatins and Metallothioneins to Heavy Metals in Garlic Seedlings

Zhang *et al.* (2005) evaluated the roles of phytochelatins (PCs) and metallothioneins (MTs) in heavy metal tolerance in garlic (*Allium sativum* L.), the cDNAs encoding a phytochelatin synthase and a type 2 MT were cloned from the seedlings of garlic using RACE method and designated *As*PCS1 and *As*MT2*a*. Semi-quantitative reverse transcriptase-PCR and PCs contents showed transcript levels of AsPCS1 in roots exposed to cadmium increased significantly within 1 h concomitant with a sharp increase of PCs. However, the RNA expression of *As*MT2*a* in roots was slightly increased within the preliminary phases of cadmium treatment and an obvious increase did not occurred until 10 h of Cd exposure. Different effects on RNA expression of *As*PCS1 and *As*MT2*a* appeared under varied stresses. Treatment with cadmium, arsenic and heat shock resulted in a strong increase of *As*PCS1 transcripts and PCs contents in roots. Theses results showed that AsPCS1 and *As*MT2*a* displayed mutual coordination under the stresses.

To understand the molecular mechanisms of garlic seedlings to conditions of heavy metal stress, first of all, we compared the effects of Cd on the expression levels of *As*PCS1 and *As*MT2*a* in roots and leaves. Fig. 6.6 shows the kinetics and dose response of the transcript levels of these two genes in response to Cd stress. A maximum increase of threefold of *As*PCS1 expression levels in roots was observed after 1 h exposure to Cd, subsequently its expression levels dropped but were still much higher than that of untreated roots and maintained at a steady-state level. However, although an obvious decrease of *As*PCS1 expression at transcriptional level in leaves was detected within 3 h of Cd stress, gradual increase of transcript levels was found after that time and 72% increase occurred at the end of the experiment compared with the control. In response to Cd, *As*MT2*a* exhibited an expression pattern distinct from *As*PCS1. Its transcript levels in roots were increased very slightly within10 h of Cd treatment and evident increase occurred after that time. *As*MT2*a* expression in leaves also presented the similar tendency as in roots with the increasing of incubation time. Dose response analysis, in which the cultures were exposed to 200 and 500 mM Cd for 24 h, revealed a trend that the increases in the expression levels of these two genes in both roots and leaves were dependent upon the Cd concentrations, with higher Cd concentrations causing larger increases in the expression levels of *As*PCS1 and *As*MT2*a*.

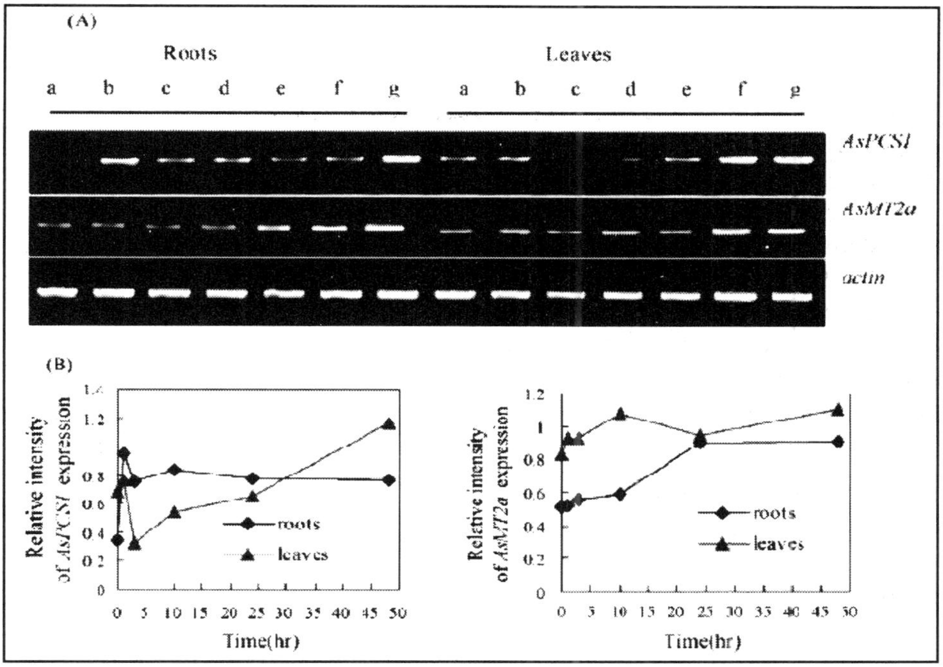

Fig. 6.6: Comparative RT-PCR Analysis of AsPCS1 and AsMT2a Expression in Roots and Leaves of Garlic Seedlings in Response to Cd Exposure

(A) Transcript levels of AsPCS1 and AsMT2a in roots and leaves from hydroponically grown plants treated for 0 h (a), 1 h (b), 3 h (c), 10 h (d), 24 h (e) and 48 h (f) with 200 mM $CdCl_2$ and 24 h (g) with 500 mM$CdCl_2$. (B) Relative amount of the normalized expression of AsPCS1 (left) and AsMT2a (right) in roots and leaves of garlic seedlings in response to Cd exposure. The expression level of actin was used as a positive internal control.

Expression of Metallothionein 3-like Protein mRNA in Sorghum Cultivars Under Chromium (VI) Stress

Many MT genes are expressed at high levels in plant tissues, at least in terms of transcript abundance. The *MT3* gene expression in roots after imposition of 100 μM Cr (VI) for 5 days in 15-day-old seedlings of two sorghum cultivars, viz. K 10 and CO 27 (susceptible and tolerant respectively, based on earlier studies on growth and antioxidant response to Cr (VI)) was studied by enzymatic amplification of RNA by polymerase chain reaction (RT–PCR), as described by Kaina *et al.* (1990). Crude RNA was extracted from stressed and control plant samples. Selective precipitation of RNA was done to remove DNA contamination.

From the results obtained it was seen that sorghum cultivar CO -27 treated with Cr (VI) had high-intensity band matching that of the gene of interest. This suggests that there could be higher transcription rates of the MT under Cr stress, particularly in the tolerant variety. It is possible that reactive oxygen species and H_2O_2 produced under Cr stress acted as a signal to induce MT mRNA transcription. Phytochelatin functions in the regulation of essential metals and in the detoxification of most toxic metals. The distinct absence of Phytochelatin has been reported in plants under Cr (VI) stress. This suggests that there could be an enhanced role for MTs in plants under Cr stress. There is a possibility that MTs could confer tolerance to plants against metal stress by binding Cr ions and rendering them non-toxic. A clear role for MTs is yet to be established, although they certainly are thought to play a role in metal metabolism. MTs may function as antioxidants and a role in plasma membrane repair is another possibility. Although MTs are expressed ubiquitously and conserved in plants, determining their function remains a future challenge.

MAMMALIAN METALLOTHIONEIN

MT genes are readily induced by various physiologic and toxicologic stimuli. Because the cysteines in MT are absolutely conserved across species, it was suspected that the cysteines are necessary for function and MT is essential for life. In attempts to determine the function(s) of MT, studies have been performed using four different experimental paradigms: (a) animals injected with chemicals known to induce MT; (b) cells adapted to survive and grow in high concentrations of MT-inducing toxicants; (c) cells transfected with the MT gene; and (d) MT transgenic and MT-null mice. Most often, results from studies using the first three approaches have indicated multiple functions of MT in cell biology: MT (a) is a "storehouse" for zinc, (b) is a free-radical scavenger, and (c) protects against cadmium (Cd) toxicity. However, studies using MT-transgenic and null mice have not strongly supported the first two proposed functions but strongly support its function in protecting against Cd toxicity. Repeated administration of Cd to MT-null mice results in nephrotoxicity at one tenth the dose that produces nephrotoxicity in control mice. Human studies indicate that 7% of the general populations have renal dysfunction from Cd exposure.

Regulation of MT Protein Degradation

Degradation of MT protein is also an important aspect of MT regulation. There are tremendous differences in the half-lives of MT synthesized as a result of chemical induction of the MT gene. For example, the half-life of Zn-MT is approximately 18-20 h, whereas that of Cd-MT is about 3 days. Studies from Kersahw and Klaassen (1992) showed that the half-life for constitutive MT in adult rats is about 4 h, whereas in neonates it is 49 h. MT induced by ethanol, $ZnCl_2$ or $CdCl_2$ also has widely different half-lives, approximately 9, 25, and 60 h, respectively, indicating that the degradation of MT is dependent on the age of the animals and the metal bound to MT.

Using cultured hepatocytes, Chen & Failla (1989) showed that the degradation of MT is primarily regulated by cellular Zn content, and it occurs in both lysosomal and non-lysosomal compartments. The importance of cathepsin B in lysosomal fraction was demonstrated when cathepsin B–specific inhibitors were found to suppress apo-MT degradation by 80%. This was further confirmed using purified cathepsin B. It was also shown that MT is degraded rapidly when there are fewer than five atoms of metal associated with each molecule of MT.

Proposed Functions of Metallothionein

Role of Metallothionein in Essential Metal Homeostasis

(i) **Zinc:** Zn is a physiologically important metal and the most abundant metal bound to constitutive MT. Zn provides essential structural and catalytic functions to a wide variety of proteins. More than 300 different enzymes depend on Zn for proper protein folding and biological function. Zn is also crucial in the regulation of gene expression because numerous transcription factors have "zinc finger motifs" that are maintained by Zn. Apo-MT (metallothionein with no metals bound) is a Zn acceptor because of the abundance of free sulfhydryl groups and their high affinity for Zn. However, the sulfhydryl groups are highly reactive, and Zn, although bound with high affinity, can undergo exchange reactions, which allows Zn to be transferred from MT to other proteins.

(ii) **Copper:** Copper (Cu) is an essential metal for structural and catalytic properties of many enzymes, such as Cu/Zn superoxide dismutase, cytochrome oxidase, and copper-responsive transcription factors. However, excess Cu can be toxic, particularly when associated with a deficit in Cu excretion. There are two diseases in humans caused by abnormal transport of Cu: Wilson's disease and Menke's disease. Wilson's disease is a hypercupremic state, whereas Menke's disease is a hypocupremic state. Wilson's disease is due to a defect of a P-type ATPase (ATP7B), which is located on autosome 13 in humans and autosome 16 in rats. As a result of the mutation in the Cu-efflux transporter, there is an inability to transport Cu across the bile canalicular membrane, and thus Cu accumulates in liver during aging.

Role of Metallothionein in Protection Against Metal Toxicity

Cadmium: Cd is an environmental pollutant toxic to a number of tissues. Acute exposure to Cd produces hepatic, pulmonary, and testicular injury, whereas chronic exposure results in renal and bone injury and cancer, as well as toxicity to other organs. Numerous studies have suggested that MT plays an important role in Cd disposition and detoxication. The factors that influence Cd absorption, distribution, and elimination are not well understood, but it is known that Cd is poorly absorbed after oral ingestion. The role of MT in Cd disposition has been examined in MT-transgenic mice. Using this model, MT does not inhibit intestinal Cd absorption, nor does it affect initial Cd distribution to various tissues. However, MT decreases Cd elimination through the bile and is a major factor for tissue retention of Cd.

Metallothionein as a Trap for Reactive Oxygen Species

MT has a high (30%) content of cysteine residues. It is reasonable to expect that sulfhydryl-rich MT may function in a manner similar to GSH, wherein MT provides an intracellular nucleophilic "sink" to trap electrophiles, alkylating MT has a high (30%) content of cysteine residues. It is reasonable to expect that sulfhydryl-rich MT may function in a manner similar to GSH, wherein MT provides an intracellular nucleophilic "sink" to trap electrophiles, alkylatingagents, and free radicals. MT can serve as a sacrificial scavenger for hydroxyl radicals and superoxide anion *in vitro* and can assume the function of superoxide dismutase in yeast.

Metallothionein Mediated Protection Against the Toxicity of Other Chemicals

Cisplatin

cis-Diaminedichloroplatinum (cisplatin) is an effective anticancer drug containing the metal platinum. Binding of cisplatin to MT has been demonstrated, but the role of MT in cisplatin resistance has been an issue of debate. Some tumor cell lines with acquired resistance to cisplatin overexpress MT, whereas other cisplatin-resistant cell lines do not have increased MT levels. Pretreatment of mice with MT-inducers, such as Zn and bismuth, protects against the lethal and nephrotoxic effects of cisplatin. However, in other studies, induction of MT in rats failed to protect against the toxicity of cisplatin.

Carbon Tetrachloride

Hepatic MT can be induced by carbon tetrachloride (CCl_4) administration, indicating a possible role for this protein in providing tolerance to CCl_4 hepatotoxicity. Induction of MT by Zn, or by inflammation, protects against CCl_4 hepatotoxicity. Similar to the binding of Cd to MT, more 14C from $14CCl_4$ is bound to MT in the MT-induced animals than in controls, with a concomitant reduction of covalent binding of 14 CCl_4 to cellular protein and lipids.

Acetaminophen MT

Acetaminophen MT is induced following acetaminophen administration, and induction of MT has been associated with protection against acetaminophen hepatotoxicity. However, there is evidence neither for the binding of acetaminophen to MT nor for an altered subcellular distribution of acetaminophen following induction of MT by Zn, or by triterpenoids. MT-I/II–null mice are more susceptible than control mice to acetaminophen hepatotoxicity.

Streptozicin, Alloxan, and Caerulein

Pancreas has the highest basal concentration of MT. Pancreatic MT can be further increased by metals and chemicals that produce diabetes. Because of the high basal levels, the percentage increase in MT is not as pronounced as in liver and kidney. Induction of pancreatic MT by Zn has been associated with protection against streptozotocin and caerulein induced acute pancreatitis but not protect against alloxan induced injury to endocrine cells of the pancreas.

Metallothionein and Protection Against Neurodegenerative Disease

MT in brain has been proposed to play a role in Zn homeostasis and neurodegenerative diseases. Brain MT-III was discovered as a growth-inhibiting factor, inhibiting neuronal sprouting in culture. MT-III was originally thought to be down-regulated in Alzheimer patients. However, further studies could not confirm the association of MT-III with Alzheimer's disease (Amoureux *et al.*, 1997). Transgenic mice that overexpress human MT-III have also been engineered. They have a ninefold increase in MT-III in cerebral cortex, a three- to fivefold increase in hippocampus, thalamus, brain stem, and olfactory bulb, and a 1.4-fold increase in cerebellum. MT-III–null mice have also been made.

YEAST METALLOTHIONEIN

A genetic approach was taken to test the function of yeast metallothionein in metal ion detoxification. A yeast strain was constructed in which the metallothionein locus was deleted (*cup*1$^{\Delta}$). The *cup*1$^{\Delta}$ strain was complemented with normal or mutant metallothionein genes under normal or constitutive regulatory control on high copy episomal plasmids. To test metallothionein protection against the toxic effects of various metals, agar plates supplemented with a variety of metal ions, metallo-drugs, or other compounds and then plated yeast transformed with the various metallothionein-expressing vectors described in Table 6.3. This directly compared metal resistance in yeast that had no metallothionein gene (*cup*1$^{\Delta}$ + YE_p 13) with yeast that had about 50 copies of the normal metallothionein gene (*cup*1$^{\Delta}$ + YE_p 36). The strain with the episomal plasmid YEP 38 was used to probe the function of the conserved amino acid sequence (Lys-Lys-Ser-Cys-Cys- Ser).

Table 6.3: Resistance to Various Metal ions by Yeast Containing Metallothionein- Expressing Plasmids

Genome + Plasmid	Concentration										
	1µM	5µM	10µM	25µM	50µM	100µM	500µM	1mM	5mM	10mM	50mM
CuCl2											
Cupl• + YEp13	+	+	+	±	–	–	–	–	–	–	
CUplΔ + YEp 13	+	±	–	–	–	–	–	–	–	–	
CUplΔ + YEp 36	+	+	+	+	+	+	+	+	–	–	
CUplΔ + YEp 38	+	+	+	+	+	+	+	±	–	–	
CUplΔ + YEp 40	+	+	+	+	+	+	+	±	–	–	
CUplΔ + YEp 42	+	+	+	+	+	+	+	±	–	–	
CdCl2											
Cupl2• + YEp13	+	–	–	–	–	–	–	–			
CUplΔ + YEp 13	+	–	–	–	–	–	–	–			
CUplΔ + YEp 36	+	–	–	–	–	–	–	–			
CUplΔ + YEp 38	+	–	–	–	–	–	–	–			
CUplΔ + YEp 40	+	–	–	–	–	–	–	–			
CUplΔ + YEp 42	+	+	+	+	+	+	+	+			
CdCl2 + 5µM $CUSO_4$											
Cupl2• + YEp13	+	–	–	–	–	–	–	–			
CUplΔ + YEp 13	±	–	–	–	–	–	–	–			
CUplΔ + YEp 36	+	–	–	–	–	–	–	–			
CUplΔ + YEp 38	+	–	–	–	–	–	–	–			
CUplΔ + YEp 40	+	–	–	–	–	–	–	–			
CUplΔ + YEp 42	+	+	+	+	+	+	+	+			
$ZnCl_2$											
Cupl2• + YEp13			+			+		+	+	±	–
CUplΔ + YEp 13			+			+		+	+	±	–
CUplΔ + YEp 36			+			+		+	+	±	–
CUplΔ + YEp 38			+			+		+	+	±	–
CUplΔ + YEp 40			+			+		+	+	±	–
CUplΔ + YEp 42			+			+		+	+	±	–

Petri plates containing 25 ml of media and the indicated concentration of metal ion were divided into 6 sectors. Yeast strains carrying the plasmid constructions were grown in a synthetic medium to A600nm = 1. Ten microliters of each culture was streaked in the appropriate sector, and plates were incubated for 2 days at 30°C. Plates were scored as follows: +, uninhibited growth (equal to the metal-free control plate); ±, stressed growth (colonies were notably fewer in number and smaller in size than the control); -, no growth. A blank indicates that this concentration was not tested.

The episomal plasmid YEp 40 was used to test *in vivo* the level of resistance bestowed by the yeast-mammalian metallothionein fusion. The plasmid YEP 42 allowed us to identify metallothionein protection from metals that do not induce synthesis of the gene. Finally, the parent strain transformed with the control plasmid *(cup*1$^{\Delta}$ + YEP 13) allowed us to compare the resistance conferred by a single chromosomal copy of the gene versus the multicopy episomal versions.

Metal resistance was compared by plating the same number of cells of all six strains on different sections of the same plate (Table 6.3). All of the metallothionein-expressing plasmids conferred dramatic copper resistance to the *cup*1$^{\Delta}$ strain. The difference in the maximally tolerated copper dose between the metallothionein-deleted strain with the control plasmid (*cup*1$^{\Delta}$ + YEp 13) and the same strain carrying the intact yeast-metallothionein-expressing plasmid (*cup*1$^{\Delta}$ + YEP 36) was approximately 1000-fold. The yeast-mammalian fusion protein (*cup*1$^{\Delta}$ + YEP 40) and the mutant yeast protein (*cup*1$^{\Delta}$ + YEp 38) each provided approximately 50% of the copper resistance as compared to the natural yeast protein (*cup*1$^{\Delta}$ + YEP 36). The yeast TDH3 promoter was less effective than the *CUPl* promoter in expression of the same gene product, as measured by copper protection (*cup*1$^{\Delta}$ + Yep 42). It is evident from the levels of mRNA and protein expression (Fig. 6.7) and from the levels of copper protection that these promoters cause high rates of transcription of both heterologous and homologous mRNA.

Yeast cultures (15 ml) were treated for 2 h with (+) or without (-) 10 μM CuSO4. Total RNA was extracted, and 10 μg was applied on a formaldehyde 1.5% agarose gel, transferred to a nylon membrane, and hybridized with ^{32}P-labeled yeast metallothionein DNA.

None of the strains were protected from cadmium toxicity except the one with high constitutively expressed metallothionein (*cup*1$^{\Delta}$ + YEp 42), which grew on plates containing 1 mM $CdCl_2$ (Table 6.3). None of the other strains survived in the presence of greater than 1 PM $CdCl_2$. Because metallothionein- mediated cadmium protection was so dramatic in the strain with constitutively expressed metallothionein, it was surprising that a small amount of cadmium protection was not observed in the strains that had episomal copies of the gene under normal regulatory control. The relatively high basal level of transcription from the *CUP1* promoter in the absence of copper (Fig. 6.7) might have provided some cadmium protection to these strains compared to the strain that had no metallothionein at all. Moreover, it was not possible to "prime" these strains with an inducing nontoxic dose of copper and observe protection from cadmium toxicity (Table 6.3).

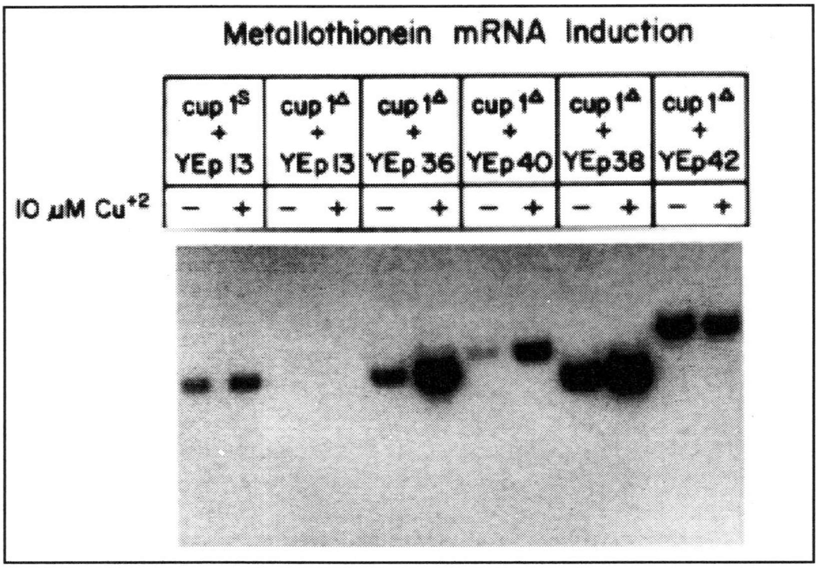

Fig. 6.7: Northern Blot Analysis of mRNA from Yeast Strains Carrying the Metallothionein Plasmid Constructions

FUNGAL METALLOTHIONEINS

From an evolutionary perspective, MTs or MT-like polypeptides have been found in all branches of the tree of life, with a remarkable conservation of the functional structure across the phyla. It has been hypothesized that ancestral MT structures evolved under selective pressure in an environment where toxic metals and free radicals were particularly abundant. Modern MTs probably have a polyphyletic origin, and during evolution might have specialized in terms of metal-binding ability and functions within each life form to adapt to different environmental niches and/or specific endogenous metabolic requirements. Two main groups of MTs have been proposed on the basis of metal-binding ability, they are Cu-thioneins and Zn-thioneins. However, some Zn-thioneins exhibit dual behaviour. For example, MTs Cup1 and Crs5 from *Saccharomyces cerevisiae* yeast have been extensively related to Cu handling, but more recently Crs5 was defined as a dual metal-binding MT significantly closer to Zn-thioneins than to Cu-thioneins (Pagani *et al.*, 2007).

Gene Expression in Heterologous Systems

Fungal MTs, research on which has been more sporadic, are usually described as Cu-binding proteins. However, few of them have been functionally characterized in terms of metal coordination chemical properties and/or by means of complementation assays in metal hypersensitive yeast mutants. Putative MTs have often been described within collections of expressed sequence tags (ESTs) simply on the basis of sequence similarity. This is the case for MT-like sequences found in mycorrhizal fungi, in particular in the ectomycorrhizal fungus *Pisolithus tinctorius*; the ericoid fungus *Oidiodendron maius* and the arbuscular mycorrhizal fungi *Gigaspora rosea, Gigaspora margarita* and *Glomus intraradices.*

Metallothioneins: A Role in Developmental Biology of Fungi Interacting with Plants

There are increasing lines of evidence for the role of MTs or MT-like proteins in mutualistic and pathogenic interactions between plants and fungi. Fungal MT genes are often transcriptionally regulated during the life stages and, in particular, during plant colonization. The first report dates back to 1995, when two genes similar to MTs were described as expressed uniquely during appressorium formation by *Colletotrichum gloeosporioides* conidia induced by the host surface wax. Similarly, two putative MT genes from the biotrophic pathogen *Uromyces fabae* are strongly upregulated in parasitic mycelium colonizing leaf tissues.

Metallothioneins and Bioremediation

To use mycorrhizal fungi for bioremediation and soil protection purposes, we clearly need to improve our understanding of the molecular mechanisms that underlie the metal-detoxification processes in these fungi. This would allow better exploitation of the mycorrhizal symbiosis. The characterization of a *P. involutus* MT is a new and important step in this regard. Data from yeast mutants, together with the fact that *Pimt1* gene expression is highly responsive to Cu, allows *Pimt1* to be defined as an important component in Cu detoxification in *P. involutus*. Transcriptional induction and yeast complementation, but not overexpression in *Hebeloma,* also suggests a role in the alleviation of Cd stress. Cadmium might also be detoxified by other intracellular mechanisms, as it is known that a variety of metal-protection strategies can coexist in a single organism; for example, *Schizosaccharomyces pombe* and *Candida glabrata* contain both PCs and MTs. The question is: does *P. involutus* have the genetic potential to synthesize additional intracellular chelators such as PCs? Biochemical studies seem to exclude this possibility at present.

CYANOBACTERIAL METALLOTHIONEIN

Differential Responses of Metallothionein Genes to Divalent Metal cations and the Oxyanions of Arsenic

Cyanobacterial cells exhibit an extraordinarily high level of resistance to arsenate. Liquid cultures of these cells are capable of normal rates of growth in the presence of 1M arsenate. This high level of resistance is due primarily to the failure of arsenate to enter phosphate sufficient cells. Arsenate may exert its toxic effects on cells by mimicking phosphate and by derivitizing essential cellular proteins. The phosphate-specific transporter (Pst) system is a slow, highly specific, inducible uptake mechanism in *E. coli* that discriminates between phosphate and arsenate under phosphate-sufficient conditions. The phosphate inorganic transporter (Pit) system is the major secondary phosphate transporter under phosphate-deficient conditions and is differentiated from the Pst system on the basis of its specificity for inorganic phosphate and the toxic anions of arsenic. We believe the phosphate-specific transport (Pst) system discriminates between phosphate and arsenate. This inducible system is the primary uptake mechanism used when phosphate is available in quantities sufficient for cyanobacterial growth. Under phosphate starvation, the phosphate inorganic transport (Pit) system becomes the major uptake mechanism for inorganic phosphate. However, this system appears not to differentiate between phosphate and arsenate. We believe that under conditions of phosphate limitation, arsenate is permitted to enter cyanobacterial cells resulting in cell toxicity.

Ybarra and Webb (1998) understand the better responses of the cyanobacterium *Synechococcus* sp. PCC7942 to divalent metal cations and the oxyanions of arsenic. First aim was to compare the transcription of genes for metallothionein and GroEL in response to these stressors. They propose that these responses should be similar. Secondly, aimed to explore the relationship between phosphate status and arsenate toxicity. Hypothesis is that arsenate is excluded from phosphate-sufficient cells and that phosphate-limited cells allow the entry of arsenate where it is then able to exert its toxic effects. Lastly, aimed to understand better the seemingly paradoxical finding that arsenate, a trivalent anion, could strongly induce metallothionein transcription, since this system responds more commonly to divalent metal cations. Their hypothesis is that arsenate covalently modifies sulfhydryl groups of the SmtB regulatory repressor protein, thus inducing metallothionein transcription. This was tested using the thiol-modifying reagent N-Tosyl-L-Lysine Chloromethyl Ketone (TLCK). We expected this reagent to induce smtA expression in a manner analogous to arsenate induction, thus providing a working model for metallothionein induction by the oxyanions of arsenic.

Ybarra and Webb (1998) focused on the effects of metal ion exposure and the oxyanions of arsenic on GroEL and metallothionein gene expression.

The general stress protein GroEL is an important aspect of cellular responses to changing environmental conditions. Metallothioneins are cysteine-rich proteins that bind metal ions and thus detoxify them by limiting their cellular availability. Additional aims were to further explore the relationship between cellular responses to arsenic oxyanions and phosphate status and to propose a mechanism for the induction of metallothionein transcription, normally controlled by divalent metal cations, by these oxyanions.

It is similar to the stress protein operon GroEL. SmtA transcription is not detectable in the control, suggesting that smtA induction is metal-dependent. Metallothionein transcription is initiated within 15 minutes and levels of transcription remain constant up to 3 hours.

The divalent cations of cadmium and zinc each elicit a stress response at concentrations of 10 micromolar, as evidenced by transcription of groEL and metallothionein genes (data not shown). Cadmium ions elicit these responses when present at concentrations as low as 1 micromolar. These findings suggest that groEL is not strictly a heat shock protein and that its transcription responds to potentially toxic metal ions. Cadmium is a highly toxic metal that quickly assimilates into photosynthetic structures and is a potent uncoupler of oxidative phosphorylation and a potent inhibitor of electron transfer in the electron transport system in photosynthesis. Cellular exposure to concentrations of this ion as low as 1 micromolar have immediate effects on electron transport, decreasing oxygen evolution by nearly one-half. Similar effects are seen with copper and zinc ions only when their concentrations are 100-fold higher (100 micromolar) (data not shown).

They have found the divalent metal cations of copper, zinc, and cadmium elicit groEL and metallothionein transcription at different concentrations. Copper ions at a concentration of 10 micromolar do not induce transcription of groEL or metallothionein (data not shown). Concentrations of this ion in excess of 100 micromolar were required to induce transcription of these genes within 15 minutes (Fig. 6.8). Again, much lower concentrations of cadmium ions (1 micromolar) were sufficient to elicit a similar transcriptional response. Figure 6.9 describes the generally accepted description of metallothionein induction by divalent cations. These ions enter the cell via transport proteins and bind sulfhydryl groups on the regulatory repressor protein. This protein then changes conformation and releases from the DNA. This allows RNA polymerase to begin transcription from smtA, resulting ultimately in metallothionein protein expression.

The second aspect of this work focused on gaining a better understanding of the extraordinarily high level of resistance to arsenate exhibited by all species of cyanobacteria examined to date. We believe that this resistance results from the failure of arsenate to enter phosphate-sufficient cells. The phosphate-specific transporter (Pst) system is a highly specific channel that selectively discriminates between arsenate and phosphate and this is the major transporter used by normally grown cells. The phosphate inorganic transporter (Pit) system is the secondary phosphate transporter which becomes a major component of phosphate-limited cells. The Pit system is differentiated from the Pst system on the basis of its specificity for inorganic phosphate and the oxyanions of arsenic, arsenate, and arsenite.

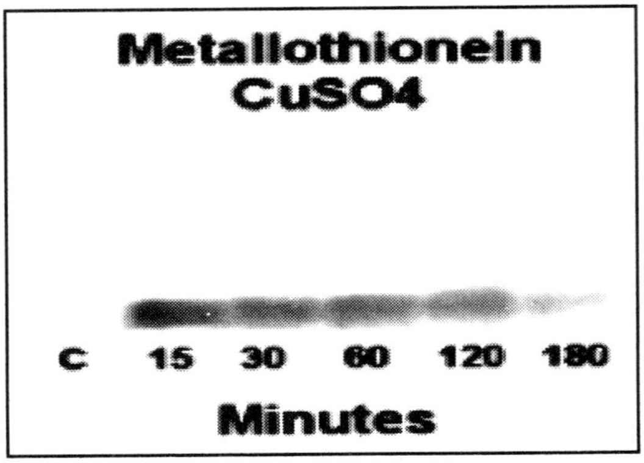

Fig. 6.8: The Transcriptional Response of smtA with Respect to Divalent Metal cations

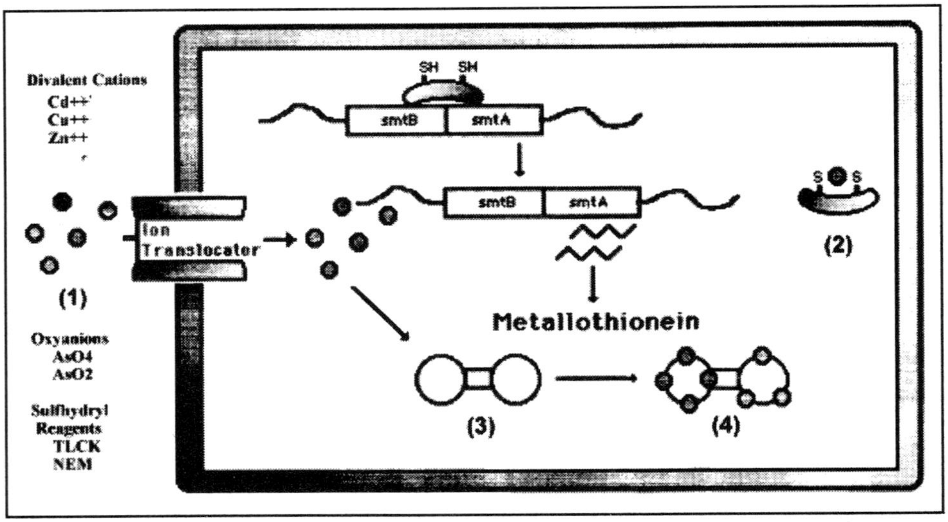

Fig. 6.9: Proposed mechanism for metallothionein induction by metal cations and the oxyanions of arsenic. (1) Divalent metal cation challenge from the environment, (2) Sulfhydryl (-SH) modification by metal or arsenate binding, (3) SmtA expression producing metallothionein proteins, (4) Metal sequestration and detoxification by metallothionein proteins.

Recombinant Metallothionein Protein from Marine Alga: *Fucus vesiculosus*

Morris *et al*. (1999) constructed a cDNA library from macro algae adapted to prolonged elevated environmental copper levels. To investigate the possible existence of a metallothionein (MT) gene, the library was screened with degenerate probes designed using plant MT cysteine-rich motifs. A gene was identified (1229 bp) with a putative open reading frame (204 bp) encoding a 67-amino-acid protein exhibiting several characteristic features of MT proteins, including 16 cysteine residues (24%) and only one aromatic residue. Although the protein sequence showed high identity with plant and invertebrate MTs, it contained a unique 'linker' region (14 amino acid residues) between the two putative metal binding domains, which contained no cysteine residues.

Putative Metal-binding Domains

The *Fucus* MT protein has two domains which contain the cysteine residues, and therefore are presumably involved in the metal-binding function. The N-terminal domain contains three Cys-Xaa-Cys motifs, and the C-terminal domain contains three Cys-Xaa-Cys motifs and one Cys-Cys-Xaa-Cys motif. An unusual feature of *Fucus* MT is the presence of a region between the two putative metal-binding domains, which contains no cysteine residues. This is a feature of plant MTs, but not of vertebrate MTs, which characteristically have a three-aminoacid linker region. In the *Fucus* MT this linker region consists of 14 amino acids, which is much smaller than the 40 residues commonly seen in plant MTs.

Expression and Characterization of the Recombinant MT Protein

To express the protein, primers flanking the coding region of the *Fucus* MT sequence were designed with additional restriction enzyme sites. The 300 bp MT PCR product was amplified from plasmid DNA and digested with the restriction enzymes *Nco*I and *Eco*RI. The MT coding region was cloned in-frame as a C terminal fusion to a sequence encoding the S-peptide (S-Tag) in the expression vector pET29a (Fig. 6.10). Induction of T7-RNApolymerase- based transcription of gene fusion was performed in the BL21 (DE3) *E. coli* expression strain by the addition of IPTG when bacterial cultures were at mid-exponential phase. Previous work had demonstrated that it is necessary to add cadmium to the medium after induction in order to stabilize MT-like clusters and prevent their degradation (Klaassen and Liu, 1998). Time-course samples were taken from the point of induction in analytical cultures; an recombinant protein accumulation was investigated by SDS-PAGE analysis of total cell extracts.

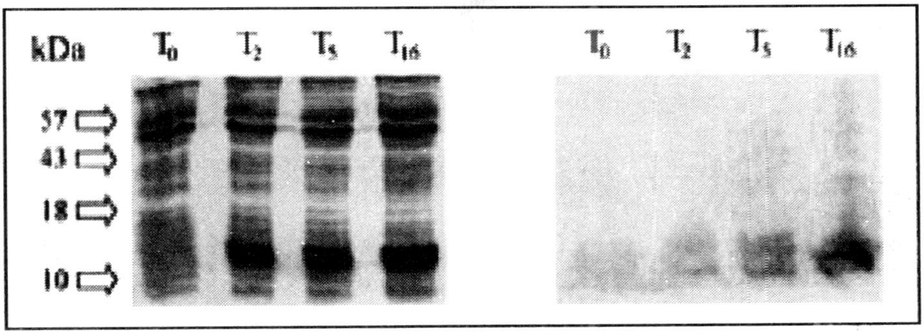

Fig. 6.10: Temporal Expressions of Recombinant *F. vesiculosus* MT

E. coli cells were harvested and prepared for electrophoresis, as described in the Materials and methods section, at the point of induction (T_0) and subsequently 2 h (T_2), 5 h (T_5) and 16 h (T_{16}) after induction with cadmium (200 μM final concentration). After size separation by SDS/PAGE (20% gel), proteins were visualized by staining with Coomassie Blue (A). An identical separation was performed in parallel and proteins were transferred to a nitrocellulose membrane. The S-peptide MT fusion was then detected by interaction with an S-protein-alkaline phosphatase conjugate (B). Arrows indicate sizes of molecular mass standards (kDa). A substantial protein component with a molecular mass of C14 kDa was clearly evident 2 h after inducing expression with IPTG, and this was still the predominant protein 16 h after induction. The identity of the induced protein was confirmed by Western blot analysis using an S-protein-alkaline-phosphatase conjugate that binds specifically to the S-peptide fusion component.

CONCLUSION

MTs are stress related protein and may be involved in essential metal homeostasis and the detoxification of excess metals during organism's developmental process. A clear role for MTs is yet to be established, although they are certainly thought to play a role in metal metabolism. MTs may function as antioxidants and a role in plasma membrane repair is another possibility. Although MTs are expressed ubiquitously and conserved in living organisms, determining their function remains a future challenge. So more work is necessary to better understand MT-metal interaction and the mechanism of MT expression.

REFERENCES

Chen, M.L and M.L. Failla. 1989. Degradation of Zinc-metallothionein in Monolayer Cultures of Rat Hepatocytes. Proc. Soc. Expt. Biol. Med., 191: 130-138.

Feng, W., F.W. Benz, J. Cai, W.M. Pierce and Y.J. Kang. 2006. Metallothionein Disulfides are Present in Metallothionein-over Expressing Transgenic Mouse Heart and Increase Under Conditions of Oxidative Stress. J. Biol. Chem., 281: 681-687.

Kagi, J.H.R and A. Schafer.1988. Biochemistry of metallothionein. J. Biochem., 27: 8509-8515.

Kaina, B., H. Lohrer, M. Karin and P. Herrlich. 1990. Over Expressed Human Metallothionein II Gene Protects Chinese Hamster Ovary Cells from Killing by Alkylating Agents. Proc. Natl. Acad. Sci. U.S.A., 87: 2710-2714.

Kohler, A., D. Blaudez, M. Chalot and F. Martin. 2004. Cloning and Expression of Multiple Metallothioneins from Hybrid Poplar. New Phytologist, 164: 83-93.

Liu, J., Y.P. Lu and N.M. Zhao. 2000. Classification and Nomenclature of Plant Metallothionein-like Proteins Based on Their Cysteine Arrangement Patterns. Acta Bot. Sin., 42: 649-652.

Messerle, B.A., A. Schaffer, M. Vasak, J.H. Kagi and K. Wuethrich. 1990. Three Dimensional Structure of Human [113Cd7] Metallothionein-2 in Solution Determined by Nuclear Magnetic Resonance Spectroscopy. J. Mol. Biol., 214: 765-779.

Morries, C.A., B. Nicolaus, V. Sampson, J.L. Harwood and P. Kille. 1999. Identification and Characterization of a Recombinant Metallothionein Protein from a Marine Alga, *Fucus vesiculosus*. Biochem. J., 338: 553-560.

Nordberg, M., Y. Kojima, J.H.R. Kagi and M. Nordberg. 1979. Metallothionein and Other Low Molecular Weight Metal-binding Proteins. In: Metallothionein, Birkhauser, Basel. pp. 41-116.

Ortiz, D.F., L. Kreppel, D.M. Speiser, G. Scheel, G. McDonald and D.W. Owe. 1992. Metallothioneins. EMBO J., 11: 3491-3499.

Pagani, A., L. Villarreal, M. Capdevila and S. Atrian. 2007. The *Saccharomyces cerevisiae* Crs5 Metallothionein Metal-binding Abilities and its Role in the Response to Zinc Overload. Mol. Microbiol., 63: 256-269.

Robinson, N.J, J.R. Wilson and J.S. Turner. 1996. Expression of the Type 2 Metallonthionein-like Gene MT2 from *Arabidopsis thaliana* in Zn^{2+}-metallothionein-deficient *Synechococcus* PCC 7942: Putative Role for MT 2 in Zn^{2+} Metabolism. Plant Mol. Biol., 30: 1169-1179.

Ybarra, G.R and R.Webb. 1998. Differential Responses of *gro*EL and Metallothionein Genes to Divalent Metal cations and the Oxyanions of Arsenic in the Cyanobacterium *Synechococcus* sp. Strain PCC7942. In: Proceedings of the 1998 Conference on Hazardous Waste Research. 76-86.

Zhang, H., W. Xu, J. Guo, Z. He and M. Ma. 2005. Coordinated Responses of Phytochelatins and Metallothioneins to Heavy Metals in Garlic Seedlings. Plant Sci., 169: 1059-1065.

Pages: 152-161

AGRICULTURE, ENVIRONMENT AND NANO-SCIENCE

Edited by: Dr. Pawan Kumar 'Bharti'

ISBN: 978-93-5056-760-9

Edition: 2015

Published by: Discovery Publishing House Pvt. Ltd., New Delhi (India)

7

Microbial Sequestration of Heavy Metals

V. Davamani; E. Parameswari and A. Rathinasamy

INTRODUCTION

The threat of heavy metal pollution to public health and wildlife has led to an increased interest in developing systems that can remove or neutralise its toxic effects in soil, sediments and wastewater. Unlike organic contaminants, which can be degraded to harmless chemical species, heavy metals cannot be destroyed. Microorganisms have co-existed with metals since early history. This is reflected in the wide range of divalent or transition metals at the active centers of many enzymes. The chemical properties of the metal have been recruited for catalyzing key reactions or for maintaining protein structure. These metals are therefore required in minute amounts for normal cell metabolism and their intake is subject to intricate homeostatic mechanisms that ensure sufficient but not excessive acquisition. Many other metals seem to serve no biologically relevant function. Instead, they cause damage, mostly due to their avidity for the sulfhydryl groups of proteins, which they block and inactivate. Thus, from a physiological point of view, metals fall into three main categories: (i) those essential and basically

Horticultural College and Research Institute, Periyakulam, Theni (Dt), Tamilnadu, (India).

non-toxic (e.g. Ca and Mg), (ii) essential, but harmful at high concentrations (typically, Fe, Mn, Zn, Cu, Co, Ni and Mo), and (iii) toxic (e.g. Hg or Cd). Further, interactions with metals depend not only on the particular element but also on its chemical speciation.

Physico-chemical methods, such as chemical precipitation, chemical oxidation or reduction, electrochemical treatment, evaporative recovery, filtration, ion exchange and membrane technologies have been widely used to remove heavy metal ions from industrial wastewater. These processes may be ineffective or expensive, especially when the heavy metal ions are in solutions containing in the order of 1-100 mg dissolved heavy metal ions/L (Volesky, 1990). Biological methods such as biosorption/bioaccumulation for the removal of heavy metal ions may provide an attractive alternative to physico-chemical methods.

Microorganisms uptake metal either actively (bioaccumulation) and/or passively (biosorption) (Hussein *et al.*, 2003). The use of adsorbents of biological origin has emerged in the last decade as one of the most promising alternatives to conventional heavy metal management strategies. Because of the absence of rational method for a priori prediction of the biosorption potential of a microorganism, the only method for identifying and developing newer and efficient biosorbents is the sustained screening of microbes (Muraleedharan *et al.*, 1995). Biosorption of heavy metals by microbial cells has been recognized as a potential alternative to existing technologies for recovery of heavy metals from industrial waste streams. Emerging technologies in this area rely on enhancing the biosorption of metals into biomass, or the precipitation of ions by exploiting some metal-related facet of bacterial metabolism (Figs. 7.1-7.2). Due to their distinct physicochemical properties, mercury and metalloids (As) can sometimes be mobilized away from polluted sites by microbes that convert them into volatile species, an alternative to the immobilization/precipitation approach.

Most studies of biosorption for metal removal have involved the use of either laboratory grown microorganism or biomass generated by the pharmacology and food processing industries or wastewater treatment units (Rao *et al.* 1993). Many aquatic microorganisms, such as bacteria, yeast and algae can take up dissolved metals from their surroundings onto their bodies and can be used for removing heavy metal ions successfully (Asku *et al.*, 1991).

GROSS RESPONSES OF MICROORGANISMS TO METALS

Microbial activity strongly influences metal speciation and transport in the environment. Different organisms exhibit diverse responses to toxic ions, which confer upon them a certain range of metal tolerance (Fig. 7.1). Eukaryotes are more sensitive to metal toxicity than bacteria and their typical mechanism for regulating intracellular metal ion concentrations is the expression of metallothioneins (MTs), a family of metal-chelating proteins.

Bacterial MTs that are functionally homologous to the short (approx. 60 amino acids) cysteine-rich eukaryotic metal binding proteins have also been reported. Prokaryotic MTs have been studied in detail only in the cyanobacterium *Synechococcus*, where they confer resistance to Zn^{2+} and Cd^{2+} (Robinson *et al.*, 2001). In fact, this production of MTs as the main mechanism of tolerance to metals is exceptional in the bacterial world. Rather, a number of specific resistance mechanisms including active efflux and sequestration or transformation to other chemical species become functional at concentrations above the homeostatic or nontoxic levels (Silver,1998) (Fig. 7.1). These tolerance mechanisms are often plasmid-borne, which facilitates dispersion from cell to cell. A prime example of heavy metal resistance is that of *Ralstonia metallidurans* CH34 (previously *Alcaligenes eutrophus* CH34). This L-proteobacterium contains resistance determinants that allow it to grow at millimolar concentrations of nine different toxic metal ions.

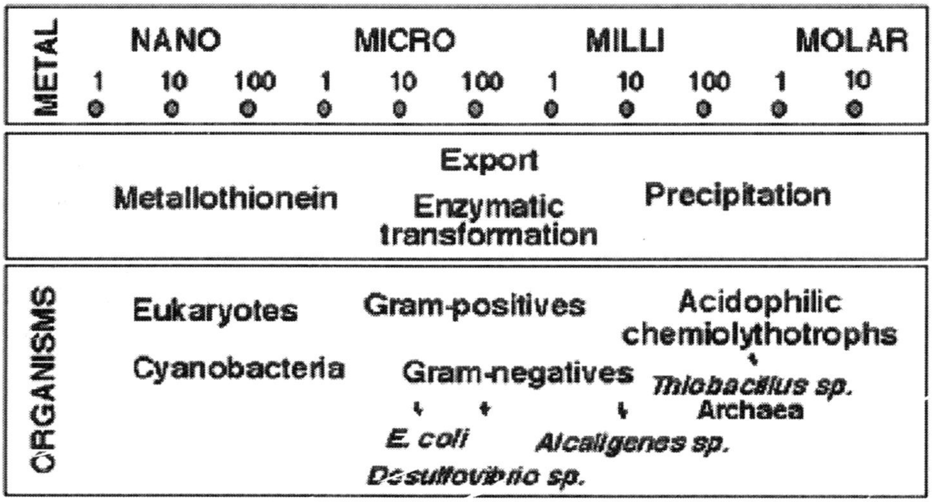

Fig. 7.1: Bacterial capacities and mechanisms of tolerance to heavy metals. Microorganisms cited in the text and the molecular strategies they exhibit to cope with metal ions are indicated. Organisms are situated in the scheme according to their tolerance towards typical toxic ions such as Cd(II) or Ni(II). Concentrations shown at the top are only indicative since metal resistance varies widely within taxonomic groups and according to the element considered (Barkay and Schaefer, 2001)

Sulfate-reducing bacteria (SRB) display a certain degree of metal tolerance (Fig. 7.1) as a secondary outcome of their metabolism. They are anaerobes that produce sulfide and immobilize toxic ions as metal sulfides. Enzymatic metal reduction might also be common in these bacteria. Finally, the organisms that grow at the highest metal concentrations are the iron and sulfur-oxidising bacteria, including the *Thiobacilli* and thermophilic archaea

(Fig. 7.1). The metal resistance of these chemolithotrophs is an adaptation to very acidic environments, where metal solubility is high. Interestingly, when the growth of *Thiobacillus ferrooxidans* is dependent on Fe(II), this bacterium is highly resistant to Al, Cu, Co, Ni, Mn and Zn (0.1-0.3 M), although it remains quite sensitive to other metal ions. Bacteria thus show a panoply of responses to metal ions and diverse bacterial groups have developed abilities to cope with these toxic elements in a variety of environments (e.g. anaerobic, aerobic, thermophilic).

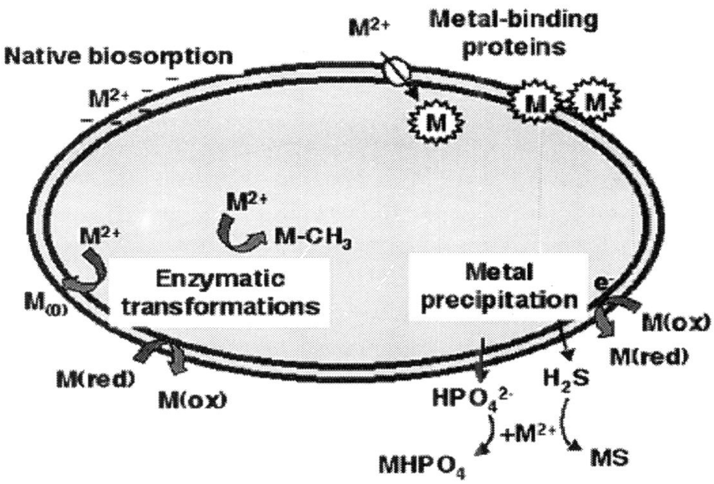

Fig. 7.2: How bacteria cope with toxic concentrations of heavy ions. The scheme summarises the various means by which bacteria react to the presence of metals (M^{2+}) in the medium, with reference to the cellular compartment that harbors the response. These mechanisms include the intra or extracellular binding (and thus immobilisation) of the metal with a cognate protein (frequently a metallothionein) or a matching anion, the biotransformation of the toxic ion into a less noxious or more volatile form, and the dissimilatory reduction of the metal

MICROBE – METAL INTERACTIONS

The chemical reactions between microorganisms and metals can be divided into six distinct processes (Ford and Mitchell,1992).

Intracellular Accumulation

Bacterial assimilation of metals may be important in detoxification, enzyme function, and physical characteristics of the cell. Extra cellular or cell wall-attached ligands are thought to bind toxic metals. These ligands transport the complexed metals through the cell wall in a slow transport step. The metals are released inside the cell, incorporated into biochemical pathways, or trapped in an inactive form by complexation with another high-affinity ligand

The protoplasm of *Escherichia coli* typically contains 0.3% trace elements, including manganese, cobalt, copper, zinc, and molybdenum. Of these, both copper and zinc are considered toxic metals. Yet these are essential for the activity of several enzymes. In addition, nickel is a component of hydrogenase in many organisms, and its addition has been found to stimulate chemolithotrophic growth. Cadmium is accumulated by a large number of organisms.

The ability of certain bacterial cells to accumulate metals intracellular has been exploited in mining practices, particularly in management of effluent treatment lagoons. Uranium has been shown to accumulate rapidly in cells of *Saccharomyces cerevisiae* and *Pseudomonas aeruginosa.*

Cell Wall Interactions

Binding of metals to cell surfaces plays a dominant role in the distribution of metals in natural waters. In addition, sorption of metals to living or dead cells is considered a practical solution to many metal contamination problems. Algal surfaces contain functional groups that have been shown to bind metals competitively with many dissolved ligands. The carboxylic amino, thio, hydroxo and hydroxy - carboxylic groups on the surface of phytoplankton cells interact coordinatively with metal ions. Bacteria possess lipopolysaccharides (LPS) in their outer membranes.

Phosphoryl groups of LPS and phospholipids are the most abundant electronegative sites available for metal binding. The polyvalent toxic metals are primarily bound to LPS molecules because of the presence of closely opposed reactive sites. It has been suggested that this many provide a mechanism to immobilize toxic metals and prevent their entry into the cell.

Siderophores

Siderophores are iron - complexing, low - molecular - weight organic compounds. Two major types are generally considered, the hydroxamate and catecholate siderophores.Siderophores vary chemically. One class is characterized by the presence of hydroxamate groups that strongly bind ferric ion. This activity is a function of the size and charge of the ion. It follows that analogs may also be strongly bound by these siderophores. For example, aluminium, gallium, and chromium form trivalent metal ions of similar size to iron. Aluminium may be a specific competitor for catecholate siderphores.

Molybdenum and copper have been shown to form strong complexes with siderophores. In particular, catecholate siderophore - molybdenum complexes may provide an important uptake mechanism for intracellular molybdenum accumulation, required for nitrogenase enzyme. Ochiai reports that a number of nitrogen - fixing bacteria secretes catecholate siderophores under molybdenum - deficient conditions.

Extracellular Processes

Organic or inorganic acids produced by microorganisms, including *Thiobacillus, Serratia, Pseudomonas, Bacillus, Penicillium,* and *Aspergillus,* are able to extract metals from solid substrates. Schinner and Burgstaller used citric acid production by a *Penicillium* to extract zinc selectively from industrial waste. Toxic metals can be mobilized under anaerobic conditions as co precipitates with iron oxides. This may be an important process, since co precipitation of toxic metals with ferric iron is a widely used treatment for high metal content waste streams.

Metals closely associated with iron (Cd and Zn) were solubilized enzymatic reduction of ferric iron, whereas others (particularly Pb) are solubilized by the indirect action of bacterial metabolites. Many metal salts are insoluble and their formation results in immobilization of toxic metals by sequestering to sediments or adsorption to soil particles. Frequently metals form insoluble complexes with, for example, hydroxides, carbonates, phosphates, and sulfides. Probably the best-known microbial immobilization process is sulfide production by the sulfate - reducing bacteria, characteristic of anoxic sediments. As a result, these sediments will often contain high concentrations of lead and mercuric sulfides.

Extracellular Polymer - Metal Interactions

Interaction between bacterial exopolysaccharides and metals has been the subject of increasing research interest. Interaction with metal ions is generally considered a direct consequence of the presence of negatively charged functional groups on the exopolymer. These groups include phosphate, hydroxyl, succinyl, and uronic acids. A pH - dependent binding of positively charged cations can rapidly occur, with stability constants in excess of those generally measured for humic substances and other naturally occurring ligands. The role of bacterial exopolymer - metal interactions in the environment is a question that has only recently been addressed.

Volatilization of Metals by Transformation

Mercuric ion resistance has been well studied. The mechanism is generally accepted to involve intracellular reduction of Hg^{2+} to Hg^{o} by mercuric reductase, with a subsequent volatilization. Mercuric reductases have been isolated from a number of microorganisms, including *Escherichia coli, Thiobacillus ferrooxidans, Streptomyces, Streptococcus,* and *Caulobacter.*

Evidence exists that certain metal - tolerant bacteria use toxic metal species as electron acceptors. Selenate has been shown to be reduced by anaerobic bacteria. Chromate reduction under anaerobic conditions has also been reported, and chromate reductase activity has been associated with a soluble protein. Undoubtedly the most studied environmentally mediated transformation of toxic metals is the methylation of mercury. Pure culture experiments have shown that many bacteria, including *Clostridium, Neurospora, Pseudomonas, Bacillus, Mycobacterium, E. coli, Aerobacter aerogenes, Bacillus megaterium,* and a number of fungi have the capability to methylate mercury. However, the sulfate - reducing bacteria (SRB) are the most significant.

Methylation has, however, been because of the arsenic, lead, selenium, tellurium, tin, thallium, and antimony. Methylation of arsenic by fungi has been studied extensively as a result of human poisoning by fungal transformations of arsenic in paints. More recent work has been concerned with transformation and mobilization in sediments and soils. The importance of biomethylation cannot be overstressed because of the potential health consequences of high methylation rates.

METHODS FOR STUDING METAL - MICROBE INTERACTIONS

Unique considerations apply when studing metal microorganism interactions. Metal concentration on a macro scale poorly reflect the toxic influences of metals on the microorganismal scale. Recall that total metal concentrations do not accurately assess the biologically degradable, it is difficult to determine whether and how a metal is being detoxified when the total metal concentration does not change. However, new and exciting technical and analytical devlopments in metal chemistry, microbiology and molecular biology are now making it possible to expand our understanding of how microorganisms influenc metal fates in the environment.

The culturing of metal resistant microorganisms in the laboratory often occurs in either nutrient rich or chemically defined media, which may contain yeast extract, phosphate buffers and amino acids that bind metal ions. Neutral medium pH is an additional factor increasing metal binding in culture media. The presence and amount of these reagents strongly influence metal bioavailability; there by influencing metal toxicity will vary. For example, it has been shown that *Tetrahymena pyriformis* can tolerate a 100 fold higher concentration of cooper (II) in a rich organic medium compared with a defined one (Maier *et al*., 2000). Consequently, several factors need to be taken into consideration when choosing a culture medium to assess microbial metal resistance. Medium nutrients need to be defined and chosen in such a way as to minimize metal binding. This applies to both carbon substrates and to buffers. For example phosphate buffers strongly precipitate metals. Recall that phosphate production in some microorganisms affords them protection from certain metals. Nonmetal binding buffers, including the sulfonic acids such as MES{2-(N-morpholino) ethanesulfonic acid ; $C_6H_{13}NO_4SCH_2O$}, Pka= 6.15 and PIPES (1, 4 piperazinediethanesulfonc acid; $C_8H_{18}N_2O_6S_2$), pKa=6.80, optimize metal bioavailability in culture media. Finally, pH strongly influences metal bioavailability. Metal readily precipitate as carbonic salts at pH >7. Therefore, medium pH should be kept slightly acidic (pH 6.0) to maintain metal solubility.

To experimentally determine the relationship between metal bioavailability and toxicity and to determine the rate and extent that microbes sequester metals, one must be able to determine both total and soluble metal concentrations. Total metal concentration is determined by digestion of the sample with hot acid such as nitric or perchloric acid. This process dissolves soil particles and release even tightly bound metals. Soluble metal determination often involves extraction with the weak acid DTPA (Diethylene Triamine Penta Aceticacid) or extraction with deionized water to release loosely bound, readily exchangeable metals. In either case, metal concentrations in the extract are determined using atomic absorption spectroscopy.

When studying metal resistance, it is assumed that a decrease in the soluble metal concentration corresponds to the amount of metal sequestered by the cell. However, care must be taken in interpreting these data since metals often precipitate with culture medium components and in addition, may bind to the walls of flasks and test tubes. Metal controls with no inoculum are therefore crucial distingishing between biological and chemical metal removal. It should be noted that while is this relatively easy to determine a macro scale of bioavaliability in the environment. Such an estimate does not necessarily reflect micro scale metal concentrations. So even if very low soluble levels of metal are measured, it is likely that in some microspores (where most soil microorganisms live) substantial levels of bioavailable metal may be encountered. This would explain why microorganisms with no detectable soluble metal may exhibit extreme resistance.

Flame or flameless atomic absorption spectroscopy (AAS) and inductively coupled plasma atomic emission spectroscopy (ICPAES) are easy, efficient techniques for determination of a metal ion in solution. Ion – selective electrodes (ISEs) available for some metals such as cadmium, lead and arsenic provide a quick way to determine metal concentrations in solution to approximately 10^{-6} M). Ion- exchange columns can be used to chromatographically separate metal species in a sample. Metals are bound to the ion exchange resin and are removed using a metal complexing solution.

Where as the methods discussed so far can detect the presence of a metal, transmission electron microscopy (TEM) provide s an effective means of locating and visualizing suspected metal deposits associated with microorganisms. This technique is particularly useful for determining whether microbes sequester metals inside or outside of the cell. When TEM is coupled with energy –dispersive X-ray spectroscopy (EDS), the metal element can be identified by signature spectral lines. High and low magnification TEM micrographs can help distinguish between intracellular and extra cellular metal interactions depending on the location of metal deposition.

Advantages

1. Biosorption of heavy metals can prove less expensive than other technologies that are used for cleanup of contaminated sites.
2. Bioremediation can often be carried out onsite, often without causing a major disruption of normal activities.

Disadvantages

1. Biological processes are often highly specific. Important site factors requires for success include the presence of metabolically capable microbial population, suitable environmental growth conditions and appropriate levels of nutrients and contaminants.
2. It is difficult to extrapolate from bench and pilot scale studies to full scale field operations.
3. Research is needed to develop and engineer bioremediation technologies that are appropriate for sites with complex mixtures of contaminants that are not evenly dispersed in the environment. Contaminants may be present as solids, liquids and gases.
4. Bioremediation often takes longer than other treatment options, such as excavation and removal of soil or incineration.
5. There are some concerns that the products of biodegradation may be more persistent or toxic than the parent compound.

CONCLUSION

The examples reviewed above indicate that remediation technologies using microorganisms are feasible alternatives to the physical cleansing of soils or the concentration of metals in polluted waters by physical or chemical means. The advantages of biological approaches include a higher specificity than the physical and chemical methods, their suitability to *in situ* methodologies (e.g. the avoidance of high energy or toxic chemical addition), and the potential for improvement by genetic engineering.

Molecular approaches may enable the design of biomass with specific metal-binding properties through the expression of metal-chelating proteins and peptides, the improvement of metal precipitation processes and the introduction of metal transformation activities in robust environmental strains. In spite of this, large-scale biological applications are still rare. The fact that the microbially mediated precipitation of metal in the form of sulfides as well as the use of biosurfactants are the objects of large-scale commercial development holds the promise that other biotechnologies could be used in the field of metal decontamination.

REFERENCES

Asku, Z; Kutsal, T; Gun, S; Haciosmanoglu, N and Gholminejad, M. 1991. Investigation of Biosorption of Cu (II), Ni (II), and Cr (VI) ions to Activated Sludge Bacteria. Environ. Technol., 12: 915-921.

Barkay, T. and Schaefer, J. 2001 Metal and Radionuclide Bioremediation: Issues, Considerations and Potentials. Curr. Opin. Microbiol., 4: 318-323.

Ford,T., and Mitchell. R 1992. Environmental Microbiology. Wiley –liss. Massachusetts. pp. 83-97.

Hussein, H; Farag, S. and Moawad, H. 2003. Isolation and Characterisation of Pseudomonas Resistant to Heavy Metals Contaminants. Arab J. Biotechnol., 7: 13-22.

Maier, R.M, Pepper, I. Gerba. C. P. 2000. Environmental Microbiology. Academic Press, New York. pp. 403-423.

Muraleedharan, T.R; Iyengar, L and Venkobachar, C. 1995. Screening of Tropical Wood-rotting Mushrooms for Copper Biosorption. Appl. Environ. Microbiol., 61(9): 3507-3508.

Rao, C.R.N; Iyengar, L and Venkobachar, C. 1993 Sorption of Copper (II) from Aqueous Phase by Waste Biomass. J. Environ. Eng., 119: 369-377.

Robinson, N.J., Whitehall, S.K. and Cavet, J.S. 2001. Microbial Metallothioneins. Adv. Microb. Physiol., 44: 183-213.

Silver, S. 1998. Genes for all Metals a Bacterial View of the Periodic Table. The 1996 Thom Award Lecture. J. Ind. Microbiol. Biotechnol. 20: 1-12.

Volesky, B. 1990. Removal and Recovery of Heavy Metals by Biosorption. In: Biosorption of Heavy Metals. Boston, USA, CRC press. pp. 7-43.

Pages: 162-173

AGRICULTURE, ENVIRONMENT AND NANO-SCIENCE
Edited by: Dr. Pawan Kumar 'Bharti'
ISBN: 978-93-5056-760-9
Edition: 2015
Published by: Discovery Publishing House Pvt. Ltd., New Delhi (India)

8

Biotechnology for Biodiversity Conservation

Ashansha Kuksal[1]; Resham Bhalla[2] and G.D. Mhaske[3]

ABSTRACT

The biggest threat to biodiversity is habitat destruction. The ever increasing spread of cities and the accompanying expansion of agriculture must be held largely responsible. Humid tropical forests are particularly valuable reservoirs of biodiversity and are currently being seriously threatened. As the human population expands, the need for food is expected to double in the next 30 years with the ensuing threat of massive habitat destruction particularly in the less developed countries. Increasing crop productivity on the land already under cultivation would prevent or at least reduce habitat destruction. One of several measures aimed at increasing yields is the use of better seeds, including those enhanced by modern biotechnology. Many other measures in

[1 & 3] Department of Biotechnology, HPT Arts and RYK Science College, Nashik - 422 005, M.S., (India).

[2] Department of Zoology, LVH Arts, Science and Commerce College, Panchavati, Nashik - 3, M.S., (India).

the technical, socio-economic and political fields need to be taken at the same time in order to balance intensification and sustainability of modern agriculture.

Modern biotechnology offers new means of improving rather than threatening biodiversity. If properly tested for both risks and benefits to humans and the environment, transgenic crops are more likely to increase agricultural biodiversity and help maintain native biodiversity rather than to endanger it, in contrast to the claims of many environmental groups. Such applications need to be judged by the criteria of improved sustainability and compared to current as well as alternative farming practices.

Key words: Biodiversity, Biotechnology, Transgenic crops, Conservation.

ESSENCE OF BIOTECHNOLOGY

Biodiversity is the multitude of different living beings in a particular ecosystem or on the whole earth. Biodiversity can be seen and studied at different organizational levels: genetic, organism and ecological. It touches both upon native environments on land and sea as well as agricultural and other man made surroundings.

The biodiversity we observe today is the result of 3.5 billion years of evolution. Through the processes of mutation and selection all living organisms we know today, as well as those that ever lived before, developed from one single-cell micro-organism. How this first living being arose 3.5 billion years ago is still a matter for speculation. This unitary origin explains why all organisms share the same basic chemistry: DNA is always the storage molecule of genetic information and the complex process of protein biosynthesis is virtually the same in all organisms. Metabolic pathways too, are similar in all organisms.

Dinosaurs are the only creatures of the past that became extinct: far more organisms lived at some time on our earth than are living here today. The vast majority, probably more than 99%, of species that arose on this globe, disappeared again. This shows that evolution is an ongoing process, with species coming and going. In the long term view, there has never been any stability of life on earth - only change. However, these changes were very slow compared to the length of a human life, or even compared to the time humans have existed.

The number of species of plants, animals and eukaryotic micro-organisms is probably around 10 million today, but only 1.4 million have been characterised and given a name by scientists. Virtually all of the 40'000 vertebrate animals are known and most of the 300'000 vascular plant species as well. On the other hand, there are likely to be over a million species each of fungi and nematodes, of which only 70'000 and 13'000 have been named. With prokaryotes the situation is even more extreme: about 5000 bacteria and viruses have been named individually, yet the total number in both of these two groups may go up to one million. All the different species of plants and animals are not living an independent existence, but are associated in specific communities and ecosystems to form more or less stable associations. One such association is, for instance, the humid (and dry) tropical forest which is generally thought to have the highest degree of biodiversity, with more tree species per km^2. Biodiversity needs not only to be considered in qualitative terms of the species present, but also in quantitative terms considering how many individuals of certain species of plants and animals are present. With large mammals this is quite easy to determine, but impossible with micro-organisms. Often the number of species found in a given ecosystem is taken as a measure of the biodiversity of that system: other criteria are more difficult to apply.

AGRICULTURAL BIOTECHNOLOGY

In addition to biodiversity in the wild, there is the biodiversity of organisms used for farming and other human activities. In agriculture, 7000 species of plants are used by farmers somewhere in the world, but only 30 species provide 90% of our calorie intake. Within these preponderant crop species there are many hundred thousand varieties adapted to local climates, farming practices, cultural predilections like taste, colour, structure, ability to store the products etc. Much of this large crop diversity is important for providing starting material for breeding However, it must be recalled that the genetic diversity found in crops is much less broad than the genetic diversity observed in plants or animals living in the wild, which points to the importance of wild species for agricultural breeding programmes.

The top three crops worldwide are wheat, rice and maize (corn) with around 500 million tons annual production each. Traditional breeding brought us in the trap of narrowing down the genomes, and wisely used biotechnology could bring back at least that part of genetic diversity which enhances pest resistance and perhaps yield There are many indications that mixtures of varieties of a crop or of different crops may give higher yields and be more resistant to pests and diseases than monoculture. However, even in mixed cultures high quality, well defined varieties and pure seeds are required and the sustainability of mixed cropping related to pest management has still to be proven. In addition, it is still not clear, whether in natural, non-agricultural habitats yield is basically dependent on biodiversity. On the basis of the same experiments, some researchers claim that loss of species leads to a reduction in biomass, while others disagree, as demonstrated by Hector and by Kaiser.

HUMAN POPULATION EXPANSION

The one species that is still globally expanding in numbers are humans. The world population has gone up from 2.5 billions in 1950 to 6 billion today;

it is expected by the UN to reach 8 billion in 2015 and 9-10 billion in 2050. Over 95% of the expected population increase will be in the less developed countries (LDCs). In those countries, most of the population growth will occur in the cities. The additional population will require more space to live in, more water, more energy, more food and more services. The HIV/AIDS epidemic with an estimated 65 million infected today worldwide. Areas with low economic growth is dropping by around 1% per year because of HIV/AIDS as estimated by Bread for the World. In the context of this paper it is important to realise that the FAO estimates that there are globally over 800 million people who do not have enough to eat today and it is imperative that more food be produced and made available to them.

INTERNATIONAL AGREEMENTS

In view of the importance of biodiversity for the future of mankind, several international agreements have been reached. Since this has only occurred in the last few years, the long term impact of these agreements cannot yet be estimated.

THE CONVENTION ON BIOLOGICAL DIVERSITY (CBD)

Recognizing that biodiversity of organisms in the wild should be maintained both for their own intrinsic value, but also on practical grounds, the United Nations prepared this Convention and succeeded in having it adopted in 1992. It entered into force in 1993.This is the first time that a large majority of States, though not the USA, have agreed to a legally binding instrument for biodiversity conservation and the sustainable use of biological resources. A radical change brought about by the CBD is the recognition that States have a sovereign right over biodiversity within their own territory, while previously organisms were considered the common heritage of mankind. Living organisms or their products may, under the terms of the CBD, only be removed from a country under mutually agreed conditions. The CBD is a comprehensive approach to biodiversity conservation of both wild and domesticated species. It aims at conservation at the genetic, species and eco system levels.

The regulations of the CBD have only been in operation for a few years. It is too early to assess their long term effects. As far as biotechnology and "bioprospecting" is concerned, it will take more time to establish smooth administrative procedures to allow simple routine implementation of close collaborations. Only if national authorities from countries rich in biodiversity as well as pharmaceutical or other companies see the mutual advantages to be gained from such collaboration, this system will spread.

THE CARTAGENA PROTOCOL ON BIOSAFETY

The CBD provided a basis for developing and formulating a further international agreement, namely one regulating primarily the trans-boundary movement of living GMOs. After much debate in 1999, the new protocol was agreed on in early 2000 under the name of the "Cartagena Protocol on Biosafety". The "Intergovernmental Committee for the Cartagena Protocol on Biosafety" had its first meeting in Montpellier in December 2000. It paved the way for launching a pilot phase of the "Biosafety Clearing House", a centre for information exchange. The latest meeting (COP-MOP3) took place in Curitiba, Brazil in March 2006 as seen on the web site of the Convention on Biological Diversity.

The Protocol is a world-wide regulation for the transfer, handling and use of living GMOs, particularly crop plants that may have an adverse effect on biodiversity, also taking into account risks to human health and focusing on transboundary movements. It makes explicit reference to the precautionary approach. The Protocol does not pertain to pharmaceuticals or other non-living products made by genetic modification.

In practice, the Protocol will be most important for the import of transgenic seeds. It requires a risk assessment by the national authorities and allows countries to reject GMOs. The protocol specifies that "lack of scientific certainty due to insufficient scientific information and knowledge regarding the extent of the potential adverse effects shall not prevent the party from taking a decision:" This may or may not be in agreement with the WTO rules, but will need to be tested in the courts. If there are disputes between the interpretation of the Protocol and the WTO regulations, which allow for trade barriers virtually only if there are scientific reasons to do so, the outcome of such disputes will depend to a considerable degree on the quality of scientific data assessing benefits and risks of GMOs. The Protocol has become operational in 2003, after ratification by 50 nations and has now been signed by over 100 (excluding, importantly, for instance the US).

LOSS OF BIODIVERSITY AND CONSERVATION

Losses of biodiversity are undoubtedly occurring in many parts of the globe, often at a rapid pace. These losses require counter measures such as an increased effort towards conservation by many different means.

CAUSES OF REDUCTION IN BIODVERSITY

The loss of biodiversity can be measured by a loss of individual species, groups of species or decreases in numbers of individual organisms. In a given location the loss will often reflect a degradation or a destruction of a whole ecosystem. Recently the Subsidiary Body on Scientific, Technical and Technological Advice (SBSTTA) of the CBD ranked the priority of threats to global biodiversity in the following manner: first comes habitat loss (most of it through the expansion of cultivated land), second comes the introduction of exotic species. Habitat loss comes not only from taking more land under the plough, but also from expanding cities and road building. In addition, habitats can be damaged by flooding, lack of water, climate changes, salination etc., all phenomena, which may be both natural and man-made. Since tropical humid forests are particularly rich in biodiversity, their destruction is disproportionately damaging to biodiversity. It is estimated by Pimm and Raven that of the original 16 million km^2 of these forests known a century ago, only half are left, with about one million km^2 being destroyed every 5 to 10 years. Burning and selective logging may damage an even greater area. Biodiversity is not homogeneously distributed over the humid tropical forests, rather there are hotspots with a particularly high level of biodiversity. The hotspots are according to Myers of particular interest for the implementation of conservation measures.

The second most important reason for loss of biodiversity is invasion by exotic plants and animals. Knowingly, or unknowingly, imported plant species threaten the native ones by being highly competitive and often by lacking local predators, such as insects or birds. One of the most extreme examples is seen in the pampas of Argentine, flat grassland with a moderate climate, from which nearly all the native grasses have disappeared and have been replaced by European plants. This invasion was brought about by European farmers, importing animals and crops, as well as accidentally spreading many different weeds. This phenomenon was already noted in 1833 by Charles Darwin, as recorded by Crosby. Still today, droves of gardeners transport seeds all over the globe and never think of the possible threat to biodiversity, as suggested by Ammann in 1997. It is estimated by Sukopp & Sukopp that one in ten imported plants may spread in a modest way and that one in a hundred may turn into a nuisance weed. Even in today's Europe invasion by exotics may threaten ecosystems. In the Ticino region of Southern Switzerland Robinia pseudoacacia, a native of North America, is displacing chestnut and oak trees, whilst in the Northern regions of the country Solidago canadensis is replacing native Irises in swampy areas. Islands are particularly threatened by invaders, as is well documented for Hawaii, New Zealand or the Galapagos Islands. For North America it has been estimated that damage caused by exotics amount to137 billion dollars a year, as calculated by Pimentel. Although such calculations are fraught with uncertainties, there is no doubt that the costs of exotics are tremendous.

Exotic biological control agents are often introduced into agricultural ecosystems on purpose, in order to control pests or weeds without resorting to chemical controls agents. Whilst there are some success stories, Strong pointed out that such systems may also go wrong. One example is the introduction of the seven-spot ladybird which was intended to fight the Russian wheat aphid. The consequence, however, was the disappearance of the native ladybirds, for which the seven-spot import was a competitor and an actual predator. Another example is the decimation of the large American moths, which are killed by European Compsilura flies, introduced nearly a century ago to control the gypsy moth. Field experiments recently done by Jensen showed that caterpillars of the American moth Cecropia were killed by massive infestations with Compsilura maggots. Whether transgenic plants are specifically prone to spread in the long term, cannot be said today on the basis of experimental evidence. However, one would not expect this to be the case unless the transgenic plant had an increased fitness. There is no good argument why crops that have for centuries depended for survival on human care should become weeds just because of the addition of one or a few well characterised genes, in addition to the many thousands of genes they already carry. However, this issue needs to be studied in a case by case manner, keeping in mind that the absence of a negative effect can never be proven with absolute certainty under all circumstances. The results of a fairly long-term study of the performance of transgenic crops in natural habitats were recently presented by Crawley. Four different crops (oilseed rape, potato, maize and sugar beet) were grown in 12 different habitats and monitored over a period of 10 years. In no case were transgenic plants found to be more invasive or more persistent than their conventional counterparts, in agreement with the general hypothesis put forward.

APPLICATIONS OF BIOTECHNOLOGY AND ITS EFFECT ON BIODIVERSITY

The methods of biotechnology can be applied to the study of virtually any biological phenomenon and will in some cases have practical applications for maintaining biodiversity. Conversely, threats to biodiversity by biotechnology also need to be considered.

BIOTECHNOLOGY FOR THE ACQUISITION OF KNOWLEDGE

There are two quite different applications of biotechnology or of molecular biology, that are relevant. The first is to use biotechnology as a tool for acquiring knowledge, whilst the second is to use biotechnology to directly intervene in plant and animal breeding, in particular to transfer genetic information from one sort of organism to a particular crop or to a farm animal to make it transgenic. Today biological research can hardly be conducted without using biotechnology in one way or another. This is useful for ex situ conservation of plants and micro-organisms. In seed banks, genetic fingerprints are used to establish the origin of a seed or the relatedness of one plant variety to another. A rational classification of most micro-organisms has only become possible with these biotechnological methods. This is important to the many collections of micro-organisms that exist around the world. Biotechnology has also proven useful for following genetic markers in plant and animal breeding. Here animal or plant varieties are crossed by conventional, sexual means. By analyzing a few cells of the newly born calf or of the newly sprouted crop, one can predict some of the expected properties of the progeny, by looking at the presence or absence of certain forms of genes. This enables one to predict a phenotypic property, which will only show up later in life, for instance certain characteristics of a cow's milk or the crop's expected resistance to an infectious plant disease. Using in vitro fertilisation of animals, the laboratory test can be done even before the embryo is implanted. This is called pre-implantation diagnostics.

The availability of genome sequences will be a boost to research. The first two complete plant genome sequences determined were those of Arabidopsis and rice. The 120 million base pair (MBP) of the small brassica Arabidopsis were sequenced by an international academic consortium and the data made publicly available as reported by both Adam and also Dennis and Surridge.

DIRECT GENE TRANSFER TO CROPS AND FARM ANIMALS

Since all genes consist of DNA and the information in this DNA molecule is read in the same way in all organisms in order to make proteins, it is in principle possible to take any (single) gene from any organism and transfer it into any other organism so that the recipient should produce a protein normally made only in the donor. The resulting organism is called transgenic. From the time this simple strategy was devised it took molecular biologists about twenty years until the first transgenic plants were made in 1985. Ten years later the first transgenic crop appeared in supermarkets in the USA, the "Flavr Savr" tomato.

The reason US farmers have adopted the transgenic crops surprisingly quickly is because of the economic benefits they offer. In most surveys done by different researchers in different parts of the US, the yields were the same or somewhat higher with the new seeds. The most noticeable difference to the farmers was the saving on herbicides. Gianessi and others also found the new crops needed less frequent sprayings and allowed" no till" management. These benefits mostly offset the initial higher cost of the transgenic seeds, but it is also so that farm profits, with or without modern biotechnology, vary a great deal from year to year and region to region. It is important to remember that a large number of transgenic crops are still in the development stage and will only come onto the market in a few years from now. They are likely to show benefits for the consumers and some may be of particular interest to farmers in tropical countries. Two rice varieties with anticipated consumer benefits are those containing Vitamin A or an increased level of iron in the product have been developed by Potrykus and Beyer. Despite traditional preventative measures (distribution of free vitamin A, encouragement to eat more fruit and vegetables) 130 million youths are vitamin A-deficient, 1-2 million die annually as a consequence of vitamin A-deficiency and 500'000 turn blind irreversibly every year. A bowl of 300 g of this cooked rice is thought by Gura to be enough to overcome to a significant degree the vitamin A-deficiency. Similarly iron-deficiency, particularly prevalent in pregnant women, can potentially be alleviated by rice containing an increased amount of iron in its endosperm. Such rice varieties have been successfully developed in the laboratory, but are far from commercialization, for both scientific and political reasons.

AGRICULTURAL BIODIVERSITY AND BIOTECHNOLOGY

Possibly not only wild plants, but also old landraces might be threatened by transgenic crops. It needs to be recalled that vertical gene transfer by pollen has always occurred between different old landraces and between different new varieties of crops. Despite this, varieties of apples or cereals have been stable over many years and specific traits have not disappeared. Pollen has always flown. What has become far more precise is the method of analysis. Thanks to gene probes and to GMOs it has become much easier to follow gene flow, since one is no longer dependent on visible traits, but can follow a specific gene Can newly introduced transgenic crops transfer genes vertically to native wild plants and thereby change important characteristics of the wild plants? Vertical gene transfer between cultivars and wild plants has always occurred within the limits of species, if the two types of plants were in close proximity and flowered at the same time. No new problems can be expected from transgenic plants, except if the gene transferred from the GMO to the wild plant significantly increased the fitness of the recipient. Herbicide resistance transfer from a herbicide tolerant, transgenic crop to a close relative can occur in the field, as has been shown for canola by Mikkelsen in Denmark. However, this would be of major significance only if the recipient weed was controlled by this herbicide in this farm setting.

Small farmers in many LDCs use a remarkable number of landraces of many different crops. These are often well adapted to the local climate and topography, and are used to produce foods for different cultural purposes. In the Andes region of South America, dozens of different varieties of potatoes are grown, often side by side on small plots. In Europe different varieties of potatoes are used for the industrial production of chips and for preparing Rösti in the home.

The rapid consolidation in the global seed market too is a concern for the maintenance of agricultural biodiversity: a decreasing number of companies controls the global seed and agrochemical markets. Anti-trust legislation needs to prevent the formation of overly powerful monopolies. This concern is not a consequence of the introduction of agricultural biotechnology, but a consequence of globalization. New technologies have in many areas, not only biotechnology, made large companies more powerful and more visible. It may be possible that modern breeding methods based on molecular genetics will per se reverse the trend of variety losses, since the insight in genomics may bring back respect for landraces and the need to conserve them.

SOCIAL CONSEQUENCES

The introduction and spread of new technologies generally have social consequences with winners and losers. For biotechnology this has led to intense public debate on many different facets, among them ethical, economic, legal and emotional.

ECONOMIC CONSIDERATIONS

One may wonder under what economic conditions biotechnology will benefit agricultural productivity, prevent the expansion of farm land and thereby help the preservation of biodiversity. It is worth remembering that the green revolution, which improved wheat and rice production in Asia, was initiated through work done in the public sector, namely in the Philippines at the International Rice Research Institute (IRRI) and in Mexico at the Centro Internacional de Mejoramiento de Maiz y Trigo (CIMMYT), both institutions which belong to the Consultative Group of International Agricultural Research (CGIAR). Today, innovative research in agricultural biotechnology is largely done by a few large companies, with smaller contributions from the public sector. That companies strive for intellectual property rights (IPR) through patenting or other protective mechanisms is understandable and largely unavoidable, if innovation is to be maintained. However, provisions need to be made, so that the agricultural research institutions of LDCs obtain easy access to the patented materials and procedures as well as to knowledge they need in order to improve the position of poorer farmers as proposed for instance by IRRI.

A very limited number of transfers of specific patents has already occurred, such as from Monsanto to the Kenyan Agricultural Research Institute for producing virus-resistant sweet potatoes discussed by MacIlvain or another to IRRI for the promoter genes used in golden rice reported by Normile. This approach, including the possibility of forced licensing, is more practicable than wanting to overthrow the world's patenting system withthe slogan"No patents on life". The patenting system does, however, need to be adapted in order to do justice to the complexity of living organisms.

At the level of the individual human being, the lack of food appears to be, and is, largely a problem of distribution: there is not sufficient food available, where it is needed. In addition, the poor simply do not have the money to buy sufficient food. Since in LDCs most of the poor still live on the land, it is there, that more income has to be generated, so that there is not only enough for survival, but a surplus which can be sold on the market. Increasing agricultural productivity is the most effective way to do this and should, according to economists such as Lipton, embrace modern biotechnology as an important component.

ETHICAL CONSIDERATIONS

The issues involved in the interaction between biodiversity and biotechnology have far-reaching consequences and need to be subject to an open and knowledge-based dialogue in society. The heated public debate, seen primarily in Europe in the last couple of years and which in some circles led to near hysteria, is according to Leisinger not sufficient to solve the underlying problems. The dialogue needs to include many different stakeholders, including farmers of LDCs, diverse scientists, policy makers and communicators. Cultural values involved in farming and food productions need to be taken into consideration, just as much as the emotional side of eating and drinking.

A significant aspect of ethical behaviour is openness. Transparent information is required both from scientists in non-commercial settings as well as from industry. Although competition from fellow researchers and from industries does not allow immediately divulging all research results, both groups should make concessions to the interested public and to policy makers. The questions put forward by ethicists need to answered on the basis of concrete scientific knowledge, using comparisons with other, established agricultural practices.

It will be important to see ethics not as a stable set of principles but rather a discursive process, which will be apt to cope up with the growing speed of new developments as discussed by Ammann and Ammann. The Nuffield Council of Bioethics recently came to the conclusion that" The moral imperative for making GM crops readily and economically available...is compelling", if well-informed governments of LDCs want to introduce them. This imperative should be taken seriously and treated with urgency: every day 20'000 children die of malnutrition and 30'000 humid tropical forest are destroyed.

A CASE STUDY: BIOTECHNOLOGY INDIA

By setting up a National Biotechnology Board in 1982 and a Department of Biotechnology in 1986, the Indian Government has demonstrated its belief in biotechnology. The country has spent 15 million $ on plant biotechnology. Prasantha Kumar Ghosh, chairman of the committee that grants permits for field trials, says he would like to see transgenic crops playing a major role in Indian agriculture. Cotton is of particular interest, since 45% of pesticides used in India are for this crop alone. It is possible that cotton will become the first commercialised transgenic crop, but this is not yet the case. Several NGOs oppose any releases of GMOs, at least as long as the new varieties come from foreign multinational companies, as reported by Jayaraman and by Sharma.

A National Plant Genome Research centre has been established at Jawaharlal Nehru University, whilst in other academic settings there are also many biotechnology groups. The Indian Academy of Sciences joined the Science Academies of China, Mexico, the United Kingdom, Brazil and the USA, to study risks and benefits of transgenic plants and their significance for world agriculture. The final text, which was published in July 2000 is an extensive and differentiated report essentially saying that the world needs these new crops, but that the socio-economic conditions have to be such, that the poorest people in the poorest countries will also benefit.

REFERENCES

Agrawal S.F. (1998): Environmental Biotechnology. APH publishers New Delhi.

Asthana D.K., Meera Asthana (1999): Environment, Problems and Solutions, S. Chand & Company, New Delhi. 16: 221-263.

P.D. Sharma (2001): Ecology and Environment, Rastogi Publications, Shivaji Road, Meerut, India. pp. 623-645.

Santra S.C. (2001): Environmental Science, New Central Book Agency, Calcutta (India). 6: 70-101.

Subbarao N.S. (1993): Biofertilizers in Agriculture and Forestry-IIIrd Edition. Oxford and IBH Publishing Co. New Delhi.

Pages: 174-185

AGRICULTURE, ENVIRONMENT AND NANO-SCIENCE
Edited by: Dr. Pawan Kumar 'Bharti'
ISBN: 978-93-5056-760-9
Edition: 2015
Published by: Discovery Publishing House Pvt. Ltd., New Delhi (India)

9

Environmental Biotechnology and its Applications

Chitralekha Bagul[1]; Resham Bhalla[2*] and G.D. Mhaske[3]

ABSTRACT

The term "Environment" is defined as our surroundings which includes the abiotic component (the non living) and biotic component (the living) around us. The abiotic environment includes water, air and soil while the biotic environment consists of all living organisms – plants, animals and microorganisms. Environmental pollution broadly refers to the presence of undesirable substances in the environment which are harmful to man and other organisms. In the past decade or two, there has been a significant increase in the levels of pollution mostly due to direct or indirect human activities. With the simultaneous increase in cases of cancer, autoimmune diseases, and infections caused by antibiotic resistant microorganisms, the healthcare system was left depleted of professionals able to manage the situation. Public

1 & 3 Department of Biotechnology, HPT Arts and RYK Science college, Nashik, 422 005, M.S., (India).

2 Department of Zoology, LVH Arts, Science and Commerce College, Panchavati, Nashik - 3, M.S., (India).

health has become a major concern throughout the world and many countries have created incentive programmes in order to motivate professionals to advance their career towards a master's degree in Public Health, a field that is in very high demand among government agencies and private organizations, such as hospitals and the medical research industry. These professionals are expected to perform in high-level, leadership positions where the skills learned through their education can be used to identify the impact of different sources of environmental pollution to human health.

Controlling the environmental pollution and the conservation of environment and biodiversity are the major focus areas of all the countries around the world. In this context the importance and impact of biotechnological approaches and the implications of biotechnology has to be thoroughly evaluated. There have been serious concerns regarding the use of biotechnology products and the impact assessment of these products due to their interaction with the environmental factors.

A lobby of the environmentalists has expressed alarm on the release of genetically engineered organisms in the atmosphere and have stressed on thorough investigation and proper risk assessment of these organisms before releasing them in to the environment. The effect of the effluents from biotechnological companies is also a cause of concern for everyone. The need of the hour is to have a proper debate on the safety of the use of the biotechnological products.

Key words: Environment, biotechnology, bioremediation, biodegradation etc.

INTRODUCTION

The major sources of environmental pollution are– Industries, Agricultural sources (mainly rural area), anthropogenic sources (man related activities mainly in urban areas), biogenic sources etc. The pollutants are chemical, biological and physical in nature. The Chemical pollutants include- gaseous pollutants (hazardous gases like sulfur dioxide, nitrogen oxide), toxic metals, pesticides, herbicides toxins and carcinogens, etc.

The physical pollutants are heat, sound, radiation, and radioactive substances. The pathogenic organisms and some poisonous and dangerous biological products are the biological pollutants.

To solve all types of environmental problems knowledge of biotechnology is important.

This aspect highlight on the use of biotechnology to protect the environment from pollution but also to use it to conserve the natural resources. As we all know that microorganisms are known natural scavengers so the microbial preparations (both natural as well as genetically engineered) can be used to clean up the environmental hazards.

Development of Alternate Cleaner Technologies Using Biotechnology

Biotechnology is being used to provide alternative cleaner technologies which will help to further reduce the hazardous environmental implications of the traditional technologies. E.g. some Fermentation technologies have some serious environmental implications. Various biotechnological processes have been devised in which all nutrients introduced for fermentation are retained in the final product, which ensures high conversion efficiency and low environmental impact.

In paper industry, the pulp bleaching technologies are being replaced by more environmentally friendly technologies involving biotechnology. The pulp processing helps to remove the lignin without damaging valuable cellulosic fibres but the available techniques suffer from the disadvantages of high costs, high energy use and corrosion. A lignin degrading and modifying enzyme (LDM) was isolated from Phanerochaete chrysosporum and was used, which on one hand, helped to reduce the energy costs and corrosion and on the other hand increased the life of the system. This approach helped in reducing the environmental hazards associated with bleach plant effluents.

In Plastic industry, the conventional technologies use oil based raw materials to extract ethylene and propylene which are converted to alkene oxides and then polymerized to form plastics such as polypropylene and polyethylene. There is always the risk of these raw materials escaping into the atmosphere thereby causing pollution. Using biotechnology, safer raw materials like sugars (glucose) are being used which are enzymatically or through the direct use of microbes converted into alkene oxides.e.g. Methylococcus capsulatus has been used for converting alkene into alkene oxides.

BIOREMEDIATION

Bioremediation is defined as 'the process of using microorganisms to remove the environmental pollutants where microbes serve as scavengers. The removal of organic wastes by microbes leads to environmental cleanup. The other names/terms used for bioremediation are biotreatment, bioreclamation, and biorestoration. The term "Xenobiotics" (xenos means foreign) refers to the unnatural, foreign and synthetic chemicals such as pesticides, herbicides, refrigerants, solvents and other organic compounds. The microbial degradation of xenobiotics also helps in reducing the environmental pollution.

Pseudomonas which is a soil microorganism effectively degrades xenobiotics. Different strains of Pseudomonas that are capable of detoxifying more than 100 organic compounds (e.g. phenols, biphenyls, organophosphates, naphthalene etc.) have been identified. Some other microbial strains are also known to have the capacity to degrade xenobiotics such as Mycobacterium, Alcaligenes, Norcardia, etc.

FACTORS AFFECTING BIODEGRADATION

The factors that affect the biodegradation are: the chemical nature of xenobiotics, the concentration and supply of nutrients and O_2, temperature, pH, redox potential and the capability of the individual microorganism. The chemical nature of xenobiotics is very important because it was found out that the presence of halogens e.g. in aromatic compounds inhibits biodegradation. The water soluble compounds are more easily degradable whereas the presence of cyclic ring structure and the length chains or branches decrease the efficiency of biodegradation. The aliphatic compounds are more easily degraded than the aromatic ones.

BIOSTIMULATION

It is a process by which the microbial activity can be enhanced by increased supply of nutrients or by addition of certain stimulating agents like electron acceptors, surfactants etc.

BIOAUGMENTATION

It is possible to increase biodegradation through manipulation of genes i.e. using genetically engineered microorganisms and by using a range of microorganisms in biodegradation reaction.

Depending on the method followed to clear up the environment, the bioremediation is carried out in two ways:

(A) In situ bioremediation - In situ bioremediation involves a direct approach for the microbial degradation of xenobiotics at the site of pollution which could be soil, water etc. The adequate amount of essential nutrients is supplied at the site which promotes the microbial growth at the site itself. The in situ bioremediation is generally used for clean up of oil spillages, beaches etc. There are two types of in situ bioremediation:

1. *Intrinsic bioremediation:* The microorganisms which are used for biodegradation are tested for the natural capability to bring about biodegradation. So the inherent metabolic ability of the microorganisms to degrade certain pollutants is the intrinsic bioremediation.
2. *Engineered in situ bioremediation:* When the bioremediation process is engineered to increase the metabolic degradation efficiency (of pollutants) it is called engineered in situ bioremediation. This is done by supplying sufficient amount of nutrients and oxygen supply, adding electron acceptors and maintaining optimal temperature and pH. This is done to overcome the slow and limited bioremediation capability of microorganisms.

Advantages of in situ Bioremediation

(a) The method ensures minimal exposure to public or site personnels.

(b) There is limited or minimal disruption to the sitc of bioremediation.

(c) Due to these factors it is cost effective.

(d) The simultaneous treatment of contaminated soil and water is possible.

Disadvantages of in situ bioremediation

(a) The sites are directly exposed to environmental factors like temperature, oxygen supply etc.

(b) The seasonal variation of microbial activity exists.

(c) Problematic application of treatment additives like nutrients, surfactants, oxygen etc.

(d) It is a very tedious and time consuming process.

(B) Ex-situ bioremediation - In this the waste and the toxic material is collected from the polluted sites and the selected range of microorganisms carry out the bioremediation at designed place. This process is an improved method over the in situ bioremediation method. On the basis of phases of contaminated materials under treatment ex-situ bioremediation is classified into two: (a) Solid phase system; and (b) slurry phase systems.

(a) *Solid phase treatment:* This system includes land treatment and soil piles comprising of organic wastes like leaves, animal manures, agricultural wastes, domestic and industrial wastes, sewage sludge, and municipal solid wastes. The traditional clean-up practice involves the informal processing of the organic materials and production of composts which may be used as soil amendment. Composting can be done in open system i.e. land treatment and/or in closed treatment system. The hazardous compounds reported to disappear through composting includes aliphatic and aromatic hydrocarbons and certain halogenated compounds. The possible routes leading to the disappearance of hazardous compounds include volatilization, assimilation, adsorption, polymerization and leaching.

(b) *Slurry phase treatment:* This is a triphasic treatment system involving three major components- water, suspended particulate matter and air. Here water serves as suspending medium where nutrients, trace elements, pH adjustment chemicals and desorbed contaminants are dissolved. Suspended particulate matter includes a biologically inert substratum consisting of contaminants and biomass attached to soil matrix or free in suspending medium. The contaminated solid materials, microorganisms and water formulated into slurry are brought within a bioreactor i.e.

fermenter. Biologically there are three types of slurry-phase bioreactors: aerated lagoons, low shear airlift reactor, and fluidized-bed soil reactor. The first two types are in use of full scale bioremediation, while the third one is in developmental stage.

Advantages of ex-situ Bioremediation

(a) As the time required is short, it is a more efficient process.

(b) It can be controlled in a much better way.

(c) The process can be improved by enrichment with desired and more efficient microorganisms.

Disadvantages of ex-situ bioremediation

(a) The sites of pollution remain highly disturbed.

(b) Once the process is complete, the degraded waste disposal becomes a major problem.

(c) It is a costly process.

Use of Genetic Engineering and Genetic Manipulations for more Efficient Bioremediation

In recent years, efforts have been made to create genetically engineered microorganisms (GEMs) to enhance bioremediation. This is done to overcome some of the limitations and problems in bioremediation. These problems are:

(a) Sometimes the growth of microorganisms gets inhibited or reduced by the xenobiotics.

(b) No single naturally occurring microorganisms has the capability of degrading all the xenobiotics present in the environmental pollution.

(c) The microbial degradation is a very slow process.

(d) Sometimes certain xenobiotics get adsorbed on to the particulate matter of soil and thus become unavailable for microbial degradation.

As the majority of genes responsible for the synthesis of enzymes with biodegradation capability are located on the plasmids, the genetic manipulations of plasmids can lead to the creation of new strains of bacteria with different degradative pathways. In 1970s, Chakrabarty and his team of co-workers reported the development of a new strain of bacterium Pseudomonas by manipulations of plasmid transfer which they named as "superbug". This superbug had the capability of degrading a number of hydrocarbons of petroleum simultaneouslysuch as camphor, octane, xylene, naphthalene etc. In 1980, United States granted the patent to this superbug making it the first genetically engineered microorganism to be patented.

A new strain of Pseudomonas sp. (strain ATCC 1915) has been developed for the degradation of vanillate (which is a waste product from paper industry) and sodium dodecyl sulfate (SDS, a compound used in detergents).

Biotechnological Method to Reduce Atmospheric Carbon Dioxide (CO_2)

Carbon dioxide is the gas that is the main cause of green house effect and rise in the atmospheric temperature. During the past 100-150 years, the level of CO_2 has increased about 25% with an increase in the atmospheric temperature by about 0.5% which is a clear indication that CO_2 is closely linked with global warming. There is a steady increase in the CO_2 content due to continuous addition of CO_2 from various sources particularly from industrial processes. It is very clear that the reduction in atmospheric CO_2 concentration assumes significance. Biotechnological methods have been used to reduce the atmospheric CO_2 content at two levels:

(a) *Photosynthesis:* Plants utilize CO_2 during the photosynthesis which reduces the CO_2 content in the atmosphere. The equation for photosynthesis is:

sunlight

$6CO_2 + 6H_2O \rightarrow C\ 6\ H12\ O6 + 6O_2$

Chlorophyll

The fast growing plants utilize the CO_2 more efficiently for photosynthesis. The techniques of micropropagation and synthetic seeds should be used to increase the propagation of such fast growing plants.

Further, the CO_2 utilization can be increased by enhancing the rate of photosynthesis. The enzyme ribulose biphosphate carboxylase (RUBP-case) is closely linked with CO_2 fixation. The attempts are being made to genetically manipulate this enzyme so that the photosynthetic efficiency is increased.

Some microalgae like Chlorella pyrenodiosa, Spirulina maxima are known to be more efficient than higher plants in utilizing atmospheric CO_2 for photosynthesis and generate more O_2 than the amount of CO_2 consumed.

The growing of these microalgae near the industries and power plants (where the CO_2 emission in to atmosphere is very high) will help in the reduction of polluting effects of CO_2. Using genetic engineering, attempts are going on to develop new strains of these microalgae that can tolerate high concentrations of CO_2. A limited success has already been reported in the mutants of Anacystis nidulans and Oocystis sp.

(b) *Biological Calcification:* Certain deep sea organisms like corals, green and red algae store CO_2 through a process of biological calcification. As the $CaCO_3$ gets precipitated, more and more atmospheric CO_2 can be utilized for its formation. The process of calcification is as follows:

$H_2O + CO_2 \rightarrow H_2CO_3$

$H\ 2CO3 + Ca\ 2+ \rightarrow CaCO_3 + CO_2 + H_2O$

Treatment of Sewage Using Microorganisms

The sewage is defined as the waste water resulting from the various human activities, agriculture and industries and mainly contains organic and inorganic compounds, toxic substances, heavy metals and pathogenic organisms. The sewage is treated to get rid of these undesirable substances by subjecting the organic matter to biodegradation by microorganisms. The biodegradation involves the degradation of organic matter to smaller molecules (CO_2, NH_3, PO_4 etc.) and requires constant supply of oxygen. The process of supplying oxygen is expensive, tedious, and requires a lot of expertise and manpower. These problems are overcome by growing microalgae in the ponds and tanks where sewage treatment is carried out. The algae release the O_2 while carrying out the photosynthesis which ensures a continuous supply of oxygen for biodegradation.

The algae are also capable of adsorbing certain heavy toxic metals due to the negative charges on the algal cell surface which can take up the positively charged metals. The algal treatment of sewage also supports fish growth as algae is a good source of food for fishes. The algae used for sewage treatment are Chlorella, Euglene, Chlamydomnas, Scenedesmus, Ulothrix, Thribonima etc.

Use of Biotechnology for Toxic site Reclamation

In order to solve the problem of soil pollution caused due to extensive use of herbicides, pesticides and insecticides, the bioremediation of soil using microorganisms is being carried out. The most common pollutants are: hydrocarbons, chlorinated, solvents, polychlorobiphenyls and metals. The bioremediation of soil involves two processes:

(a) **Biostimulation**: Biostimulation involves the stimulaton of microorganisms already present in the soil. This can be done by adding nutrients e.g. nitrogen, phosphorus etc., by supplying co-substrates e.g. methane which can degrade trichloroethylene, or by adding surfactants to disperse the hydrophobic compounds in water.

(b) **Bioaugmentation**: Addition of specific microorganisms to the polluted soil constitutes bioaugmentation. Some of the pollutants like polychlorobiphenyls (PCBs), trinitrotoluene (TNT), polyaromatic hydrocarbons (PAHs) etc are not degraded by only native soil microorganisms so a combination of microorganisms referred to as "consortium" or "cocktail" of microorganisms is added to achieve bioaugmentation.

(c) **Bioventing**: Bioventing involves aerobic biodegradation of pollutants by circulating air through sub-surfaces of soil and is one of the very cost effective and efficient technique used for the bioremediation of petroleum contaminated soils. It is very effectively used for degradation of soluble paraffins, and polyaromatic hydrocarbons.

(d) **Phytoremediation**: Bioremediation by using plants is called phytoremediation. Certain plant species which have the capability to stimulate biodegradation of pollutants (specially near the soil adjacent to roots- rhizophere) are cultivated near the sites of polluted soil. This is a cheap and environmentally friendly process but takes a long time to finish the clean up process.

(e) **Land farming**: Land farming is a technique for the bioremediation of hydrocarbon contaminated soils. In this the soil is excavated, mixed with microorganisms and nutrients and spread out on a liner just below the polluted soil.

(f) **Use of slurry - phase bioreactors**: In this process, the excavated polluted soil is subjected to bioremediation under optimal controlled conditions in specifically designed bioreactors.

Use of Biotechnology in the Removal of Oil and Grease Deposits

The oil spills from oil tankers on land surface as well as in seas and oceans are a major environmental hazard. This not only kills the aquatic flora and fauna by destroying the habitat but also creates health problems for the local inhabitants. Traditionally chemical dispersants are being used as remediation efforts. However these chemical dispersants are also toxic in nature and they persist in the environment for a long time. The present techniques of washing the oil off the gravel and cleaning the area of oil spills, is very expensive and time consuming. In order to overcome some of these problems, the oleophilic fertilizers are being developed which allow rapid growth and multiplication of microbes which further leads to the increase in the biodegradation process for removal of oil. In recent years, using genetic engineering, oil utilizing microorganisms have been produced which can grow rapidly on oil. The genetically engineered microbes for cleaning oil spills are mixed with straw. At the site of oil spill, the straw mixed with microbes are scattered over the oil spilled area. The straw soaks the oily water and the microbes break the oil into non-toxic and non polluting materials thereby cleaning up the site.

Some of the oil utilizing microbes can also produce surface active compounds that can emulsify oil in water and thereby removing the oil. A strain of Pseudomonas aeruginosa produces a glycolipid emulsifier that reduces the surface tension of oil-water interface which helps in the removal of oil from water. This microbial emulsifier is nontoxic and biodegradable and has shown promising results in the laboratory experiments.

Some of the microorganisms which are capable of degrading petroleum include pesudomonads, various corynebacteria, mycobacteria and some yeasts. The two methods for bioremediation of oil spills are: (a) using a consortium of bacteria; and (b) using genetically engineered bacteria/ microbial strains.

Use of Biotechnology in Reducing the Use of Chemical Pesticides, Herbicides and Fertilizers

A lot of debate is going on the overuse of chemical herbicides, pesticides and fertilizers. They become an environmental hazard because they undergo degradation by microorganisms and ultraviolet light which releases toxic chemicals in the environment. Using biotechnology, bacterial pesticides and viral pesticides are being developed which will help in reducing the use of chemical pesticides. Several companies in USA like Monsanto, Mycogen, Ecogen, Repligen, Zoecon etc are actively involved in the development of biological pesticides. The trials are going on to use the genetically engineered live soil bacteria for coating seeds before planting. Another method being tried is to kill the recombinant bacteria and apply them to the leaves of crop plants. Both these approaches protect the toxin from degradation by microbes or ultraviolet rays once applied to the crop plants.

The company Ecogen Inc. was involved in developing biological pesticides against the two major crop pests budworm and ballworm by transferring a gene from Bacillus thuringiensis (Bt), into either a naturally occurring soil bacterium or in to a strain of Pseudomonas. Bt insecticides are already being marketed for past few years and in future these will be modified using genetic engineering and will be used against a variety of insects.

Genetically engineered insect resistant plants have been successfully produced which will further help in reducing the use of insecticides in the future.

The experiments are going on to develop environmentally safe herbicides. In order to use these herbicides for crop protection programme, genetically engineered herbicide resistant plants have been produced in a variety of crop plants. This will ensure the use of environmentally safer herbicides.

BIOFERTILIZERS

Biofertilizers are also being used in place of chemical fertilizers to further reduce the environmental hazards caused due to chemical fertilizers. The term biofertilizers is used to refer to the nutrient inputs of biological origin to support plant growth which is generally achieved by the addition of microbial inoculants as a source of biofertlizers. Biofertilizers broadly includes the following categories:

(A) **Symbiotic nitrogen fixers**: The diazotrophic microorganisms are the symbiotic nitrogen fixers that serve as biofertilizers e.g. Rhizobium sp., Bradyrhizopium sp.

(B) **Asymbiotic nitrogen fixers**: The asymbiotic nitrogen fixing bacteria can directly convert the gaseous nitrogen to nitrogen rich compounds. On the death of these nitrogen fixers, the soil becomes enriched with nitrogenous compounds thereby serving as biofertilizers e.g. Azobacter sp., Azospirillum sp.

The blue green algae, multiply in the water logging conditions and fixes the nitrogen. They accumulate the biomass which helps in improving the physical properties of the soil. This is useful for reclamation of alkaline soils besides providing partial tolerance to pesticides. The most common blue green algae are Azobacter sp. and Azospirillum sp. Azolla, which is an aquatic fern contains an endophytic cynobacterium Anabaena azollae in the leaf cavities providing symbiotic relationship. Azolla with Anaebaena is useful as biofertilizer.

(C) **Phosphate solubilising bacteria**: Some bacteria like Thiobacillus, Bacillus are capable of converting non-available inorganic phosphorus present in the soil to organic or inorganic form of phosphate. These bacteria can also produce siderophores, which chelates with iron, and makes it unavailable to pathogenic bacteria. Siderophores are iron-binding low molecular weight (400- 1,000 Daltons) peptides synthesized by some soil bacteria.

(D) **Organic fertilizers**: Certain types of organic wastes are used as fertilizers e.g. animal dung (cow dung, elephant dung etc.), urine, urban garbage, sewage, crop residues and oil cakes. All these wastes can be converted in to organic manures.

Advantages of using Biofertilizers

- Biofertilizers improve the tolerance of plants against toxic heavy metals.
- It is possible to reclaim saline or alkaline soil by using biofertilizers.
- Use of biofertilizers helps in controlling environmental pollution.
- Fertility of soil is increased year after year.
- Low cost and easy to produce.
- Biofertilizers increase the physico-chemical properties of the soil, soil texture and water holding capacity.

Some of the limitations encountered while using the biofertilizers are that they alone cannot meet the total needs of the plants for nutrient supply and also they do not produce the spectacular results as observed in synthetic fertilizers. It is important to evolve an approach which can maximize the use of biofertilizers and reduce the dependency on the chemical fertilizers in the near future with out affecting the crop productivity. This will help us to solve the environment related problems caused due to overuse of chemical fertilizers.

Use of Biotechnology in the Conservation of Biodiversity

The extinction of wild species due to the destruction of habitats and ecosystems has raised serious concerns about the biodiversity in general. Biodiversity provides genes from wild species for biotechnology exercises and experiments hence biotechnology and biodiversity are interrelated. Besides taking steps to minimize and regulate the factors responsible for causing loss of biodiversity, efforts are on to develop the techniques of conservation of biodiversity. One of the methods involves the establishment of "gene banks" leading to "in situ conservation and ex situ conservation. The in situ conservation involves the conservation of plants and animals in their natural habitat and ecosystems. The ex situ conservation includes conservation of species away from their habitats. The ex situ conservation uses sample populations and establishes the "gene banks" which includes resource centers, zoos, botanical gardens, national parks, culture collection centers etc.

Biotechnology offers special methods to conserve both animal and plant genetic resources especially in the conservation of endangered plant species. The tissue culture method is being used to multiply an endangered plant species. The method of embryo transfer and artificial insemination is used for the multiplication of endangered animal species.

REFERENCES

A.K. Chatterji. (2005), Introduction to Environmental Biotechnology, Prentice Hall of India, New Delhi. 4: 60-63.

Agrawal. S.F. (1998): Environmental Biotechnology. APH Publishers New Delhi. pp. 1-389.

S.N. Jogdand. (2006): Environmental Biotechnology, Himalaya Publishing House, Girgaon, Mumbai. 6: 115-128.

Santra S.C. (2001): Environmental Science, New Central Book Agency, Calcutta (India). 29: 477-494.

Subba Rao N.S. (1993): Biofertilizers in Agriculture and Forestry-IIIrd Edition. Oxford and IBH Publishing Co. New Delhi, 8: 129-135.

Index

C